American Virtues

American Political Thought
edited by
Wilson Carey McWilliams and Lance Banning

American Virtues
Thomas Jefferson on the Character of a Free People

Jean M. Yarbrough

University Press of Kansas

Published by the University Press of Kansas (Lawrence, Kansas 66049),
which was organized by the Kansas Board of Regents and is operated and
funded by Emporia State University, Fort Hays State University, Kansas State
University, Pittsburg State University, the University of Kansas, and Wichita
State University.

Library of Congress Cataloging-in-Publication Data

Yarbrough, Jean M.
    American virtues : Thomas Jefferson on the character of a free
people / Jean M. Yarbrough.
        p.   cm. — (American political thought)
    Includes bibliographical references and index.
    ISBN 0-7006-0906-7 (cloth : alk. paper)
    1. Jefferson, Thomas, 1743–1826—Political and social views.
2. United States—Politics and government—Philosophy. 3. Social
values—United States. 4. National characteristics, American.
I. Title. II. Series.
E332.2.Y37   1998
973.4'6'092—dc21   98-18597
                                                              CIP
British Library Cataloguing in Publication Data is available.

Printed in the United States of America

10 9 8 7 6 5 4 3 2 1

For Dick
Husband, Colleague, Dearest Friend

Jefferson is one of the great men whom this country has produced, one of the men who has contributed largely to the formation of our national character—to much that is good and to not a little that is evil in our sentiments and manners.

John Quincy Adams

Contents

Acknowledgments

To alter only slightly Paul Valéry's marvelous quip, "A book is never finished, merely abandoned." But a book on character, especially, cannot be abandoned without first expressing gratitude to those institutions and individuals who through their generosity, encouragement, and sage advice have done so much to make it better. It is, therefore, a pleasure to acknowledge at long last the financial support of the Earhart Foundation, the National Endowment for the Humanities, and Bowdoin College. I should also like to thank the Department of Political Science at the University of Toronto for inviting me to present an early draft of chapter 3 on the relationship between agrarian virtue and the moral sense. Special thanks to Melissa Butler, Thomas Pangle, and Clifford Orwin for their comments and hospitality. Finally, I am happy to thank the Liberty Fund for organizing so many splendid conferences over the last fifteen years and bringing together such a wonderful mix of American historians, legal scholars, and political theorists. I have benefited enormously from the readings and discussion sections, and most of all from the friendships that developed during the notorious "hospitality" hours stretching well into the night. I am especially grateful to Peter Onuf of the University of Virginia for his constructive comments and encouragement on the manuscript as a whole. His occasional warnings that my arguments were anachronistic, the historian's favorite complaint, saved me from one of the occupational hazards of my own discipline. My colleague and friend Paul Franco also read the entire manuscript and offered perceptive criticisms throughout. Paul Rahe of the

University of Tulsa performed yeoman service, reading several drafts of the first four chapters and offering, as usual, keen analysis and myriad suggestions for further reading. My first and only graduate student from the days when I was teaching at Loyola University of Chicago, Peter C. Myers, now at the University of Wisconsin, Eau Claire, helped me early on to think more clearly about the overall design of the project. And just as I was about to tackle Jefferson's religious views, my dear friend and colleague William Watterson presented me with a collector's copy of *The Life and Morals of Jesus of Nazareth.* Working with this beautiful leather-bound edition added a distinctively Jeffersonian pleasure to my labors. I would also like to thank two librarians at Bowdoin College, Guy Saldanha and Virginia Hopcroft, for their assistance in obtaining all the interlibrary materials I needed and for exercising patience and understanding when I ignored their recall notices. Special thanks to Ginny Hopcroft for her initiative and ingenuity in obtaining much-needed, but hard to come by, sources. For assistance in dealing with a complete computer crash and instruction on using my new, vastly improved but bewildering model, as well as for help in preparing this manuscript for final editing, I would like to thank Leilani Goggin at the Academic Computing Center of Bowdoin College. I cannot begin to express my appreciation to my able and industrious research assistants over the last four years, Seth G. Jones, Sean P. Cronin, and Amanda Norejko, who spent untold hours tracking down notes, rounding up articles, making "house calls," and generally getting this manuscript into shape. I should also like to thank my editors, Lance Banning of the University of Kentucky and Wilson Carey McWilliams of Rutgers University, for giving so freely of their time and accumulated knowledge at every step of the way, and especially at the end when I needed them most. Finally, I should like belatedly to acknowledge my teachers at the Graduate Faculty of the New School for Social Research, especially the late Howard B. White and the late Hannah Arendt, for first introducing me to the study of things American.

In a sense, my children's characters have been formed, for better or worse, by the demands of this book. No doubt I neglected them at times when they needed me, but I would like to think they also learned patience, self-restraint, and independence from the hours I spent sequestered in my study. Such are the self-deceptions to which working mothers in particular are prone. And thanks more than I can say to my parents, Mary R. and Ralph J. Yarbrough, who, by the power of their example, have taught me the virtues of hard work and self-reliance. Extending the circle beyond my immediate family, it is a pleasure to acknowledge the encouragement and unfailing support of Erica Aronson and Ernest Stern, both of Chicago. They know all that they did, and they know how grateful I am.

But my greatest debt is to my husband, Richard E. Morgan, who back in the winter of 1991 encouraged me to return to this project, in the full knowledge that, for however long it took, we would have to give up lunching together. No *liebespiel* can adequately express all that I owe to him.

Introduction

This book began life more than a decade ago, when, as an NEH Bicentennial Fellow in 1984–85, I received a yearlong grant to investigate the moral foundations of the American Republic. At the time, I expected to contribute my small part to the ongoing liberal-republican debate by examining the competing claims of self-interest and virtue as the ground of our political morality. But gradually I came to realize that the dispute was really part of a larger and more important question: What kind of character must Americans as a people cultivate in order to ensure their freedom and happiness? In other words, the question is not simply about whether we *as a political community* are bound together by appeals to self-interest or to civic virtue, but how a free society might develop and nurture in its members the full range of human excellences both public and private, moral and intellectual, which will vindicate the honor and dignity of the American experiment.

Seen from this perspective, the first mistake of both liberals and so-called classical republicans was to try to explain the American character by looking only at its public philosophy without regard to the virtues that are fostered in our private and social lives. But, compounding the initial error, both sides tended to exaggerate the significance of their preferred principles. By emphasizing only the egoism of the natural rights doctrine announced in the Declaration of Independence and focusing exclusively on appeals to self-interest and institutional checks in the federal Constitution, at the same time that they ignored the role of the states in fostering the virtues necessary to self-government, the most eloquent defenders of the liberal view unduly narrowed the moral foundations of our public philosophy. All too often they gave the impression that the Founders sought to invent a "machine that would go of itself," spontaneously channeling men's selfish interests and passions in the direction of the public good, and no longer having to worry about the character of the people or their leaders.

If defenders of the liberal interpretation underestimated the importance of virtue to the Founders, supporters of the classical republican tradition erred in the opposite direction. Having started from the sensible premise that republican government, more than any other form of government, cannot survive without a virtuous people, they made virtue, rather than the protection of natural rights, the central principle of the Founding. Moreover, in focusing exclusively on virtue, they mistakenly concluded that virtue meant primarily civic virtue. Thus, they tended to exaggerate the importance of political life for the moral and intellectual perfection of the individual, wrongly attributing to the Founders Aristotle's observation that man is by nature a *zoon politikon*. But even for Aristotle, and certainly for the Founders, there are other, even more important, virtues that flourish outside the public realm. Benevolence, friendship, and wisdom, to name only the most important of these virtues, all presuppose a vibrant private sphere where individuals freely choose to exercise these virtues without being coerced by government. It is precisely the glory of modern *liberal* republicanism (as opposed to the ancient republics of Greece and Rome) that the perfection of the individual is not exclusively or even primarily bound up with political activity.

When, after a hiatus of several years, I returned to this project in earnest in 1991, I was able to draw on recent scholarship in political philosophy, history, and public policy to move beyond the original liberal-republican debate. Important new studies in political theory and history, especially Paul Rahe's magnificent three-volume survey *Republics: Ancient and Modern*, persuasively argued that modern republicanism was essentially a variation on the liberal project rather than a genuine alternative to it. Nor were the revisions all on the republican side; liberalism, too, came in for reexamination. Where only a decade before, liberalism was viewed exclusively as a philosophy of "possessive individualism," taking its bearings from the "low but solid" pursuit of individual self-interest and bereft of any genuine moral principles, a new generation of scholars, led by Nathan Tarcov, now argues that there are indeed such things as liberal virtues. Locke, in his educational writings, sought to instill them; so, too, in slightly different form, did Adam Smith and David Hume. Indeed, Scottish moral sense philosophy, like civic republicanism, turned out to be not so much an alternative to liberalism as liberalism in a different key.

Indeed, the big news in the nineties was that the concern for virtue was everywhere, not only in modern liberalism, civic republicanism, and Scottish moral sense philosophy but also in contemporary politics. When William J. Bennett's *Book of Virtues* appeared in 1993, it immediately soared to the top of the best-seller lists, and stayed there. A year later, *Newsweek*'s cover story was "The Politics of Virtue." Meanwhile, back in the academy, advocates of "civil society" and communitarians like Michael J. Sandel joined forces against "procedural" liberals, whose vision of the polity as a collection of "unencumbered selves" threatened to dissolve the community into an atomistic mass. At the same time, still other theorists, led by William Galston and Stephen G. Salkever, set to work at developing a composite of the virtues appropriate to a modern liberal republic, drawn selectively from Aristotle, Locke, Smith, Tocqueville, Mill, and Kant. In applying these virtues to contemporary politics, these theorists often relied on the findings of public policy analysts, who themselves, after a silence of several decades, were rediscovering the importance of character and virtue for the health of the polity. Indeed, with the publication of James Q. Wilson's *The Moral Sense* (1993), public policy and moral theory came together in a single powerful voice.

Thinking about these developments, it seemed to me that examining the political thought of the Founding or, more precisely, of one particular Founder with respect to the problem of character would be a fruitful place to pick up my inquiry. In contrast to the original liberal-republican debate, character has to do with the full range of moral and intellectual virtues, and not simply those that relate to public life. To think about character is to think about the duties we owe to ourselves, to others, to God, as well as to our country, and to put them in right relation to each other. For a people that elevates patriotism and love of country above all else will be very different from a people that prizes individual freedom and self-development, and both will differ from a people that places service to others or duty to God at the top of the moral hierarchy. Finally, to think about character is to think about the role of government in cultivating virtue and enforcing moral obligation. Here again, a people that uses the power of the laws to enforce its conception of the good life will be very different from a people that relies principally on the family, religion, education, and other social institutions to form the character of its citizens.

But even if, as in America, we look first to the family and society to cultivate the virtues we associate with happiness and the good life, government still has a role to play. Some virtues, especially justice, *must* be enforced by political power. Others, ranging from the lowly personal virtues of independence and self-reliance to the more estimable social and intellectual virtues, can either flourish or wither depending on whether government indirectly promotes or discourages them. This, in turn, raises still another question: How much can prudent statesmanship do to shape the character of a nation? In an era of globalization and interdependency, does it even make sense to talk about deliberate policy choices, or are we, as a people, subject to powerful transnational economic and social factors beyond our conscious control? Is there anything anyone can do about the collapse of the family, the decline of public education, the apathy and cynicism about our political institutions, the loss of vitality in our communities? Although character is sometimes regarded as a conservative issue, these questions suggest that the concern with the moral well-being of Americans transcends ideological or partisan divisions; liberals, no less than conservatives, have a stake in the outcome.

While political theory and public policy have done much to focus our attention on character and virtue in the broadest sense, almost nothing has been done to apply the most recent scholarship to our own political tradition, and especially to the political thought of the Founding. By focusing on the political thought of Thomas Jefferson, I hope to show that the concern with character has from the outset been on the minds of our greatest statesmen and that their insights still have much to teach us. Moreover, by looking at the virtues in the context of our own political tradition, I seek to correct the ahistorical tendencies that characterize even the best discussions of "liberal virtue" in the abstract.

Why Jefferson? First, because Jefferson believed that virtue was not merely useful but also natural to human beings and essential to their happiness. Second, because Jefferson thought broadly about the full range of virtues that would perfect the American character. The moral sense virtues of justice and benevolence; the "agrarian" virtues of industry, self-reliance, patience, moderation, and independence; the civic virtues of vigilance and spirited participation; the Epicurean virtues of wisdom and friendship; the secularized virtues of charity, toleration, and hope—all figure in his conception of character. Third, because Jefferson actively sought to pursue those social and economic policies and strengthen those institutions that would reinforce his moral vision. Family and friends, work and property, universal education and political participation, statesmanship and philosophical inquiry, all play a role in fostering the virtues necessary to the distinctively American view of happiness and freedom. Finally, because Jefferson is (in Merrill Peterson's apt metaphor) the mirror in which each generation finds reflected its most urgent moral and political concerns. Thus, at a time when questions of character are once again uppermost in the minds of many Americans, it is not surprising that supporters and detractors alike return to Jefferson, not only to revisit *his* character but also, as in the present study, to consider his vision for the American character.

Still, at the outset it must be acknowledged that there is something paradoxical about looking for guidance to the one Founder who, above all others, warned against the folly of looking to the past for wisdom and guidance. As Jefferson would probably be the first to admit, his generation failed spectacularly to solve the greatest moral dilemma of the day, with consequences that can still be felt today. But at least Jefferson knew that slavery was a blot upon the American character, since it so clearly contradicted the political morality he himself set forth in the Declaration. By contrast, Jefferson never understood what was so insidious about his "scientific" investigation of racial differences. Nor did he recognize that his private war against revealed religion and his insistence on a "wall of separation" between church and state might, if carried to extremes, have far-reaching and detrimental effects on our moral character. Conversely, some of the things Jefferson feared, such as manufacturing and banks or the political equality of women, have had a more benign effect on the American character than he supposed. But it is not just that Jefferson was mistaken about particular policies. His sunny view of human nature and his faith in progress often led him to slide over the tensions between the duties we owe to ourselves, to others, and to God. One suspects that Jefferson's easygoing morality masks a certain flatness of soul or, as Gordon Wood suggests, that it lacks a tragic dimension. And finally, although Jefferson *thought* more about the virtues Americans would need to cultivate than perhaps any other Founder, he did not, as Benjamin Franklin so charmingly did in his *Autobiography,* place his table of virtues before the public. Nor did he ever address the assembled leaders of the country and their wives on these matters, as James Wilson did in his famous Lectures on Law. Much of what we know about Jefferson's understanding of virtue and character comes from his private correspondence, or indirectly through his efforts to shape public policy, rather than from his public statements. Considering the opportunities he was given to speak out on these matters, Jefferson's attempt to shape the American character cannot be judged an unqualified success.

So, at the outset we are warned not to expect that Jefferson got everything right, or that, if we could but apply his teachings wholesale to our own day, all would be well. In some very important respects, ours is a better country today than in Jefferson's day—but not in every respect, and perhaps not even in the most decisive respects. For in place of Jefferson's belief in a permanent, unchanging human nature, which envisions a free people exercising their rights in such a way as to vindicate the honor and dignity of mankind, we stumble along without direction. Postmodern doubt about the very existence of moral and spiritual truths coupled with a reflexive tolerance (at least among elites) for almost any "lifestyle"; the triumph of materialism in the family and consumerism in education; the widespread and debilitating growth of an entitlement mentality and a refusal to accept the inevitable risks inherent in a free society—all contribute to a peculiarly American form of demoralization. By exploring in a serious and critical way Jefferson's understanding of the virtues that modern republicanism encourages and on which it depends, we may be in a better position to address some of the most pressing moral and political problems of our own day.

So far I have sketched out the genesis and the aim of this project. Let me now outline the direction of my argument. The book opens with a reconsideration of the principles Jefferson sets forth in the Declaration of Independence. At first sight this might seem a strange way to begin a book on character, since the Declaration speaks almost entirely of rights and has almost nothing to say about duty, save for the duty to throw off oppressive governments. The Declaration never mentions the word "virtue." But this is exactly the point: the Declaration sets forth what we as a political community hold most dear, namely, our equal rights. Thus, I begin by exploring where these rights come from, what they mean, and how our understanding of them shapes our character. My aim is to show that, properly understood, Jefferson's conception of rights encourages much that is admirable in the American character. Thus, in contrast to those who insist that our rights are historically conditioned, I argue that our most fundamental rights are grounded in a permanent and unchanging human nature. But against those who assert that all our natural rights can be traced back to the single Lockean desire for comfortable self-preservation, I maintain that the rights set forth in the Declaration are grounded in three distinct passions: the selfish desire for a secure and comfortable life, a healthy democratic pride in the capacity of human beings for moral and political self-government, and the social (unselfish) passion of benevolence. Turning from the ground of these rights to an examination of the rights themselves, I again take issue with those who argue that the right to the pursuit of happiness lacks any definite content and leaves each individual free to define what best contributes to his or her own happiness. Nor do I believe that in talking about happiness Jefferson means merely to reintroduce the Lockean right to property by the back door. At the same time, I also reject the suggestion that Jefferson here signals his agreement with the classical, either Aristotelian or Epicurean, conception of happiness. Instead, I argue that, for Jefferson, happiness is indeed bound up with the practice of virtue, but it is the modern social virtues, rather than the classical concern with intellectual virtue, or wisdom, that most contribute to our happiness. Thus, a proper understanding of the relationship of these passions and of the meaning and limitations of our rights is essential to the kind of character Jefferson envisioned. For in this complex rendering, interest tames

pride and pride ennobles interest, while at the same time the concern for others enlarges our self-interest, and interest restrains the
desire to do good within reasonable bounds. Yet precisely because
the relation between these rights is so complex, Jefferson should
have taken greater pains to help Americans understand their true
meaning. Partly because he failed to do so, future generations have
strayed even further from the original conception of rights outlined
in the Declaration. The contemporary preoccupation with rights as
entitlements or procedural safeguards, unrestrained by any reference to nature as both the source and the limitation of these rights,
is now a distinctive aspect of our national character, but it is not
what Jefferson intended. Indeed, in many ways the prevailing conceptions of rights work against the Jeffersonian virtues by undermining self-reliance and independence and by sapping our pride in
our capacity for self-government.

Turning from the public principles that shape our character,
chapter 2 continues the exploration of human nature begun in
chapter 1, here focusing on the role of the moral sense in making
known our duties and obligations to others. In particular I explore
the innate moral sentiments that give rise to the distinctive virtues
of justice and benevolence. I argue that the virtues sketched in
chapter 2 represent the peak of human excellence for Jefferson,
since he ranks the social virtues that teach us our duties to others
and, above all, benevolence, higher than the moral and intellectual
virtues that perfect us as individuals. I look first at how these
virtues are to be inculcated, since the mere existence of the moral
sense is no guarantee that moral impulses leading to justice and
benevolence will triumph over the more powerful selfish passions,
especially when these latter combine forces with calculating reason. For Jefferson, the lessons of justice and benevolence begin in
the family, where these innate moral sentiments are strengthened
through habit and example. But is there also a place for government in fostering these virtues? The answer here is mixed. In the
case of benevolence the answer is emphatically no. Precisely because benevolence stands at the top of the moral hierarchy, liberal
governments have no business enforcing this virtue. The perfection
of the moral character must always be an act of free will. By contrast, justice, understood as the equal protection of rights, is the
virtue that preserves, rather than perfects, us in our relations with

others. Unlike benevolence, justice must be enforced by government, since this is the reason individuals enter civil society in the first place.

Chapter 3 moves from a consideration of the "most estimable" social virtues to a discussion of "agrarian virtue" and, more broadly, the way in which work, property, and the economic system shape our moral character. I begin by exploring what, specifically, Jefferson means by agrarian virtue and then consider how the virtues that grow out of the cultivation of the land, and that focus on the independence and self-sufficiency of the individual, are related to the more noble social virtues recommended by the moral sense. I then examine the effect of slavery, as well as the growing commercialization of agriculture, on agrarian virtue and the American character. In the second section, I consider Jefferson's opposition to Hamilton's economic program. Although Hamilton clearly understood the emerging economic order better than Jefferson, Jefferson's instinctive distrust of "licentious commerce" anticipates many of the vices to which an advanced capitalist society is prone. As this section makes clear, especially in a liberal republic where citizens spend most of their time at work rather than participating in politics, economic matters can never be divorced from moral considerations. The chapter concludes with a discussion of the particular virtues that private property promotes: industry, hospitality, liberality, but above all justice, understood as the equal right of all the fruits of their labor.

Chapter 4 takes up civic virtue and statesmanship, or the duties we, as members of the political community, owe to our country. While civic virtue no longer represents, as it did for the classical republicans, the *akmē* of human perfection, it still stands high on Jefferson's list of virtues. For more than any other Founder, Jefferson was convinced that republican government depends for its preservation not merely on institutional arrangements but also on a certain kind of spirit in the people. I explore what precisely Jefferson means by this "spirit" and consider his various proposals for keeping it alive. While this "spiritedness" has often been condemned as violent and destructive, I argue that when restrained by prudent statesmanship and properly channeled into political organizations where citizens have a genuine interest in the issues, civic spirit does indeed act as a positive force in preserving republican self-government. At the same time, however, I recognize that Jefferson's ambivalence toward public service, especially at the highest levels, undermines the life of the statesman and thus makes the cultivation of civic virtue more problematic.

Chapter 5 concludes with a consideration of the moral duties we owe to ourselves, the role of the intellectual virtues in developing the American character, friendship, and the duties we owe to God. As such, it goes beyond the discussion of the duties we owe to ourselves and the "agrarian" virtues cataloged in chapter 3. Since it is in the elaboration of the moral duties we owe to ourselves that Jefferson finds the ancient moralists most compelling, I first take up the Epicurean virtues of temperance, fortitude, justice, and prudence. I then consider the place of intellectual virtue or wisdom in the perfection of the American character and explore the tension between Jefferson's embrace of Epicurean philosophy and his endorsement of the "sublime" morality recommended by the Gospels. From there, I consider how different kinds of friendships, especially political and philosophic friendships but also sentimental friendships, perfect the moral and intellectual character. Here again I emphasize the tension between Jefferson's endorsement of a life of "active utility," or doing good to others, and his own preference for the life of a private man, pursuing the pleasures and cultivating the virtues of wisdom and friendship. In the penultimate section, I take up the duties we owe to God and argue that here, too, Jefferson glosses over the tension between the different branches of morality by attempting to reduce them all to the obligations we owe to others. In place of piety, the duties we owe to God are tolerance and charity toward others. Still, Jefferson's more limited conception of tolerance is superior to our contemporary understanding because it does not extend toleration to moral matters or to actions Jefferson believes we know to be wrong. Finally, I conclude with a brief reflection on that most Jeffersonian and, indeed, American, of virtues, hope. Because Jefferson's hopes are completely centered on the pursuit of happiness in this world, they very much depend on the renewal of the American character and a restoration of those virtues that both preserve and perfect the republican experiment.

Chapter One

The Declaration and
the American Character

Americans are a notoriously rights-loving people, and no Founder is more closely identified with this aspect of the American character than Thomas Jefferson. As the celebrated author of the Declaration of Independence, Jefferson immortalized the distinctively American trilogy of rights, declaring the rights to life, liberty, and the pursuit of happiness to be the sole objects of legitimate government. And throughout his political career and into his long retirement, he remained a devoted and outspoken champion of "the rights of man." Reflecting on the significance of the Declaration near the end of his life, Jefferson concluded that the principles contained therein embodied the very "soul of our country."[1]

How, precisely, does the Declaration's commitment to natural rights shape the American character? Does the belief that all human beings are endowed with equal natural rights encourage us to treat others with greater justice and humanity? Or does it push us toward our own private and hedonistic conceptions of the good? What does it mean that we as a nation tend to view moral questions overwhelmingly in terms of individual rights and to speak so sparingly of our duties? Does the primacy of rights lead to proud self-assertion or instead foster dependency and a sense of entitlement? Is the contemporary preoccupation with "rights talk"[2] the inevitable outgrowth of Jefferson's political philosophy, as certain conservative critics have from the outset supposed,[3] or a corruption of it?

To answer these questions, it is necessary first to consider what Jefferson understands by inalienable rights. To assert that rights are inalienable means that they are so firmly rooted in our nature that

1

we can never willingly give them up. What is it, then, in human nature that serves as the ground of these rights: is it reason or the passions, and if the passions, is it exclusively the selfish passions, as
Locke argues, or, as the Scots maintain, some combination of the
selfish and the social passions? Jefferson's view of human nature
will, in turn, influence what he means by the rights to life, liberty,
and the pursuit of happiness.

For much of our history, it has been taken for granted that the
Declaration is merely a restatement of Lockean liberalism.[4] Except
for the inconsequential substitution of the pursuit of happiness for
property, so this interpretation goes, Jefferson merely echoes the argument of the *Second Treatise*. In this view, the rights to life, liberty,
and property are all reducible to one single passion: the desire for
a secure and comfortable life. Because this is what humans beings
desire most, and what they can never voluntarily surrender, they
are said to have an inalienable right to preserve and secure this object. Still, where individuals are free to act on their impulses, they
tend to invade each other's rights. Thus, men must consult with
reason, which is "the law of nature," to figure out how they can
best secure what they most desire. Reason directs them to establish
a government to ensure that each individual respects the same
rights in others as he claims for himself. Seen from a political perspective, this is supposedly the great realism of Lockean liberalism,
for grounding rights on this single selfish passion marries rights to
self-interest and thereby increases the odds that a government devoted to this end will succeed.

Yet when viewed from the moral perspective, this "selfish system" becomes more problematic. For even if we grant that mutual
recognition of rights bestows upon what were initially purely selfish claims a certain "moral quality,"[5] such reciprocity never rises
above the level of enlightened self-interest. "I agree to respect your
rights because I want you to respect mine." While this principle can
usually be relied upon, it does not work in those cases where individuals conclude that respecting the rights of others would somehow endanger their own. This, of course, was the great moral
dilemma posed by slavery.[6] In 1776, the issue was not whether to
introduce slavery but what to do about an institution that already
existed, the abolition of which Southerners believed would
threaten the enjoyment of their own rights. As Locke observed, we

are bound to respect the rights of others only when our own preservation is not at stake.[7] If, however, the rights in the Declaration rest on no higher moral principle, does it make sense to speak of the "soul" of America, or is it more accurate to mourn its "lost soul"?[8]

Alternatively, in talking about Jefferson and formation of the American character, we might reject Locke's influence on the Founders generally and minimize the significance of rights altogether in favor of republican virtue.[9] Or we might look to the Scottish school, to Kames and Hutcheson, Smith and Hume, to discover, in the more generous passions, a less selfish foundation for moral action. But how this would affect our interpretation of rights is debatable. Certainly it would not, as Garry Wills has argued, mean that government must actively promote benevolence and the common good at the expense of liberty and individual rights.[10] The rights and duties of benevolence do indeed stand at the top of the Scottish moral hierarchy, but precisely for this reason a liberal republic cannot compel individuals to exercise them.

How, then, should we understand rights in relation to the American character? In what follows, I shall argue that the way in which Jefferson understands the trilogy of rights in the Declaration is something of a hybrid, for while the rights are in large part reducible to the selfish passions, they are not *exclusively* rooted in them. Jefferson's political psychology departs from the orthodox Lockean account in three important respects. First, Jefferson, following the Scots, starts with a more amiable view of human nature, one in which self-interest and moral duty are brought into closer alignment through the operation of an innate moral sense. Or, as he famously puts it, no man has a "natural right in opposition to his social duties."[11] Second, Jefferson rejects the Lockean hierarchy of the passions, which elevates the desire for comfortable self-preservation as the single source of all our rights.[12] But he does so partly in the name of another *selfish* passion, pride in the capacity for self-government, which also serves as the ground for our right to liberty. In this sense, Jefferson's conception of rights departs from the *Second Treatise* by taking a more expansive view of self-love, but it follows Locke in retaining the selfish passions as an important source of our rights. Third, Jefferson, in contrast to Locke and again following the Scottish school, does not ground all of our rights on the selfish passions. As Jefferson understands it, the right of each individual to pursue happiness does not arise solely from the selfish part of our constitution; it is also suggested to us by the generous desire to do good to others, or what the Scots called benevolence. Thus, the conception of rights in the Declaration is not reducible to the Lockean desire for comfortable self-preservation, but seeks to combine two different, and to some extent competing, selfish passions on the one hand with benevolence on the other.

If Jefferson's conception of human nature departs from the orthodox Lockean view, it would follow that his understanding of rights would also differ to some extent. And it does, though not in the way that some scholars suppose. The appeal to pride in the capacity for self-government suggests a view of liberty that is more "positive," or republican, than classical liberalism. Similarly, the appeal to the social as well as selfish passions points to a different conception of happiness. Whereas Locke in the *Essay on Human Understanding* links happiness with the desire to avoid pain and seek pleasure, Jefferson, while nowhere denying that happiness is bound up with pleasure (and, indeed, later on affirming it), also insists that happiness is allied with virtue. And, in keeping with his view of human nature, the virtues Jefferson admires are more generous and benevolent.

The Jeffersonian State of Nature: Moral Implications

It is likely that Jefferson, like countless other readers of the *Second Treatise*, misunderstood Locke's true teaching about human nature and attributed to him the more benign view of Thomas Hooker, whom Locke so frequently quotes. Locke, after all, had gone out of his way to give the impression that he shared Hooker's view of men as naturally inclined by bonds of affection to seek the "communion and fellowship" of others.[13] Moreover, the view of man as a social animal would have accorded with the position of the Scottish moral sense philosopher Henry Home, Lord Kames, whose writings Jefferson owned and greatly admired.[14] At an early age, Jefferson had copied into his *Commonplace Book* the following observation from Kames's tract on property: "Man, by his nature is fitted for society, and society by it's [*sic*] conveniences is fitted for man."[15]

Jefferson, too, begins with the assumption that human beings are naturally social. "We consider society as one of the natural wants with which man has been created."[16] By this Jefferson does not mean that human beings always act in ways that affirm their social nature; he seems to accept Kames' observation that primitive people are capable of treating each other with great brutality and cruelty. Rather, he means that as human beings gradually develop the capacity to recognize and act on their innate moral feelings, they can live together without law and government, guided only by their moral sense. Sometimes Jefferson offers the American Indians as empirical confirmation of the "real" as opposed to the hypothetical state of nature: "Our Indians are evidently in that state of nature which has passed the association of a single family; and not yet submitted to the authority of positive laws, or of any acknowledged magistrate. Every man, with them, is perfectly free to follow his inclinations."[17] In his most optimistic moments, Jefferson apparently considers these inclinations benign (and, when belligerent, controllable without resort to government), for on at least one occasion he wonders whether such a prepolitical society may not be the *best* condition for human beings.[18]

At other times, Jefferson remains more cautious. Although he believes that the Benevolent Creator who has destined men for society has at the same time endowed every individual with the capacity to recognize his moral obligations to others, he does not conclude from this that most people are capable of acting spontaneously on the dictates of the moral law. The generous affections, by themselves, are no match for the more selfish passions. Here too, the Indians' treatment of their women provides empirical evidence. Left to the promptings of the moral sense alone, Indian men exert their superior force to impose an "unjust drudgery" on their women.[19] Without "civilization" to enforce the equal rights of those who are physically weaker, natural societies tend to slide into "barbarism." From this perspective, it is a question of whether no government or too much government is the greater *evil*.

But if human beings need government to compel the triumph of sociality, how does Jefferson's view of human nature differ from Locke's suggestion that we are naturally selfish? If sociability does not lead individuals to respect the rights of others or make them better, what good is it? Jefferson's argument differs from Locke's in two important respects. First, although the moral sense by itself is weak, the fact that it exists at all means that the task of government can be limited to reinforcing the more generous social impulses that are already present in some inchoate form within human nature. And for Jefferson this will require, even by the standards of Lockean liberalism, only a modest role for government in securing rights.[20] Sociability provides the moral grounding for Jefferson's confidence in the capacity of the people for self-government. Second, and closely related, sociability means that our rights and duties are neither reducible to the selfish passions, even the selfish passions broadly construed, nor merely conventional, the result of utilitarian calculation. Generosity, compassion, and benevolence are also part of our moral constitution.[21] Thus, while Jefferson starts from self-love, he moves beyond it to the social affections, hoping in this way to bridge the gap between rights and right.

One might object that self-interest and moral obligation often pull in opposite directions, and Jefferson himself admits this at times.[22] But on the whole he believes that republican institutions, universal education, and an agrarian economy will improve, if not actually transform, human nature and so minimize the tension between the two. "Our interests soundly calculated, will ever be inseparable from our moral duties."[23] By this, he does not mean the Lockean argument that our moral duties to others can be rationally deduced from our selfish interests alone, but, on the contrary, that our deepest interests, if correctly understood and carefully cultivated in the proper republican environment, can spontaneously approach our genuine moral obligations. In short, Jefferson's assertion that human beings are social points to a less egocentric view of human nature than that suggested by Locke. Jefferson's political psychology seeks to combine the realism of an expanded self-interest with the moral dignity of benevolence and, in so doing, subtly transforms Locke's understanding of the liberal virtues.[24] Where Locke emphasizes those virtues that promote peaceful acquisition and the accumulation of wealth, Jefferson's understanding of rights and his treatment of virtue tend to be more spirited and more philanthropic.

The Right to Life

If Jefferson does not make the desire for self-preservation, especially the softer Lockean desire for *comfortable* self-preservation, the sole foundation of all our rights, he nevertheless accords it a special prominence. As the first of our inalienable rights, the right to life, or more precisely the right to preserve life,[25] is the law of our nature. In the Declaration, Jefferson deliberately obscures whether our right comes directly from nature or whether it is the gift of God[26]; nor does he identify the passion or desire upon which this right is based. But elsewhere he makes it clear that the ground of this right is our natural desire for self-preservation. How strong is this passion?

In A Bill for Proportioning Crimes and Punishments, Jefferson observes that self-preservation is not always the most powerful of the passions. Parental love is "the strongest affection known . . . greater than even that of self-preservation."[27] In times of great national emergency, moreover, spirited self-assertion or pride can also vitiate the concern with self-preservation, as the pledge that concludes the Declaration makes clear. Less admirably, darker passions, such as hatred and revenge, may on other occasions overpower the rational pursuit of our self-preservation. Of English foreign policy in 1786, Jefferson observes ruefully that "interest is not the strongest passion."[28] But however mighty these other passions may prove in particular circumstances, they are limited in their applicability, and none but pride, and only then if it is domesticated and directed toward the capacity of individuals for self-government, can plausibly give rise to reciprocal claims on which rights may rest.

Thus, although the desire for self-preservation is not always and in every circumstance the most powerful passion, Jefferson recognizes that it is usually so. Accordingly, the right to life takes precedence over our moral obligations to others. As if to underscore the unevenness of the conflict, Jefferson develops this point in the very document where he introduces the phrase "moral law of our nature." In the Opinion on the French Treaties, Jefferson acknowledges that "when performance of an obligation becomes self-destructive to the party, the law of self-preservation overrules the laws of obligation to others."[29] The best he can do is to interpret this exception to the moral law narrowly. Although we are not obliged to perform a duty that will result in our own destruction, we "will never read there the permission to annul [our] obligations for a time or forever, whenever they become dangerous, useless, or disagreeable; certainly not when merely useless or disagreeable. . . . Yet the danger must be imminent, and the degree great."[30] Nevertheless, even this rule of interpretation proves more porous than it at first appears. For all individuals and nations must judge for themselves when these obligations become self-destructive. As a last resort, Jefferson reminds us that we must all answer to "the tribunal of our consciences," but he leaves unresolved whether conscience or what he elsewhere calls the moral sense is sufficiently powerful by itself to override the more selfish and subjective determinations of when a danger is "great, inevitable, and imminent."

The question, therefore, is what in Jefferson's understanding of human nature might offset the power of self-interest to eclipse all other moral considerations. We are not talking now about the grave and immediate danger to life, for Jefferson recognizes that in such circumstances the right to life almost always takes primacy. What we mean here is the tendency to construe every limitation on our liberty as a dire threat to our self-preservation. As Herbert J. Storing has pointed out, the tendency of the modern natural rights doctrine, insofar as it is rooted exclusively in the selfish passions, is "for justice to be reduced to self-preservation, and for self-preservation to be defined as self-interest, and for self-interest to be defined as what is convenient and achievable."[31] Indeed, Jefferson himself in his letter to John Holmes provides unwitting testimony to this tendency to view indirect and distant threats to one's own rights as imminent and life-threatening. When Jefferson, commenting on how the Missouri Compromise might affect emancipation efforts in Virginia, makes his famous observation, "We have the wolf by the ears, and we can neither hold him nor safely let him go. Justice is in the one scale and self-preservation in the other,"[32] he does not mean only that emancipation in some cases posed an immediate and grave danger to the lives of Virginia slaveholders. As the rest of the letter makes clear, he also means that Virginians would not support emancipation unless they could first significantly reduce the number of slaves in Virginia by allowing their owners to take them *as slaves* into the newly developing territories.

Virginians would be persuaded to end the "moral abomination" of slavery when they were convinced it was not only safe but also in their interest to do so.

If, however, Jefferson's understanding of rights so far seems vulnerable to the kind of criticism both Jaffa and Storing have leveled against the Lockean conception of natural rights, his understanding of both liberty and the pursuit of happiness may each, in their own way, help to mitigate the egoism these critics properly deplore.

The Right to Liberty

For Jefferson liberty is the natural condition of human life. "The God who gave us life, gave us liberty at the same time: the hand of force may destroy, but it cannot disjoin them."[33] Liberty in the first instance is a corollary of the natural right to life; it refers to the right of each individual to defend himself against the willful and destructive passions of others.[34] And once civil society is established, liberty includes the right to be free from governmental encroachments on both persons and property as well. But for Jefferson, the natural right to liberty includes much more than the absence of physical restraint.

The purpose of civil society is to preserve the broadest possible sphere of "rightful liberty" to each individual, requiring only that each individual respect the equal rights of others.[35] Thus, the natural right to liberty extends to the full range of activities that individuals may innocently pursue in cultivating their natural faculties and sensibilities.[36] It includes those rights connected with self-development, such as the "rights of thinking and publishing our thoughts by speaking and writing," as well as "the right of personal freedom"[37] and freedom of conscience. In addition, it encourages personal enrichment by recognizing the right to immigrate, to trade freely, to choose a vocation, and to labor for a livelihood.[38]

The natural right to liberty raises two questions that bear particularly on the American character. First, does Jefferson mean the phrase "all men" to apply to blacks, and, if so, what obligations does this lay on whites? As the original draft of the Declaration makes clear, Jefferson considers the slaves to be men, and he denounces the king for denying them their rights to life and liberty. Although these passages were omitted from the final draft, Jefferson, along with most of the signers, repeatedly appealed to the Declaration's principles to condemn the institution of slavery and to lay the ground for its eventual extinction.

But if the principles of the Declaration set in motion the forces that would ultimately abolish slavery, these same principles did not require Americans to extend the rights of full citizenship to emancipated blacks. That all men are created equal and are endowed with certain inalienable rights does not mean that everyone has an equal right to become a member of a particular polity. All that the Declaration requires is that blacks be restored to their natural liberty to form themselves into a distinct people. They do not have the right to join an existing polity unless that people chooses to admit them.[39] Thus, expatriation is consistent with the Declaration's principles, but so, too, are the Fourteenth and Fifteenth Amendments.

The second question is: Does Jefferson's enlarged conception of liberty, especially when taken in conjunction with his deliberate exclusion of property as a natural right, lay the ground for the steady expansion of rights, first in economic matters and then on moral issues, and the use of a vastly more activist government to secure them? While this interpretation first gained force during the Progressive Era,[40] there are two problems with it. First, the natural right to liberty, as Jefferson understands it, applies only to the exercise of one's own faculties to satisfy one's own needs; it does not (except in unusual circumstances, as, for instance, when laborers are denied their fundamental right to labor for a living) extend to a claim on the faculties and property of others.[41] To argue as the Progressives do that government ought to redistribute wealth in order to promote greater socioeconomic equality is to misunderstand the most powerful impulses that lead individuals to form civil societies in the first place. What men seek before everything else is "the *guarantee* to every one of his industry and the fruits acquired by it."[42]

Thus, although Jefferson declines to elevate property to an inalienable natural right, his understanding of the connection between liberty and property is not fundamentally different from Locke's and appears to be rooted in the same desire for a secure and comfortable life. Consequently, it is only those rights that conform to this passion that can be justified. As Eva T. H. Brann has argued, these rights "would, in general, be the rights which are the conditions of possibility of gaining goods rather than those which give access to goods directly."[43] This is Jefferson's point exactly, as his observations on the limited role of government in the First Inaugural make clear: "A wise and frugal government which shall restrain men from injuring one another, shall leave them otherwise free to regulate their own pursuits of industry and improvement, and shall not take from the mouth of labor the bread it has earned."[44]

The second problem relates to the more recent debate over what might be called "lifestyle" questions. Here again, in contrast to contemporary liberals, who argue that human beings are autonomous and ought to be given the broadest possible freedom in moral matters as long as they do not harm anyone else, Jefferson believes that all our rights are founded on an unchanging and universal conception of human nature. And nature establishes certain limits to human freedom. Thus, the natural right to liberty does not, for example, extend to what are today called the "privacy" issues, such as homosexuality, or to what Walter Berns has called "the right to think, speak, and print unguided by moral principle."[45] Indeed, as Jefferson understands it, the natural right to liberty does not even require equal civil rights for women. This does not mean that political societies may not extend certain civil rights to their citizens beyond the natural rights Jefferson deduces from the Declaration, but these rights should accord with "the law of nature and nature's God."

If, in these important respects, Jefferson's understanding of liberty so far tracks Locke's argument, there is one important way in which it departs from him. To secure the rights of the people, Jefferson seeks, far more than Locke, to restrict the powers of government[46] and, as a further safeguard, to organize citizens in local associations to keep a jealous eye on their elected representatives. This expansion of liberty to include the "natural right of self-government" after civil society has been established is one of the distinctive features of Jefferson's conception of rights and raises the question of how we are to interpret it. Is the natural right of self-government grounded exclusively in the desire for a comfortable life, which is the source of so many of our private liberties, or is it at least partly rooted in some other passion?

At first sight, the right to self-government does seem to be an extension of the desire for comfortable self-preservation: one reason the people insist on retaining the right of self-government is because they cannot always trust their elected representatives to protect their rights. According to this view, the right of self-government is nothing more than a means of securing our selfish interests. But there is a second and more positive, or "republican," aspect to Jefferson's expansion of liberty to include the right of self-government. Men seek to govern themselves not simply because it promotes their interest but because it gratifies their pride and vindicates their "sacred honor."[47] Jefferson's expanded conception of liberty seems at least partly to be grounded in pride and its associated passions, the love of honor, ambition, and self-assertion, which attend the spirited, as opposed to the appetitive, dimension of human nature. Moreover, in contrast to the classical liberalism of Hobbes and Locke, Jefferson seeks to channel these more spirited passions not only into economic but into political activity. Indeed, one of the more striking aspects of Jefferson's understanding of character is the extent to which he views spiritedness in distinctively political terms. While spiritedness may be directed toward the cultivation of the land or the taming of the wilderness, it manifests itself most fully in the proud determination to live freely under laws that citizens have established for themselves. For this reason, Jefferson will later define a republic solely by whether it reserves to the people some opportunity to exercise their natural right of self-government on those matters which are "nearest and most interesting" to them.[48]

That the natural right to liberty is not simply reducible to the acquisitive desires (liberty is not simply the freedom to grow as rich as we can) is also clear from Jefferson's repeated warnings that the rising tide of prosperity would sap the springs of republican virtue. Long before Alexis de Tocqueville warned of the danger of excessive materialism and its corrosive effects on civic life, Jefferson worried that the American preoccupation with making money would drain the public realm of its vital spirit and energy. Thus, although he would vigorously defend the right to acquire and possess private property, unrestrained acquisitiveness, especially when it joined forces with modern commercial institutions, remains far more problematic for him than for Locke.

But what does it mean for Jefferson that there are two passions, each linked to a distinct and somewhat competing element in human nature, which ground the natural right to liberty? Does pride act as a counterweight to the desire for comfortable self-preservation, inspiring citizens to cherish their freedom and capacity for self-government, or does it encourage people to assert themselves even more vigorously on behalf of their selfish and narrow interests? Pride is a dangerous passion. Where it is not restrained, as in the case of many Southern slaveholders, it can play a destructive role, emboldening them to "trample" on the rights of their slaves. But this is not the whole story. As we shall see in chapter 4, Jefferson believes that a properly cultivated pride exercises a generally positive effect on the American character. The proud determination of citizens to govern themselves rightly serves to temper the otherwise private and acquisitive aspects of liberty and generally dignifies the life of free men. To use the words of Harvey C. Mansfield, Jr., in a different context, by grounding liberty on these two irreducible passions, Jefferson "tempers our pride with our interests, yet ennobles our interests by combining them with pride."[49]

And the Pursuit of Happiness

The pursuit of happiness remains the most elusive of the rights announced in the Declaration. Does Jefferson mean basically to reaffirm the Lockean right to property using other language,[50] and if so, is this substitution an improvement upon the original? In the opinion of at least one scholar, if this is what he intended, the right to property might have been preferable, since the pursuit of happiness introduces an element of radical subjectivity into the heart of the Declaration's principles. In place of the solid Lockean right to acquire property through labor, Americans today commonly understand the term to mean the Veblenian passion for consumption, fun, and self-actualization.[51] Or perhaps Jefferson means to signal his agreement with the Locke of the *Essay on Human Understanding*, where Locke develops at length the notion of the "pursuit of happiness."[52] If this is so, what is the connection between Locke's understanding of happiness as the enjoyment of pleasure without uneasiness and his argument in the *Second Treatise* that the purpose of government is to protect property? Does happiness mean "the pursuit, not of material advantages, but of the life of reason and human nature,"[53] or does it lay the ground for a materialistic hedonism?[54]

At the same time, other scholars have ventured beyond Locke to discover in the phrase a far grander vision "of man and of man's *telos*."[55] But what precisely is this vision? Does it indicate a return to the classical, i.e., Aristotelian, conception of happiness,[56] or does it point to a more modern understanding?[57] Finally, what does it matter how Jefferson understood happiness, if we understand the term to mean something different? Nothing in the Declaration denies us the right to pursue happiness as we understand it.

Here it may be useful to recall the warning of philosophers from Plato and Aristotle through Locke and the Scottish school that if we misunderstand what it is that makes us truly happy, our pursuit will be largely in vain.[58] Jefferson's understanding of happiness has much to teach a generation of Americans taught to believe that happiness can be found primarily in the gratification of bodily and material desires, or that it is relative and subjective. For while Jefferson acknowledges the variety of human talents, inclinations, and situations, which inevitably lead individuals to pursue different objects, he also insists that the core of happiness is permanent and universal: there can be no genuine happiness without virtue. "The order of nature is that individual happiness shall be inseparable from the practice of virtue."[59]

At the same time, however, Jefferson's conception of happiness is not simply moralistic. No one who lived and entertained as well as he did could fail to appreciate the material prerequisites of the good life. But he never made the mistake of believing that wealth, power, good birth, or even bodily well-being could, by themselves, without the cultivation of virtue, bring true happiness. For Jefferson, the "greatest happiness" requires what Aristotle calls virtue and equipment; it depends on "good conscience, good health, occupation, and freedom in all just pursuits."[60]

Nevertheless, the attempt to move beyond this general formulation raises several difficulties. First, Jefferson never systematically explores what he means by happiness in general or the pursuit of happiness in particular. Nearly all of his comments about happiness occur in private correspondence addressed to a wide variety of family, friends, acquaintances, and even strangers, in which the meaning of happiness is often casually treated. And, of particular significance in trying to understand the meaning of the pursuit of happiness in the Declaration, before 1785 even these sources are limited.[61] Second, and closely related to this last point, although Jefferson consistently maintains that virtue is the essential component of happiness, his conception of virtue undergoes a major change, from an early classical emphasis on individual excellence to be achieved through stoic resignation and control of the passions, to a later Scottish and Christian emphasis on the social virtues, especially benevolence. Thus, even if Jefferson means to link the pursuit of happiness with the practice of virtue when he substitutes this right for property in the Declaration, it is difficult to know precisely which virtues he has in mind in 1776.[62]

Third, even if these matters can be explained, if not systematically at least plausibly, by reference to Jefferson's writings, there remains the question of how the *right* to pursue happiness can be read as implying moral *duties* either to ourselves or to others. In a document justly celebrated as a declaration of *rights*, and one that never mentions virtue, this reading of the pursuit of happiness is far from obvious.

Fourth, and finally, Jefferson insists that the purpose of the Declaration is not "to find out new principles or new arguments, never before thought of, not merely to say things which had never been said before." Is there any evidence that Americans in Jefferson's time understood the pursuit of happiness in this way? Does the equation of happiness with virtue express what Jefferson believes to be the "common sense of the subject"?[63]

Beginning with the last objection, it should be noted that although the connection between virtue and happiness may strike the modern reader as far-fetched, it was very much a part of the eighteenth-century English heritage shared by Americans. As Herbert Lawrence Ganter has argued: "In the literature of eighteenth century England, the discussion about 'virtue' and 'vice,' and their bearing upon human happiness, occupies about the same relative position in the thought of the time as that accorded to capital and labor, individualism and collectivism, in our day. Every work on moral philosophy—and at that time, government and political economy were still branches of moral philosophy—dwells upon this problem of human happiness."[64]   And Howard Mumford Jones, in his classic study of the term, makes the same point, only more broadly. It was not only eighteenth-century Englishmen and Americans who equated happiness with "a knowledge of moral duties," but the entire Western tradition beginning with the ancient Greek and Roman moralists.[65]

It is not surprising, therefore, that the equation of happiness with virtue had seeped into the Virginia culture. Indeed, in the years immediately preceding the Declaration, Jefferson could read a number of essays on such topics as "The Pursuit after Happiness," "Happiness," "Essay on Happiness," and "The Character of a Happy Life," all published in the *Virginia Gazette*.[66] Although most of these essays tend to emphasize the Christian argument that true happiness can never be achieved in this world, all of them equate happiness with the practice of virtue.

If, however, in maintaining that "without virtue, happiness cannot be,"[67] Jefferson is merely echoing the prevailing beliefs and "harmonizing sentiments" of his day, we still need to know which virtues Jefferson associates with happiness, and how this might help us better to understand the meaning of our rights. In his earliest years, Jefferson's conception of happiness seems to have been strongly influenced by the ancient moralists, especially Cicero and the Stoics. Jefferson's letter to John Page, written in 1763 when he was twenty, contains perhaps the fullest statement of his youthful philosophy. Although we can never expect perfect happiness in this world, we can nevertheless approach it by "a perfect resignation to the Divine Will, to consider that whatever does happen, must happen, and that by our uneasiness, we cannot prevent the blow before it does fall, but we may add to its force after it has fallen."[68] Nothing could be further from the Lockean pursuit of happiness as the perpetual flight from the "uneasiness of desire" than Jefferson's stoic acceptance of life's calamities and misfortunes.

Jefferson's *Literary Bible*, which was compiled during his youth and early adulthood, suggests a similar interest in the ancient moralists and poets. By far the greatest number of abstracts are from Cicero's *Tusculan Disputations*, in which the Roman statesman observes that wisdom is the highest virtue; that human beings naturally incline toward virtue and happiness; that virtue can be attained only through discipline and control of the passions; and that it is our duty to strive for such self-mastery.[69]

That we have duties not just to ourselves but to our country is the theme of several other entries. Quoting from Pope's translation of Homer, Jefferson apparently identifies with the noble disdain for death in the service of one's country.[70] Other entries also hint at a certain aristocratic pride in good birth that enables noblemen to overcome base passions and fears. "Eternal honor" and "well-deserved glory" are the just rewards for rising above "vulgar indolence" and a mere animal existence.[71] Finally, an abstract from Horace on the joys of the pastoral life suggests a tension that runs throughout Jefferson's thought between the private and the public life as the source of greater happiness: "Happy the man who . . . keeps away from the Forum, and the proud threshold of the powers that be."[72]

Despite the considerable sway these ancient moralists continued to exercise over Jefferson throughout his life, it would be a mistake to try to reconstruct the meaning of the pursuit of happiness based exclusively on abstracts from the his several commonplace books. Jefferson began to record selections when he was still an adolescent in school, continued during his college years and had essentially completed the books by the time he married in 1772.[73] Although it makes sense to argue, as Gilbert Chinard does, that Jefferson agreed with the selections he included, the obverse does not hold up. As Douglas Wilson has observed, "It will not follow that . . . whatever is not included is rejected."[74]

During these years, Jefferson read widely and began to acquire books for what was to be the first, and then the second, of his three great libraries. A letter in 1771 to his future brother-in-law, Robert Skipwith, in response to the latter's request for assistance in compiling a library, sheds considerable light on the range of Jefferson's reading. In particular, it suggests that Jefferson was already familiar with the main outlines of Scottish moral philosophy, for among his recommendations are Thomas Reid on the human mind, Adam Smith's theory of moral sentiments, and Lord Kames on natural religion.[75] That Jefferson would have included books he had not read is unlikely. Indeed, E. Millicent Sowerby has argued that the copy of Kames's *Natural Religion* probably dates back to the first, or Shadwell, library (most of which was destroyed by fire in 1770) because it contains a marginal notation by Jefferson "in an early hand" commenting favorably on one aspect of Kames's treatment of the moral sense.[76] Thus, it is likely that Jefferson was already familiar with Scottish moral sense philosophy when he wrote the Declaration. Moreover, in contrast to the selections in the *Literary Bible*, which emphasize the intellectual virtues, the letter to Skipwith offers as examples of virtue the moral virtues of charity and gratitude, and discusses virtue in terms of our duties to others, rather than individual perfection through stoical control of the passions.

What all this suggests is that when Jefferson included the right to the pursuit of happiness in the Declaration, he had come to no clear conclusion about the rank ordering of the intellectual and social virtues. Throughout this early formative period, classical and modern conceptions of virtue continued to overlap and to present themselves as models of human excellence. It is not clear that Jefferson was even aware of the tension between the two.

Because this period is so unsettled, it makes sense to look to those later writings that expand on earlier arguments, the implications of which he no more than dimly perceived when he included the right to the pursuit of happiness in the Declaration. While any such interpretation elevating the social virtues over the intellectual virtues must remain tentative and provisional, Jefferson's numerous remarks suggest that it is not arbitrary. Nor would such a reading rule out the practice of the intellectual virtues for those who are naturally inclined to pursue them. Indeed, Jefferson's own life testifies to the power of the intellectual virtues and their capacity to charm and delight. The point here is not to get bogged down in an argument about the precise ranking of the virtues (we shall return to this question in chapter 5) but to consider how our conception of rights, and herewith our character, might be different if we understood happiness as being in at least some broad way connected with the cultivation of virtue.

The Ascendancy of the Social Virtues

One of the more explicit acknowledgements of the battle waging in Jefferson's mind between the classical virtues of wisdom, tranquillity, and self-sufficiency and the Scottish emphasis on philanthropy, benevolence, and service to others is his letter to Maria Cosway in 1786.[77] In this celebrated dialogue between the head and the heart, the lines are clearly drawn. Taking what in effect is the side of antiquity, the head begins by cautioning against too passionate an involvement with Mrs. Cosway, warning that the greater the friendship, the more dangerous "to our tranquillity." But then, not altogether consistently, the head suddenly drops its stoic concern with tranquillity and self-control, sliding into the Epicurean argument that happiness is pleasure, and pleasure is the absence of pain. The surest way to avoid pain is to withdraw from worldly involvements and to depend solely on ourselves for our own happiness: "The most effectual means of being secure against pain, is to retire within ourselves, and to suffice for our own happiness. Those which depend on ourselves are the only pleasures a wise man will count on: for nothing is ours which another may deprive us of. Hence the inestimable value of intellectual pleasures." Speaking for the moderns, the heart contemptuously dismisses these counsels as nothing more than the ravings of a "sublimated philosopher," pursuing "visionary happiness." The wisdom so prized by the ancients turns out to be "supreme folly"; it "mistake[s] for happiness the mere absence of pain."

The significance of the letter is that here, for the first time, Jefferson tentatively reverses the classical hierarchy, which equates happiness with intellectual virtue, substituting for it the moral or social virtues that are known by the heart. The heart, it turns out, not only is the center of true happiness but also has its own more genuine calculus of pleasure. Unlike the head, which chooses intellectual pleasures because it mistakenly believes they are the purest and most self-sufficient, the heart knows there is "no pleasure without alloy."[78] Since there are no pure pleasures, those pleasures that are shared with others are greater than those enjoyed singly; conversely, those burdens that are shared with others are lighter. By this calculation, friendship brings greater pleasure than wisdom.

What began as a playful contest between the head and the heart, the intellectual and moral virtues as the ultimate source of human happiness, eventually ends in a rout. Returning to the morality of the ancients more than a decade after the famous dialogue, Jefferson now finds that Seneca and Cicero place far too much emphasis on individual perfection and not enough on the moral duties we owe to others. As he explains in a letter to Benjamin Rush:

> Of the ten heads in Seneca, seven relate to ourselves, viz., *de ira, consolatio, de tranquilitate, de constantia sapientis, de otio sapientis, de vita beata, de brevitate vitae*; two relate to others, *de clementia, de beneficiis*; and one relates to the government of the world, *de providentia*. Of eleven tracts of Cicero, five respect ourselves, viz., *de finibus; Tusculana, academica, paradoxa, de Senectute*; one, *de officiis*, relates partly to ourselves, partly to others; one, *de amicitia*, relates to others; and four are on different subjects, to wit, *de natura deorum, de divinitatione, de fato*, and *somnium Scipionis*.[79]

Although Jefferson continues to admire their precepts relating "chiefly to ourselves and the government of those passions which, unrestrained, would disturb our tranquillity of mind," he now believes they are "short and defective" in elaborating the duties we owe to others. It is not that the ancients ignored the social virtues altogether, for, as Jefferson immediately adds, "they embraced, indeed, the circle of kindred and friends, and inculcated patriotism, or the love of our country in the aggregate, as a primary obligation: towards our neighbors and countrymen they taught justice, but scarcely viewed them within the circle of benevolence."[80]

If, then, Jefferson comes to believe that the essence of virtue is benevolence or "doing good to others," it would follow that benevolence lies at the heart of his understanding of happiness. But where in human nature is there a foundation for this conception of virtue and happiness, and how is it connected to our rights? Perhaps the fullest discussion of this first question occurs in a letter to Thomas Law, written in 1814.[81] Although this is nearly forty years after the Declaration was written, it enlarges on themes Jefferson had already been exploring when he wrote the Declaration and so may provide some clue to the ground of this third and most elusive right.

The letter to Law seeks to locate the "foundation of morality" in human nature. Following the Scottish school, Jefferson rejects the argument of Hobbes and his followers that the moral duties we owe to others are ultimately reducible to the promptings of self-love. At the same time, he rejects the alternative claims of the rationalists (Reid, Clarke, and Wollaston) that virtue is grounded in reason, truth, or some notion of fitness. Neither truth, nor the love of God, nor the love of the beautiful, nor self-love provides a true "foundation of morality." Jefferson devotes special attention to the enlightened form of self-interest put forth by the French philosopher Helvetius, who had argued that we do good for others because we receive pleasure from such acts. Jefferson agrees with Helvetius, "one of the best men on earth," that these good acts do indeed give us pleasure. But he here denies that this is the reason we approve of such acts or perform them. Retreating from the position staked out in the head-heart dialogue, Jefferson now insists that moral action cannot be grounded on the pleasure we receive from doing good to others because this would return moral virtue to a selfish foundation.[82] Thus, the pleasure we receive is the by-product of something more fundamental: the natural and immediate inclination, registered by the moral sense, to consider as a motive for our actions the good of others. In other words, the ground of moral virtue is the unselfish "love of others, a sense of duty to them, a moral instinct, in short, which prompts us irresistibly to feel and succor their distresses, and protests against the language of Helvetius 'what other motive than self-interest could determine a man to generous actions?'"[83] It is this view of man as a social animal, naturally endowed by a Benevolent Creator with generous passions acting upon an innate moral sense, that directs us to pursue our own happiness by promoting "the happiness of those with whom he has placed us in society, by acting honestly towards all, benevolently to those who fall within our way, respecting sacredly their rights, bodily and mental, and cherishing their freedom of conscience."[84]

So far we have shown that Jefferson believes we have a natural duty to promote the good of others, but how is this duty connected with the right to the pursuit of happiness? And how can the Declaration be interpreted to imply a duty to promote the good of others when the document speaks only of rights? If anything, the language of the Declaration would seem to reinforce the tendency to view all moral questions exclusively from the perspective of rights,[85] since it says almost nothing about duties, save for the duty to throw off oppressive governments, and never mentions virtue.

Yet this is precisely why we need to recover the true meaning and ground of our rights as Jefferson understands them. For one of the great differences between Locke and the Scottish school is that the latter insists that both our rights and our duties are grounded on the social as well as the selfish passions. As the letter to Law clearly indicates, Jefferson follows the Scots, rather than Locke, on the question of moral duties; regrettably, he nowhere directly addresses the question with respect to rights. But given his agreement with the Scots that human beings are naturally social, that the generous impulses are as much a part of our constitution as the selfish passions, and that our moral obligations to others are rooted exclusively in the social affections, it makes sense that he would ground the right to the pursuit of happiness on more than the selfish desire for comfortable self-preservation. Moreover, if the right to pursue happiness derives partly from the social passion of benevolence, this would explain how a right can also imply certain duties. For as naturally social creatures, endowed not merely with selfish but also with generous impulses, the right to pursue our own happiness and the moral duty to promote the good of others tend to be reciprocal.[86] As Abraham Lincoln observed, the Declaration embodies a "right principle of action" other than self-interest.[87]

Although the moral implications of understanding happiness in this way are profound, the impact on politics is minimal: the rights and duties connected with happiness are not the objects of governmental concern. As the Declaration makes clear, government is obliged to protect only the *pursuit* of happiness; it cannot compel us to act benevolently toward others, even if this is part of what makes us truly happy. For Jefferson, the tasks of the liberal republic are few: government ought to restrain men from committing aggression against each other, compel them to contribute to the necessities of society, and require them to submit to an impartial arbiter. "When the laws have declared and enforced all this, they have fulfilled their functions."[88] It was not then, and is not now, the purpose of government to enforce the full range of our natural rights and duties. As James Wilson, who also followed the Scots in these matters, put it in his lecture on natural rights: "The rights and duties of benevolence are but rarely, though they are sometimes, the objects of municipal law."[89] Thus, although the right to the pursuit of happiness entails certain moral obligations to others, which places it on a different moral footing from those rights that are grounded solely in the selfish passions, it does not fundamentally alter the limited role that Jefferson, speaking on behalf of all Americans, envisions government playing in our lives. The Declaration presupposes a vision of human happiness, linked to the exercise of the most exalted liberal virtues, but it leaves individuals free to pursue happiness as they see fit.

Rights, Passions, and Virtue in the American Character

If, however, each of the three great rights in the Declaration rests on a different, and to some extent, competing passion, how do these rights fit together? Is there, in Jefferson's political psychology, a hierarchy of the passions that would bind our rights into a coherent whole, without reducing human beings to mere self-seekers or requiring of them an unrealistic capacity for virtue? Or is human nature merely a bundle of contradictory desires to be acted upon by each individual as he or she sees fit? If there is no hierarchy among the passions, how can we rationally choose among our rights when they, as they sometimes do, conflict?

From his reading of the Scottish moral philosophers, Jefferson might have been aware of these questions. Taking note of the "perplexity" of competing passions that "seem to draw different ways," Francis Hutcheson had asked, "Must the generous determination, and all its particular affections, yield to the selfish one, and be under its control? Must we indulge their kind motions so far as private interest admits and no further? or must the selfish yield to the generous? or can we suppose that in this complex system there are ultimately two principles which may often oppose each other, without any umpire to reconcile the differences?"[90] Jefferson does not address these questions directly, but his scattered comments suggest that the pursuit of happiness is the most comprehensive of our rights.[91] Happiness is the end to which human beings devote their lives and liberties. And although their different circumstances, talents, and inclinations will lead them to pursue different paths, there is at bottom one good that remains constant: true happiness depends on virtue and virtue means, above all, the social virtues that bind us to one another. Doing good to others can take a variety of forms: it can mean respecting the rights of others, exercising benevolence, or at least civility, to one's fellow men, or it can mean pursuing the useful knowledge that will improve the lot of humankind.[92] For Jefferson, all the virtues, both moral and intellectual, are ultimately directed toward the good of others.

Does this mean that we are obliged to pursue the good of others over our own good? Not at all. In those few cases where our own good is at stake, Jefferson does not require benevolence to overrule self-love. But for the most part Jefferson assumes that we are so constituted that virtue and self-interest can, with the appropropriate republican institutions, be made to coincide. A Benevolent Creator has endowed us with a moral sense and has so arranged our nature that we receive pleasure from doing good to others; the exercise of the social virtues *is* our interest. Our happiness depends in part on the happiness of others.

For this equation to work, however, each of the passions must play its part. Just as pride ennobles self-interest, and self-interest tempers pride, so, too, does concern for others enlarge our conception of self-interest. At the same time, pride and self-love must be enlisted to restrain the impulse to do good within reasonable limits. It is not that the tension between these passions ever completely disappears, as Jefferson's own inability to put aside self-interest on the question of slavery poignantly attests, but it is significantly reduced by the operation of the moral sense and the constructive interplay of the passions.

Yet precisely because there are tensions among these rights, Jefferson should have taken greater pains to help Americans understand their true meaning. For whereas it may be self-evident that all human beings possess certain inalienable rights, it is by no means self-evident what these rights mean, where they come from, or how they can be fitted together. As Jefferson himself observed, the ideas expressed in the Declaration were culled from a number of sources, some popular but others, especially "the elementary books of public right, as Aristotle, Cicero, Locke, Sidney, etc.,"[93] emphatically not. Jefferson's failure to instruct Americans in the deeper meaning of the principles they share and to which he eloquently gives voice has encouraged subsequent generations even less sure of their political and moral heritage to believe that they are free to interpret their rights in whatever manner they wish, including ways that sap their independence and pride, and subject them increasingly to the dictates of a government less interested in protecting liberty and the natural right to self-government than in ensuring equality of condition and increased political power for itself.

Thus, at a time when the explosion of the "rights industry"[94] threatens to dissolve society into a mass of isolated and ever more powerless individuals and warring tribes, where parents are divided against children, women against men, the elderly against the rest of society, one race against another, and so on, it makes sense to try to recover the original ground and meaning of our rights and to explain their requirements and limitations more fully than Jefferson does. Properly understood, the conception of rights set forth by Jefferson in the Declaration helps shape the American character in the following ways.

First, it reminds us that rights are not simply wishes or aspirations but instead are grounded in the most permanent and powerful human passions. These are not the desires of a particular race, class, or gender at a given historical moment but the irresistible and universal longings of men and women everywhere. They are neither wholly nor narrowly selfish; still less are they simply altruistic. Together they form a coherent whole, originating in the desire for security and culminating in the proud pursuit of those objects that give moral meaning and purpose to life.

Second, and closely related, nature serves not only as the ground of our rights but also as a brake on their steady expansion beyond, and even in contradiction to, anything Jefferson envisioned. Thus, in contrast to contemporary liberals, who are often uneasy with the very idea of human nature because it serves as a limit on individual freedom,[95] Jefferson's conception of rights is limited by the idea of man as a rational and moral being, subject to "the laws of nature and nature's Gode." This does not mean that there are no rights beyond those that Jefferson recognized, but it does mean that there can be no "rights" that conflict with or erode the individual capacity for "rational liberty."

Third, rights, as Jefferson understands them, are claims that individuals as free moral agents assert for themselves, employing their own faculties and powers. They are not entitlements that others can assert for us on our behalf; a people too dispirited and demoralized to defend their own rights cannot look to other, more powerful groups to exercise their rights for them.[96] Of course, citizens may join together with others to exercise their rights and, in a democratic republic, where individuals by themselves are often weak, it is inevitable that they will do so. But republican self-government can flourish only where citizens are sufficiently engaged, either individually or collectively, to act for themselves.

Fourth, the exercise of equal rights leads inevitably to inequality of outcomes, most obviously in property and wealth, but also in intellect and virtue. Yet in contrast to many of today's rights advocates, Jefferson is more inclined to accept the social and economic inequalities that result from the formal possession of equal rights. To be sure, Jefferson is suspicious of great wealth. But as long as these inequalities do not become so great or so menacing as to threaten the very survival of republican government, they must be permitted because this is the reason people come together in the first place: to be able to rise as far as their different talents and efforts enable them. Jefferson's conception of rights favors equality of opportunity over equality of condition, and liberty over equality.

Finally, although Jefferson nowhere claims that individuals have a right to be happy, only that they have a right to pursue happiness, he is no moral relativist when it comes to the meaning of happiness. Although he allows considerable scope for the great diversity of human talents, desires, and situations, he never suggests that happiness is whatever an individual believes it to be. The one universal component of happiness is virtue, and virtue is always the same: doing good to others. In a liberal republic, government may not compel citizens to accept a particular view of happiness or force them to practice benevolence, but neither can government remain indifferent to these matters. This is why, for Jefferson, it is so important to exercise and strengthen the moral sense; only then will the benevolent affections that contribute to our happiness ultimately prevail.

Chapter Two

The Moral Sense Virtues and Character Formation

Jefferson's belief in the moral sense goes to the heart of his understanding of what the character of free men and women should be. For while character may be influenced by politics and rights, it is essentially about morality and virtue. Thus, for Jefferson, it involves reflection on those innate moral sentiments that, when cultivated and strengthened by steady practice and example, define the moral core of the individual. The main assumptions of the moral sense doctrine as Jefferson understands it are as follows: First, the capacity for virtue is natural to all human beings everywhere. The moral sense is the perfect expression of Jefferson's faith that human beings are naturally endowed with a capacity to perceive right and wrong that, if reinforced by habitual exercise from childhood and fortified by modest instruction in the "little rules of prudence,"[1] will enable citizens to govern themselves and to reach a level of moral perfection in their social relations hitherto reserved only for the few.

In maintaining that morality is part of our natural endowment, Jefferson does not mean to suggest that it is the whole of our constitution, or even its most powerful component. Nor does he mean to deny the influence of history and culture on the morals of a particular society. In different circumstances people may draw different conclusions about the moral sentiments all human beings feel. And everywhere these original moral impulses can be either improved by education and the right institutions or corrupted by their opposites. Still, no matter how savage, ignorant, or misguided a society might be, it is never completely bereft of moral feelings. Human beings everywhere are born with the capacity to perceive certain moral sentiments. All people desire justice, admire gratitude, honor fidelity, cultivate friendship, and approve of benevolence and generosity (at least within their own tribe or society), even if they disagree about what these things mean or how they can be combined or reconciled.[2] It is the human capacity for moral judgment, located in a distinct faculty of perception, that elevates humans above all other creatures and endows them with moral dignity.

Second, because morality arises out of certain sense impressions that the moral sense perceives and approves, virtue requires no uncommon degree of reason to give it effect. Although Jefferson does not go so far as to deny reason any role at all in the operation of the moral sense, he is drawn for political reasons to those moral philosophers who would severely restrict its province. If moral knowledge depended exclusively on right reason (as the ancient philosophers had insisted), very few individuals would be capable of independent moral judgment. "For one man of science, there are thousands who are not. What would have become of them?"[3] Yet in grounding morality on sentiment rather than reason, Jefferson insists on the primacy of the social over the selfish passions. The duties we owe to others can never be discovered by consulting our own interests or self-love. "Self-love . . . is no part of morality. Indeed, it is exactly its counterpart. It is the sole antagonist of virtue, leading us constantly by our propensities to self-gratification in violation of our moral duties to others. Accordingly, it is against this enemy that are erected the batteries of moralists and religionists as the only obstacle to the practice of morality."[4] Morality is neither a matter of reason intuiting certain principles of right action nor a function of the selfish desire to avoid pain and enjoy pleasure. It arises out of certain moral sentiments that are inherent in our nature as social beings.

Third, although Jefferson's analogy to the senses gives the impression that virtue is as automatic as seeing or hearing, it clearly is not. That nearly all human beings can perceive certain impulses from which arise their moral obligations does not mean that these feelings guarantee right action. The moral sentiments require continual exercise and encouragement to develop into the established habits and dispositions that form our character. On the other hand, Jefferson does seem genuinely to believe that the exercise of virtue is on the whole both easy and pleasant, and that, if we but follow our hearts, all will be well. It is part of nature's benevolent plan to lay "the foundation of happiness"[5] in virtue and to reward its exercise with feelings of pleasure. Missing from much of his discussion is any suggestion that virtue is sometimes painful, or that vicious things can also give us pleasure.[6] Jefferson assumes that under the right circumstances, that is, in a republican society, moral education can get most people to take pleasure from what is good.

Fourth, and finally, that we seek the approval of others and in turn pass judgment on their actions testifies to the essentially social character of the moral sense. Accordingly, the virtues that emerge as the most praiseworthy are those that preserve and perfect us as social creatures: justice ranks higher than the "frigid speculations" of philosophy,[7] and benevolence highest of all. All this Jefferson learned from the Scots, and it found powerful affirmation in his unorthodox reading of the New Testament. It is this marriage of moral sense philosophy and Christian ethics (shorn of its miraculous and nonrational elements) that Jefferson holds up as the model of virtue for republican America.

Empiricism, Egoism, and the Foundations of Morality

Jefferson was attracted to the Scottish moral sense philosophers because they attempted to resolve one of the great problems posed by modern empiricism. If, as Locke had argued, all knowledge arises out of sense impressions or in the mind's reflection on these sensations, where does morality come from?[8] Is morality derived from the selfish desire to avoid what is painful, or is there some other ground for virtue that is natural to human beings? In seeking a different foundation for moral action, but one that was compatible with Lockean empiricism, the earliest of the Scottish philosophers posited the existence of a distinct moral faculty capable of perceiving genuine moral sensations arising out of the social, as opposed to the selfish, passions.[9]

Francis Hutcheson was the first of the Scottish school to locate the seat of morality in the moral sense. Hutcheson divides moral virtue into three branches: the duties we owe to ourselves, the duties we owe to others, and the duties we owe to God. The affections or desires that give rise to these different branches of virtues are, respectively, self-love, goodwill or benevolence, and piety. Although Hutcheson acknowledges a role for self-love in perfecting the individual, this part of his moral philosophy received little attention. What attracted notice, then as now, was Hutcheson's argument that all the social virtues, or duties we owe to others, were ultimately traceable to benevolence or goodwill. It is this generous affection that moves us to seek the happiness of others independent of any selfish motives. For Hutcheson, we are so constituted by nature that the moral sense tends to "approve every kind affection either in ourselves or others and all publicly useful actions which we imagine flow from such affection, without our having a view to our private happiness in our approbation of these actions."[10]

Reacting against the "utopian" assumption that, regarding the duties we owe to others, benevolence is the sole "principle of action" of which the moral sense approves, Henry Home, Lord Kames, sought a more realistic foundation for this faculty. Kames does not deny, indeed, he agrees with Hutcheson, that "benevolence and generosity are more beautiful and more attractive of love and esteem,"[11] and that "nothing ennobles human nature more than this principle or spring of action,"[12] but he doubts that benevolence can account for all the social virtues and in particular for "justice, and every thing which may be strictly called Duty."[13] Although benevolence is natural to humankind, it is limited in its scope to family and friends. Through imagination and abstract reasoning, it may be extended beyond our immediate circle to religion or country, but it cannot be stretched to include an equal universal duty to all. Such extensive benevolence may belong to some men as individuals, but "there is no such general fondness of man to man by nature."[14] The moral sense may approve these generous sentiments, but it does not oblige us to act on them.[15]

If, however, the social virtues cannot all be traced back to the social affection of benevolence, neither are they thrown back upon "absolute selfishness." Following Hutcheson, Kames insists that human beings are endowed with both selfish and social passions; therefore, "to contend that we ought only to regard ourselves and be influenced only by the selfish passions is against nature."[16] Instead, Kames seeks to ground morality on those sentiments, or "springs of action," that give rise to a sense of duty or obligation.

As social beings who need the company of others, we naturally feel bound to honor compacts and agreements. This duty arises out of the moral sentiment of fidelity, which Kames considers a social affection. At the same time, since many of the compacts we respect preserve the sanctity of private property, this duty is not simply social. The "feeling for private property" is rooted in the natural desire for self-preservation as well as self-love. Together, these social and selfish impulses give rise to the virtue of justice. Justice, according to Kames, is "that moral virtue which guards property and gives authority to covenants."[17] The desire for justice is one of the strongest desires of human beings everywhere; it is solidly rooted in human nature. And because it is necessary for the preservation of society, justice is the one virtue that government may legitimately compel.[18]

One other aspect of Kames's theory deserves mention. Because Kames insists that the moral sense is natural to human beings at all times and in all places, he must try to account for the cruelty and brutality that primitive peoples visit upon each other. If the moral sense has always been present, why does it not restrain such behavior? Kames must satisfy those critics who argue that morality is not natural to human beings but is acquired only with civilization and education.

Kames replies that the moral sense has always existed but that conditions did not initially permit its full development. Rude and illiterate people have not yet developed the capacity for complex ideas and abstract propositions; consequently, they tend to be governed by their immediate selfish passions. Under these circumstances, he concedes, it is *as if* the moral sense did not exist, since it is still too weak to influence behavior. But gradually, as people develop the capacity to form more complex ideas and to think abstractly, they are able to act on more general principles, the seeds of which were always there. Thus, as humankind becomes more civilized, the selfish passions are brought into submission and the social affections gain ascendancy. The important point is that reason and education do not create these affections; they merely help to refine and improve them. Nurture completes, but does not replace, nature's intention; reason remains the handmaiden of feeling.

Still, the central question that Hutcheson and Kames could not convincingly answer was whether such a faculty of moral perception actually existed. If there were such a sense, where was its organ of perception? We see with the eyes, taste with the tongue, and so on; what is the analogous organ that perceives moral sensations? Moreover, even if such an organ existed, it would not function in the same way as the sense organs. Whereas we exercise the five senses automatically from birth without training or instruction (we do not need to be taught to see), virtue requires a long period of regular exercise and instruction before it develops.[19] These difficulties led David Hume and Adam Smith to reflect on the following question: If what the moral sense does is approve the moral sentiments, might we not focus directly on those sentiments and locate approval in some other known faculty of the mind, such as reason or, better still, the imagination? Acting on this insight, Hume and Smith shifted the focus of their inquiries. While retaining the phrase "moral sense," both of them tend to analyze moral knowledge in terms of the operation of the most basic human passions directly on the mind. In so doing, they move the discussion away from the moral sense as a distinct faculty of sense perception akin to hearing, seeing, and so forth, to an examination of those sentiments that prompt us to virtuous action.

For both Hume and Smith, the sentiment that moves us to moral approbation and action is sympathy. By sympathy, they do not mean pity or compassion but the more neutral propensity of human beings as social creatures to enter imaginatively into the feelings and actions of others and to approve of those actions if they meet with our sense of what is "useful and agreeable," in the case of Hume, or with propriety and merit, in the case of Smith. For both philosophers, the foundation of morality is the innate human capacity to identify with the joys and sorrows of others. It is the faculty of imagination, acting by itself or in conjunction with reason, that makes moral judgment possible.

There is, however, one important difference between the two. Hume does not believe it is possible to ground all the moral virtues on the operation of the moral sentiments. In contrast to Kames, he insists that some virtues, notably justice, have no foundation in any moral sentiment; rather, they originate *solely* in considerations of public utility. We approve of motives and actions which result in justice because we *reason* they are useful to society. Although, over time, we come to develop what may be called a "natural" regard for justice based on its "extensive utility," justice, considered from the standpoint of its origin in reason rather than an innate moral sentiment, remains in this sense an "artificial" virtue.[20]

By contrast, Smith seeks to establish a full-fledged theory of moral *sentiments*, which derives the virtues exclusively from certain innate feelings, independent of reason and calculation. Instead of reason seeking to determine what is useful, Smith asks us to *imagine* whether an Impartial Spectator would sympathize with and approve of our feelings and actions. Smith insists that we can win this approval only if we moderate our passions so that the Spectator is able to sympathize with the propriety and merit of our feelings.[21] According to Smith, this exercise in moderation, necessitated by the universal human need for approval, results in the exercise of those virtues that are useful and agreeable to ourselves and to others, but without having to compromise the primacy of the sentiments as the spring of all moral action.

Thus, by grounding his theory of moral sentiments on the imaginative capacity to sympathize with the joys and sorrows of others and to have them, in turn, sympathize with us, Smith avoids the difficulties encountered by Hutcheson and Kames. He does not have to defend the existence of the moral sense as a faculty of sense perception; nor does he derive all the social virtues from the one affection of benevolence, as Hutcheson did. Sympathy, which is rooted in human sociality and the need for the approval of others, points in several directions. It gives rise to justice, the virtue most needful to society, as well as prudence, the virtue connected with the care of the self. The moral sentiments are largely, but not exclusively, other-directed; there are certain moral virtues, like prudence, that arise out of self-love with which all human beings can and do sympathize and approve. At the same time, however, Smith reserves the highest praise for benevolence, that virtue which looks to the happiness and well-being of others. These differences are important to keep in mind as we try to figure out how the moral sense contributes to the formation of character, and what kind of character it recommends. For despite the centrality of the moral sense to Jefferson's understanding of human nature, he seldom does more than mention the faculty and only twice discusses its operation in any detail.[22] Moreover, the discussions occur in two letters separated by more than twenty-five years. In each, Jefferson does no more than sketch the broad outline of his views, and in a way that tends to emphasize the agreement between him and his correspondent.[23] Thus, the more extended analyses provided by the Scots help to fill in some, though by no means all, of the lacunae.

The Operation of the Moral Sense

Although Jefferson had alluded to certain aspects of moral sense philosophy, and had used the term without elaboration in earlier writings and letters,[24] his first discussion of the operation of the moral sense occurs in a letter to his nephew Peter Carr, written in 1787 while Jefferson was in Paris. In this letter, Jefferson describes the moral sense as a distinct faculty for perceiving right and wrong, analogous to the sense organs: "This sense is as much a part of his nature as the sense of hearing, seeing, or feeling." And Jefferson never wavered from this view, for nearly thirty years later he repeats the analogy, shifting the focus to emphasize that the occasional absence of the moral sense, like the absence of sight or hearing, "is no proof that it is a general characteristic of the species." But if the moral sense is a distinctive faculty of perception, analogous to the sense organs, what bodily organ is its seat? Jefferson can answer this question only metaphorically: the organ of the moral sense is the heart. Adopting the voice of the heart in his celebrated letter to Maria Cosway written during this same period, Jefferson has the heart reply to the head: "When Nature assigned us the same habitation, she gave us over it a divided empire. To you, she allotted the field of science. To me that of morals." It is in the "mechanics of the heart" that the social affections of sympathy, generosity, humanity, charity, benevolence, gratitude, justice, and friendship all find their metaphoric home.[25]

Just as Jefferson remains untroubled by the inability to locate the moral sense in an actual organ of perception, he seems to ignore the other previously mentioned breakdown in this analogy. Whereas we possess fully the capacity to see, to hear, to feel, and so on, from birth, the moral sense does not operate so automatically. The ability to make moral judgments develops only slowly with practice as we mature, and even then not always to full capacity. Perhaps this is why, in the very next sentence and without any sense of contradiction, he compares the moral sense to the limbs of the body: "The moral sense, or conscience, is as much a part of man as his leg or his arm." And like these bodily appendages, it "may be strengthened by exercise, as may any particular limb of the body."[26] In likening the moral sense to the arms and the legs, Jefferson can drive home the importance of regular exercise and good habits in forming moral character. But he does so at the cost of undermining his earlier analogy with the sense organs.[27]

Yet despite these difficulties Jefferson continues to view the moral sense as a distinct faculty of sense perception, whose particular task it is to approve the moral impulses of each individual and to sit in judgment on the moral actions of others. But how does this "Internal Monitor"[28] know what to approve? Is the approbation of the moral sense automatic, requiring no assistance from the faculties of reason or imagination, or are these faculties also involved? At times, Jefferson seems to deny reason any positive role in moral judgment and action. To Maria Cosway, he insists that nature never intended to rest morality upon "the uncertain combinations of the head." Indeed, when reason does become involved, it is usually to mislead the promptings of the heart. Thus, he concludes by chiding the head, "I do not know that I ever did a good thing on your suggestion, or a dirty one without it."[29] Nor is this an isolated romantic outburst, for Jefferson returns to this point some years later: "The practice of morality being necessary to the well-being of society, he has taken care to impress its precepts so indelibly in our hearts that they shall not be effaced by the subtleties of our brain."[30]

But in the letter to Peter Carr, where Jefferson explicitly discusses the operation of the moral sense, he backs away from this position. Here he concedes that the moral sense "is submitted in some small degree to the guidance of reason," though he is quick to add, "it is a small stock which is required for this: even a less one than what we call common sense."[31] These must have been something like the "prudential rules"[32] for governing our conduct in society that Jefferson offered to his grandson when he went away from home for the first time. But beyond such prudential advice, apparently nothing more is needed. Indeed, Jefferson worries that too much reliance on reason can corrupt moral judgment by leading it astray with "artificial rules."[33] The plowman is at least as good a judge of moral cases as the professor, if not a better. Acting on this belief, Jefferson advises this same nephew and later on another grandson not to waste time studying moral philosophy or metaphysics in college.[34]

At first sight, Jefferson's disparagement of reason in discovering our moral duties may seem odd for the man considered to be the foremost representative of the American Enlightenment. But on further consideration, Jefferson's position (although excessively polemical) is consistent with Enlightenment assumptions. What Jefferson objects to is not reason per se but the traditional rationalist argument that the moral and political truths necessary for men living together in society can be known *only* by reason, and in particular by intuitive reason.[35] If this were true, then the bulk of humankind whose ability to reason is limited would be dependent on the wise few for moral knowledge. And, indeed, traditional moral philosophy tended to support aristocratic, or at least non-democratic, political arrangements for precisely this reason.[36]

Stated positively, Jefferson's distrust of reason alone in discovering our moral duties rests on the premise that a Benevolent Creator is not at the same time a "pitiful bungler." Since the Creator intends men for society, He has equipped each of them with the capacity to know and act on those truths most needful for their common life together. It is the moral sense, with its instinctive feelings of virtue and vice, knowable in principle by all, that is the rightful seat of moral judgment. For Jefferson, human sociality has decidedly republican implications, in morals and epistemology no less than in politics.

Having established the primacy of the moral sense, Jefferson can then, like Kames, grant reason a supporting role, though since he never takes up the issue systematically, he sometimes gives the impression that reason is necessary only when the moral sense is defective or absent. In these unhappy cases, "appeals to reason and calculation," especially in matters of honesty, may help to supply the defect.[37] Yet it is precisely in these cases that reason seems least effective. Jefferson never explains how, lacking a basic moral sense, rational appeals to "other motives" such as the "love, or the hatred, or rejection of those among whom he lives,"[38] all of which start from the premise of human sociality and are in fact bound up with the operations of the moral sense, can restrain an individual bereft of social impulses.

Yet despite his tendency to denigrate reason, and occasionally even to blame it for corrupting the moral sense, Jefferson in fact accords reason a more positive role in moral judgment than he is prepared to admit.[39] Consider, first, the extensive comment entered into his copy of Kames's *Essays* on the perfectibility of the moral sense. Responding to Kames's suggestion that the moral sense "admits of great refinements by culture and education,"[40] Jefferson reflects on the progress made over two millennia in treating prisoners of war:

This is a remarkable instance of improvement in the moral sense. The putting to death captives in war was a general practice among savage nations. When men became more humanized the captive was indulged with life on condition of holding it in perpetual slavery; a condition exacted on this supposition, that the victor had right to take his life, and consequently to commute it for his services. At this stage of refinement were the Greeks about the time of the Trojan War. At this day, it is perceived we have no right to take the life of an enemy unless where our own preservation renders it necessary. But the ceding his life in commutation for service admits there was no necessity to take it, because you have not done it. And if there was neither necessity nor right to take his life then there is no right to his service in commutation for it. This doctrine is acknowledged by later writers, Montesquieu, Burlamaqui, etc., who yet suppose it just to require a ransom from the captive. One advance further in refinement will relinquish this also. If we have no right to the life of a captive, we have no right to his labor; if none to his labor we have none to his absent property which is but the fruit of that labor. In fact, ransom is but commutation in another form.[41]

Such abstract propositions can never be the work of the moral sense acting alone. It is, according to Kames, reason that clarifies and extends the original moral sentiments, leading to ever more delicate and refined judgment and action. In other words, although abstract reasoning is not critical in the formation of each individual's moral judgments, which seem to require only a "small stock" of reason, the ability of particular individuals to reason abstractly is essential to moral progress and helps to explain why some societies are more morally advanced than others.[42]

Utility, Reason, and the Moral Sense

There is, moreover, a second way in which reason helps to influence moral judgment, though reason in this instance involves the capacity to calculate consequences rather than think abstractly. The discussion occurs in his most extended treatment of the moral sense, where Jefferson announces that "nature has constituted utility the standard and test of virtue."[43] Commentators have seized on this statement to argue that Jefferson's last and fullest statement on the moral sense seems to contradict his earlier remarks and even his discussion of the moral sense in the same letter. For if the standard and test of virtue is now a matter of utilitarian calculation, if virtue now has to do with the "effect" of our actions, what becomes of the moral sense? In earlier letters, Jefferson had followed the Scottish school in making the approbation of the moral sense the test of virtue, while here, in the letter to Law and in another to Adams, he shifts over to calculation. Similarly, he had earlier stressed the importance of motive, while here he focuses on consequences. By invoking utility as the standard of virtue, has Jefferson rendered the moral sense superfluous?[44]

As long as we do not insist on viewing the moral sense as a faculty that operates without any assistance from reason, a position that Jefferson in his few direct discussions of the moral sense never maintained, the answer is no. So what is he doing? We can better appreciate his intention if we examine the context in which Jefferson introduces utility. In the letter to Law, and in a similar response to Adams, Jefferson is attempting to answer a particular question: If human beings everywhere perceive the same moral sentiments, why do people around the world have such different and even conflicting ideas of right and wrong, justice and injustice, virtue and vice? Anticipating the question of an imaginary critic who, observing these differences, sensibly wonders why, "if nature had given us such a sense, impelling us to virtuous actions, and warning us against those which are vicious, then nature would have designated, by some particular ear-marks, the two sets of actions which are, in themselves, the one virtuous, the other vicious. Whereas, we find, in fact, that the same actions are deemed virtuous in one country and vicious in another."[45] Similarly, in the letter to Adams, Jefferson is trying to refute the idea that the moral sense and justice are not natural to human beings because different societies hold radically different views of virtue and vice, right and wrong.

In both instances, Jefferson introduces utility precisely to defend the existence of the moral sense. His argument is as follows: all human beings in whatever circumstances are moved by impulses to duty or justice as well as benevolence; "every human mind feels pleasure in doing good to another." In every society, "the essence of virtue is doing good to others."[46] The difficulty is that under "different circumstances, different habits and regimens," these natural impulses are pulled in different directions, so that "what is good may be one thing in one society, and it's [sic] opposite in another." Although the moral sentiments are natural, they are too weak and diffuse to tell us how to act in particular circumstances. Reason, in the form of utilitarian calculation, directs the original impulses to consider the moral consequences of actions, that is, what will do good to others, under vastly different circumstances.

This is not to say that the opinions different societies form about virtue and vice are all morally equal. The French opinion that adultery is acceptable in aristocratic societies where marriages are arranged to protect property does not contribute to true human happiness.[47] Still, the moral codes that different societies have evolved are probably the best they can do under the circumstances; in any case, it is fallible reason and not the absence of the moral sense that explains why different societies have different opinions about virtue and happiness. To be sure, Jefferson's reply does not address the contradiction between his earlier assertion that it is the moral sense that determines right and wrong, and his insistence here that virtue is a matter of utility. But in the context, this is not his principal concern. Jefferson is here trying to defend the existence of the moral sense while accounting for the variety of moral codes in different cultures. Whatever the difficulties, Jefferson introduced utility to defend the moral sense, not to replace it.

As for the switch from motives to consequences in determining what is virtuous, Jefferson might have responded, as Adam Smith did, that although the theory of moral sentiments is, strictly

speaking, concerned only with motives, consideration of consequences can be explained as an "irregularity" of the moral sentiment that serves a necessary, practical purpose. Because human
beings are social, they must be concerned with the effects of their
actions on others, even if ultimately this is not the most important
moral question. That we may sometimes do the right thing for the
wrong reasons should not be judged too harshly. Conversely, vicious consequences must as a rule be punished because motives are
more difficult, if not impossible, to determine and, in any case, a
liberal society cannot punish or reward people for their intentions
alone. There are, then, good practical reasons to focus on effects,
even if the moral sense theory, strictly speaking, is concerned with
motives.[48] At the same time, the virtues remain genuine virtues and
are never admirable simply because they achieve good results.

Finally, keep in mind that Jefferson introduces utility to explain how *societies* form different opinions about right and wrong
based on different circumstances and cultural traditions. He is not
suggesting that utilitarian calculation plays a critical role in the
formation of individual moral judgment. While some small degree
of prudence and common sense may be necessary, moral imagination and habituation are far more important in shaping individual
character.

Imagination and Moral Judgment

In contrast to the "small stock" of reason required for moral judgment, imagination plays a larger and more positive role in the operation of the individual moral sense. Writing to his young
grandson who was away from home for the first time, after receiv-
ing a letter from the boy's mother confiding her fears about his
character, Jefferson explains how his own imagination had helped
him overcome the temptations of youth. When, as a fourteen-year-
old also on his own, Jefferson was uncertain how to act, he would
ask himself what the most respected and distinguished men he
knew would do, and "what course in it w[ould] insure me their approbation." Jefferson assures his grandson that "this mode of de-
ciding my conduct tended more to correctness than any reasoning
powers I possessed." For young people, in particular, imaginative

identification with men of superior moral and intellectual character is more likely than inexperienced reason to lead to a "prudent and steady pursuit of what is right."[49]

Jefferson also recognizes the power of literature to shape the moral imagination and so mold character. This is why, after advising Peter Carr not to bother with lectures in moral philosophy, he urges him to "read good books." For Jefferson, the "entertainments of fiction" are no less valuable than experience in eliciting "the sympathetic emotions of virtue."[50] When we read good literature, "the spacious field of imagination is thus laid open to our use, and lessons may be formed to illustrate and carry home to the mind every rule of moral life."[51] Jefferson is confident that every reader of "feeling and sentiment" will react with disgust to the villainy of Macbeth, just as every son or daughter will form "a lively and lasting sense of filial duty" from reading *King Lear*. Marmontel can excite in the reader a strong desire to emulate acts of "fidelity" and "generosity," while the writings of Sterne "form the best course of morality ever written."[52] Comedy, tragedy, epic poetry, even the "well-written" romance,[53] can excite our virtuous sentiments and make us feel that we are better people for having read them. And the more we exercise such dispositions, even in our imagination, the stronger they become.

Still, it is not clear that Jefferson means to confine the imagination to sympathetic identification with those whom we admire, either in real life or in literature. As social creatures, we need the love and approval of those with whom we live, and whose society is essential to our happiness and even survival. Thus, in contrast to the letter in which Jefferson tells his young grandson of how he deliberately sought to win the approval of the most respected characters, he recommends to his nephew Peter Carr a somewhat different imaginative exercise. Whenever the lad is in doubt about whether an act is right or wrong, he should imagine how he would act if "all the world" were watching.[54] When tempted to do anything in secret, he advises his nephew, ask yourself if you would do it in public. If you would not, be sure it is wrong. Without perhaps realizing it, Jefferson assumes that publicity, with its implicit appeal to majority sentiment, is the same as, or no worse than, sympathetic identification with the best.

This same confusion crops up in the letter to Thomas Law.

Here Jefferson (mistakenly) remembers Lord Kames as having taught that moral obligation arises not from "the feeling of a single individual" but from the "general feeling in a given case."[55] In other words, Jefferson tends to equate (to a far greater extent than Kames) the approval of the moral sense with the approval of those around us. In this rendering, the role of the imagination is to internalize for the moral sense the moral sentiments of the majority and not simply those we esteem and admire.[56]

At first sight, Jefferson's reliance on what will win the approval of others seems to push the moral sense in the direction of social conformity at the expense of right conduct.[57] For if the "general feeling" of the majority "in a given case" is what merits approval and, hence, determines what is right and wrong, virtuous or vicious, how can anyone ever challenge existing opinions and moral standards? How can Jefferson square such moral majoritarianism with moral reform? These questions take on added meaning when we consider that Jefferson regards Jesus as the greatest moral reformer of all time and, in his own day, antislavery Southerners found little support for emancipation in the "general feeling" of the people in their states. What the majority approves of is not necessarily right.

While this is certainly a danger, it seems likely that Jefferson does not mean to link the approbation of the moral sense with the reigning opinions in every society, but only those where the natural moral impulses of the people are encouraged by enlightened practices and benevolent institutions.[58] For although he does not often mention it, he recognizes that corrupt societies, though they cannot annihilate the moral sense, can warp and distort it. Indeed, he considers the effect of slavery on the South in just these terms. Although the "love of justice and love of country"[59] continue to plead the cause of the slaves, Southerners have ceased to feel their own moral impulses. "Nursed, educated, and daily exercised in tyranny,"[60] Southern children have learned to imitate the vices of their parents and to approve the most "boisterous" and haughty passions. Just as the moral sense can be strengthened by proper exercise, so can it be corrupted by immoral institutions that inflame and distort an otherwise healthy pride. In such circumstances, imaginative identification with those around us in society does not lead to moral action.

Perhaps this is why Jefferson continues to insist on the necessity of believing in divine rewards and punishments, and not only for those few individuals lacking a moral sense. Imagination can be put to powerful effect in summoning up the terrible vision of an avenging God, exacting retribution for the moral offense of slavery. In language that anticipates Lincoln's warning of divine retribution in his Second Inaugural Address, Jefferson asks:

> And can the liberties of a nation be secure when we have removed their only firm basis, a conviction in the minds of the people that these liberties are the gift of God? That they are not to be violated but with his wrath? Indeed I tremble for my country when I reflect that God is just: that his justice cannot sleep forever: that considering numbers, nature and natural means, only, a revolution of the wheel of fortune, and exchange of situation, is among possible events: that it may become probable by supernatural interference! The Almighty has no attribute which can take side with us in such a contest.[61]

Yet such warnings, which excite the imagination to reflect on the awful possibility of divine wrath in order to get us to do what is right, are rare in Jefferson. Although belief in a future state of rewards and punishments is the only tenet of Christianity not rationally provable on which he continues to insist,[62] Jefferson tends to emphasize the love, rather than the fear, of God and to view the Deity as a Benevolent Creator who has equipped human beings with the capacity to know and act on what is right.

The Moral Sense and the Role of Habit in Character Formation

In the two letters where Jefferson discusses the operation of the moral sense in detail, he gives the impression that this faculty functions as automatically as the five senses. The moral sense appears to perceive right and wrong as spontaneously as the eye sees an object placed before it. But in fact these letters give an incomplete and somewhat misleading picture of how moral character is actually formed. To correct this impression, recall that Jefferson compares the moral sense not only to the sense organs but also to the limbs of the body. And like an arm or a leg, the moral sense requires regular exercise, supplemented by appeals to "other motives," to develop properly. Perhaps nowhere is this clearer than in the letters Jefferson writes to his daughters, grandchildren, and other family members.[63] In attempting to teach them right and wrong, Jefferson understands that the moral impulses are too weak and diffuse to move them to moral action. These sentiments need to be strengthened by regular exercise and affectionate encouragement until they become like a second nature. It is the long process of habituation, of acquiring good manners, that ultimately results in the steady disposition to virtue that constitutes our character.[64] Thus, Jefferson advises his nephew Peter Carr to take every opportunity to exercise and strengthen his "dispositions to be grateful, to be generous, to be charitable, to be humane, to be true, just, firm, orderly, courageous, etc."[65] It is the habitual practice of these virtues, and not simply the occasional good act, that makes individuals happy and wins the esteem and approbation of others. Jefferson takes it for granted that most people, with the proper moral instruction, can learn to admire what is truly virtuous. That the greatest virtues are social, rather than intellectual, only increases the likelihood that this is so.

In his long absences from his daughters, Jefferson regularly appeals to their natural desire for his love and approval in order to encourage them to cultivate pleasing manners and virtuous dispositions. He does not scruple to say what is obvious, but is today too infrequently said out of fear of being considered "manipulative,"[66] namely, that he will love his daughters more as they prove themselves "more worthy" of his love. Jefferson never threatens to withhold his love if the girls disobey or disappoint him. When Mary fails to respond to his letters and entreaties, when Martha stalls in her Latin or falls into adolescent indolence, Jefferson's response is neither angry nor severe. He continues to encourage them, with patience and humor, to exercise their virtuous dispositions so that they will become "valuable to others and happy in [them]selves."[67] Later on, he will take the same approach with his grandchildren, promising "the more I perceive you are advancing in your learning and improving in good dispositions, the more I shall love you and the more everybody shall love you."[68] The appeal to "other motives" to reinforce the natural moral sentiments is not confined, as Jefferson elsewhere suggests, to those lacking a moral sense but is a regular part of moral development.

Thus, the process of character formation turns out to be more complicated than the letters on the moral sense, when taken by themselves, suggest. Although all human beings directly perceive certain moral sentiments of which the moral sense approves, the moral sense by itself is too weak to call forth virtuous conduct. It requires some small assist from reason, not in the form of abstract or speculative thinking but of prudence and common sense. More important still is the role of the imagination, which enables individuals from youth to put themselves in the place of others, and especially those they esteem, to determine whether they would approve of their motives and acts. Finally, good character does not result from the occasional good act; it is the result of permanent and steady dispositions. Thus, the moral sentiments must be regularly exercised and reinforced by appropriate social rewards, beginning with parental love and later extending to the approbation and esteem of those we admire. In time, the steady "exercise . . . of the moral feelings produces a habit of thinking and acting virtuously."[69]

Moral Sense and Moral Sentiments

What are the moral feelings or sentiments that move us to virtuous action, and what virtues do they recommend? Are the social virtues activated by benevolence, as Hutcheson argues; or do they arise out of other more compelling principles that the moral sense not only approves but also obliges, as Kames insists?[70] Among the students of Jefferson, Garry Wills has explored these issues in the greatest detail, but his argument severely overstates the case. Wills concludes that Jefferson followed Hutcheson in grounding morality entirely on benevolence, and that benevolence could be enforced by appropriate government action. Wills considers briefly the competing argument, advanced by Kames, that by far the greater part of morality consists in those sentiments of which the moral sense not only approves, such as benevolence, but feels dutybound to exercise, in particular, refraining from harming others and keeping our agreements. But because Wills wrongly insists that the impulse to duty is rooted exclusively in self-love, he concludes that Jefferson could not have intended this sentiment to serve as the foundation of morality. This, however, is to misread Kames, who never argued that the sense of duty is founded in self-love alone. For Kames, the duty to respect agreements and honor engagements partakes of both the selfish and the social principles of action; it is midway between benevolence and self-love. And it is massively to distort the political implications of benevolence in Hutcheson's thinking in order to justify the use of public power to enforce Wills's own vision of the good.[71] Yet in fact Jefferson seems not to have noticed, or, if he noticed to have cared, that Hutcheson and Kames differ in their moral psychology. In his eclectic analysis, benevolence and the impulse to duty each gives rise to different social virtues. Moreover, Jefferson understands, as Wills does not, that these two moral sentiments are not both enforceable by government.

To support his interpretation, Wills focuses on those passages where Jefferson equates the moral sense with the "love of others." Thus, for example, in the letter to Thomas Law, Jefferson asserts that "nature hath implanted in our breasts a love of others, a sense of duty to them, a moral instinct in short, which prompts us irresistibly to feel and succor their distresses."[72] In this instance, the "sense of duty" does seem to refer back to the benevolent impulse to relieve the suffering of others. But in other letters Jefferson makes it clear that the impulse to duty is also related to justice. In a letter to Francis Gilmer, which Wills fails to mention, Jefferson seems to have Kames's argument unambiguously in mind when he observes that because we are social beings the "sense of justice" must be part of our "natural organization."[73] And to John Adams, Jefferson seems almost to equate the moral sense with justice: "I believe [that justice] is instinct, and innate, that the moral sense is as much a part of our constitution as that of feeling, seeing, or hearing."[74]

What this suggests is that, unlike Hutcheson but like Kames, Jefferson believes there are several moral sentiments or "principles of action" that present themselves to the moral sense for its approval. Depending on the particular context, Jefferson emphasizes one or the other of these sentiments, and the social virtue to which each gives rise. Thus, for example, in the letter to Gilmer, where

Jefferson is discussing the legitimate scope of political power and what actions government may compel, he focuses solely on the "sense of justice." Because justice is essential to the preservation of society, it is the one virtue a liberal republic must enforce. In other letters, which concentrate more directly on morality, and especially in those that examine the relative merits of different moral codes, Jefferson can and does acknowledge the importance and, indeed, the primacy of benevolence.[75]

Justice

In thinking about the origin of justice, Jefferson rejects the Hobbesian notion that justice is merely conventional, that it comes into being only with the establishment of civil society and is whatever the sovereign declares it to be. He criticizes the projected treatise on morals by Destutt de Tracy (whose economic writings he much admired) for adopting "the principles of Hobbes or humiliation to human nature; that the sense of justice is not derived from our natural organization, but founded on convention only."[76]

With Hutcheson and Kames, Jefferson insists that man is by nature social. And part of his endowment as a social creature is a natural sense of justice. Jefferson offers his view in the form of a "syllogism": "Man was created for social intercourse; but social intercourse cannot be maintained without a sense of justice; then man must have been created with a sense of justice."[77] Since this sense of justice belongs to man as a social being, Jefferson seems to agree with Kames that this principle of action cannot be traced exclusively to the selfish passions. Justice, understood as the mutual recognition of personal and property rights, does not arise solely out of the selfish desire to have our own rights respected. Justice also arises out of the realization that, as social beings, we are bound by certain "moral duties which exist between individual and individual in a state of nature, and accompany them into a state of society."[78] Chief among these are honoring engagements, observing compacts, and respecting the equal rights of others. Justice in this sense is natural because it is rooted in the impulsive duty each individual feels to perform those obligations that are necessary to the peace and order of society. At the same time, justice remains an essentially negative virtue, a list of things we may not do. Indeed, it is precisely because government can force us to fulfill our obligations, and does not leave them to our free will and moral choice, that justice is not the highest virtue. For Jefferson, who here again follows the Scots, the peak of the moral virtues can be found in uncoerced acts of benevolence that take place beyond the reach of government.

Benevolence

Jefferson's belief that we are by nature social beings who depend for our happiness and well-being on the approval of others means that the most praiseworthy virtue will be that which perfects, rather than merely preserves, us in our dealings with others. For Jefferson, it is the innate "love of others," variously described as the natural impulse to charity, generosity, humanity, compassion, and benevolence, that moves us to the "most sublime" virtue, benevolence.[79] Benevolence is more noble than justice because it is always freely chosen. Whereas government must enforce "equal and impartial justice" as its "sacred duty,"[80] it cannot demand that its citizens exercise benevolence. The perfection of the moral character must be an act of free will. As such, benevolence is always accompanied by the greatest pleasure and approval. Conversely, the failure to act benevolently may disappoint, but it cannot, like the breach of justice, be punished.[81]

If Jefferson learned from the Scots that benevolence was the "most beautiful" of the virtues, it was not principally from them that he came to appreciate its true meaning and extent. Thus Wills is particularly misguided when he tries to explain what Jefferson means by benevolence with reference to Hutcheson. For Jefferson, the model of true benevolence is to be found in the life and teachings of Christ. Of course, it is not orthodox (Trinitarian) Christianity that Jefferson embraces; this he regards as mere superstition, invented by unscrupulous priests to gain power and control over the unsuspecting multitude.[82]

It is Jefferson's discovery of the writings of the English Unitarian Dr. Joseph Priestley that enables him to consider religion in a new light.[83] In his two-volume *History of the Corruptions of Christianity* (which Jefferson read sometime after 1793), Priestley argues

that Jesus is not the son of God but merely an exemplary moral reformer to whom God had granted the power to work miracles as a
sign of his own divine approval. Christianity can be reduced to a
few straightforward moral principles concerning our duties to one
another. Following Priestley, Jefferson now views Christ as a
human being and true Christianity as a moral code knowable by
reason and the moral sense alone. Religion merely ratifies those
moral precepts the Benevolent Creator has instilled in human nature so that men may live together peaceably in society.[84]

What is it that "true religion" teaches, and in what way is it superior to other moral systems? A decade later, and again following
Priestley's lead, Jefferson sets out to compare the morals of Jesus
with the ancient moralists he admired as a youth.[85] Having read
Priestley's most recent "treatise" on this subject, favorably comparing Jesus with Socrates, Jefferson confides in a letter to Dr. Benjamin Rush that he, too, has come to regard Jesus' teachings as
superior. Not only does Jesus emphasize the duties we owe to each
other, rather than the duties we owe to ourselves, but he takes a
more expansive view of these obligations. When the ancient moralists speak of our duties to others, they tend to think in terms of patriotism and justice, "but scarcely viewed them [our neighbors and
countrymen] as within the circle of Benevolence. Still less have they
inculcated peace, charity, and love to our fellow men, or embraced
with benevolence the whole family of mankind."[86] It is, then, precisely because Jesus extends our moral obligations beyond justice
to benevolence, and benevolence "not only to kindred and friends,
to neighbors and countrymen, but to all mankind," that Jefferson
considers the "genuine" teachings of Christ as the "most perfect
and sublime that has ever been taught by man."[87]

Moreover, in contrast to the ancient moralists, who (as Jefferson now reads them) lay most of their emphasis on men's acts,
Jesus teaches that our motives must be as pure as our acts. "He
pushed his scrutinies into the heart of man, erected his tribunal in
the region of his thoughts, and purified the waters at the fountain-
head."[88] It is this common emphasis on motive, along with the ele-
vation of benevolence as the highest moral virtue, that encourages
Jefferson to blend the moral doctrines of Christ with those recommended by the Scottish school. From this syncretism, Jefferson reaf-
firms his belief that a Benevolent Creator has endowed human

beings with a faculty that will enable them, once they are instructed by the example of Christ, to acts of benevolence even more extensive than the most "utopian" of the Scots had proposed.

What precisely does Christianity understood as a moral code require of men as social and moral beings? To answer this question, Jefferson compiles his forty-page digest of the New Testament,[89] in which he proposes to separate the genuine moral teachings of Jesus from the fraudulent and fantastic accounts of the Evangelists. Undaunted by the complexity of the task, Jefferson repeatedly insists that the genuine teachings of Jesus are as easy to distinguish as "diamonds in a dunghill."[90] In keeping with Jefferson's general view that religion teaches only "the moralities of life and the duties of a social being,"[91] which can be known by reason and the moral sense, Jefferson omits all references to "the immaculate conception of Jesus, His deification, the Creation of the world by Him, His miraculous powers, His resurrection and visible ascension, His corporeal presence in the Eucharist, the Trinity, original sin, atonement, regeneration, election, orders of Hierarchy, etc."[92] For Jefferson, the essential teaching of Christianity is contained in the two commandments: to "love our neighbors as ourselves and to do good to all men."[93] In answer to the question Who is our neighbor? Jefferson offers the Parable of the Samaritan, which he commends as "true Benevolence."[94] Elsewhere in the table of contents, he includes Luke 14:12–14, which exhorts us to invite to the feast those who can never repay us, subjoining to it the comment "the merit of disinterested good." And he endorses Luke's view (17:7–10) that we cannot discharge our duties to others simply by fulfilling our legal obligations, adding his own comment: "mere justice no praise." Among other selections Jefferson includes without comment are Matthew 5:44 ("Love your enemies, bless them that curse you, do good to them that hate you, and pray for them that despitefully use you") and the Sermon on the Mount. Although Jefferson offers no comment on the latter selection at the time, years later he would express the wish that "all the Christian religions would rally to the Sermon on the Mount, make that the central point of Union in religion, and the stamp of genuine Christianity, since it gives us all the precepts of our duties to one another."[95] As Jefferson abridged them, the Gospels of Jesus contain the "most sublime and benevolent code of morals which has ever been offered to man,"[96] enjoining upon each individual the duty to relieve the suffering of others and to do good.

Yet precisely because the true teachings of Jesus would require the most heroic exertions, which are far beyond the natural feelings registered by the moral sense, we are justified in wondering whether such universal benevolence can reasonably be expected of the mass of citizens, and whether this is what Jefferson has in mind when he links the pursuit of happiness with virtue. The question gains force in the kind of liberal republic Jefferson helped to create, where benevolence cannot be compelled by legislation, and where the commitment to private property and individual rights runs counter to such selfless virtue. The advice in Matthew 6:25, "Take no heed for your life, what ye shall eat, or what ye shall drink; nor yet for your body, what ye shall put on," or Matthew 19:21, "If thou wilt be perfect, go and sell what thou hast, and give it to the poor, and thou shalt have treasure in heaven," both of which Jefferson includes in his digest, seems well beyond the reach of a democratic society. The problem is not that Jefferson lacks a vision of human excellence but, on the contrary, that at its highest it may be too exalted and self-denying for a liberal republic.

Jefferson's appropriation of Christian benevolence for his own social and political purposes helps us to appreciate both the strength of his moral vision and the defects to which it almost inevitably gives rise. Although the model of Christian love that Jefferson recommends as the *akmē* of purely "human excellence" remains beyond the reach of most individuals, it does continue to inspire the imagination and to evoke the greatest admiration and esteem whenever, in all its purity and innocence, it appears. Instructed by carefully chosen Gospel stories, the moral sense reserves its highest approbation for those sentiments that inspire voluntary acts of extensive benevolence.

Yet at the same time, there is the danger that Jefferson's use of the Bible for purely social and political ends may encourage its own particular form of corruption. The reduction of religion to a mere moral code concerned principally with our obligations in this world may inspire political idealists to use the innate "love of others" for their own ends. Failing to recognize that benevolence is a virtue only when it is uncoerced, and divorcing the practice of virtue from the duties owed to God, such moralists may be tempted to remake the world by compelling others to exercise benevolence and compassion. The model of universal philanthropy set forth in the Gospels and endorsed by Jefferson sets no geographic or political limits to such aspirations.[97]

Jefferson himself avoids this danger through moderation and common sense. Although the Gospels offer the "most sublime" moral principles known to humankind, Jefferson does not realistically expect most men and women to model their lives on the Good Samaritan. Indeed, it is striking that in his letters to his daughters and (later) his grandchildren, he never mentions these Bible stories or holds them up as a model of moral conduct. As far as his own daughters are concerned, the duties of benevolence extend no further than to their families and those immediately around them: "The circle of our nearest connections is the only one in which a faithful and lasting affection can be found. . . . It is therefore the only soil on which it is worth while to bestow much culture."[98]

Within this circle, Jefferson advises his daughters to cultivate those pleasing dispositions that will win them the approval and admiration of their family and friends: "Never be angry with any body, nor speak harm of them, try to let every body's faults be forgotten, as you would wish yours to be; take more pleasure in giving what is best to another than in having it for yourself, and then all the world will love you, and I more than all the world."[99] It is altogether an agreeable portrait, in which individuals are linked through the natural bonds of affection and goodwill, and each understands that her own happiness is linked to the happiness and well-being of others. And in a further concession to realism, Jefferson acknowledges that even within the family the exercise of these virtuous dispositions will not always be as easy as he elsewhere suggests.[100] Although the benevolence he seeks to instill in his daughters is considerably less demanding than the extensive philanthropy held up in the Gospels, even this more limited virtue requires considerable practice and effort to bring the desires into alignment with what is right.

Finally, despite the model of extensive benevolence Jefferson admires in the Gospels, he recognizes that for all but the most liberal minds, the further most people move from their intimate attachments, the weaker the impulse to do good. Thus, backing away from the most "sublime" moral teachings of the New Testament, Jefferson advises his grandson that he owes nothing more than good humor or, failing even that, the "artificial" virtue of politeness to mere acquaintances and strangers. Indeed, it is precisely the mark of good humor that it "deprive[s] us of nothing worth a moment's consideration"; it demands nothing more than the sacrifice of "the little conveniences and preferences." No wonder Jefferson can exclaim: "How cheap a price for the goodwill of another."[101] In practice, the biblical proclamation "goodwill toward men" turns out, for most people, most of the time, to be little more than a call to civility and good manners.

The Enduring Appeal of Jefferson's Moral Vision

It is easy to criticize a moral vision that ranges from the exalted to the quotidian, in which all human beings are simultaneously called to the most extensive benevolence and yet praised for their amiability and mere politeness. Thus, Thomas L. Pangle and Lorraine Smith Pangle object that Jefferson's moral sense doctrine leaves no room for magnanimity; it seems to cut off at the roots the psychological motivation of the great-souled man, who acts for others not out of any moral sentiment directed toward their well-being but out of a sense of his own superior nature and what is due him.[102] But magnanimity of this sort cannot regularly be expected in a liberal republic, founded on the proposition that "all men are created equal." It properly belongs to an earlier, more aristocratic age, like the one Jefferson deliberately set out to overthrow.

At the opposite extreme, Gordon Wood lays bare what some revolutionaries regarded as the residual hierarchical assumptions of benevolence. Although benevolence is intended to replace earlier relations of hierarchy and dependence by uniting people on the basis of so-called natural affections, the obligation of gratitude to which benevolence gives rise masks a lingering inequality and dependence. In the end, benevolence must give way to the more powerful and radical forces of democratic equality.[103]

But what has been the effect of this more radical idea of equality on the American character? We have moved from Jefferson's faith in the capacity of ordinary men and women to discipline their selfish desires and bring them under the governance of the moral sense to a postmodern doubt about the very possibility of moral judgment. Under this dispensation, we have seen the virtual extinction of politeness and civility, even as the voices calling for the public enforcement of benevolence have become more insistent.

As Americans struggle with these problems today, Jefferson's moral vision has much to recommend it. More than any other Founder, Jefferson speaks to the republican hope that human beings can act as responsible moral agents. But at the same time, he reminds us that virtue and good character depend on instruction and practice. Human beings may have a natural instinct for virtue, but this instinct requires training and development before it bears fruit. Moreover, the task of building character is, and in a liberal republic must remain, primarily the responsibility of the family, and of economic arrangements and social institutions that operate outside the sphere of the government. We turn now to a consideration of how work and property help to shape the American character.

Chapter Three

Work, Property, and Character: Agrarian Virtue and Commercial Virtue

While acknowledging the primacy of the family in developing the moral character of the young, Jefferson recognizes that broader cultural forces also influence the kind of people Americans will become. He sees clearly that the habits and attitudes engendered by different kinds of work shape the soul of the individual and of the Republic in fundamentally different ways. Whether a man is his own master or labors for another; whether he tills the soil, performs simple repetitive operations in the workshop, or speculates in markets has implications that reach beyond the purely economic. So, too, do the laws and mores bearing on property and wealth. A society that protects the right to own, inherit, and freely dispose of property, or that encourages citizens to acquire and increase their wealth and possessions, fosters habits and virtues quite different from one that subordinates material gratification to moral, spiritual, or political concerns. And refining the issue still further, *how far* a society encourages its citizens to increase their wealth and possessions also affects their character.

Jefferson's reflections on work, property, and character can be grouped around three related issues: first, a decided preference for agriculture not merely as an occupation but as a morally superior way of life; second, a fear that a more fully developed commercial society will corrupt the American character by encouraging unwholesome occupations, consolidating and expanding political power, and promoting the rise of cities; and third, a defense of private property rights, and especially small-scale land ownership, as a means of fostering those virtues appropriate to a modern liberal republic.

Agriculture and Character:
The Intellectual and Martial Virtues

Jefferson's praise of agrarian life in Query XIX of the *Notes on Virginia* is arguably his most famous pronouncement on virtue, and among the most controversial. Unlike the moral sense doctrine, currently enjoying a revival in political and moral discourse, Jefferson's insistence that "those who labour in the earth are the chosen people of God, if ever he had a chosen people," stands as a direct rebuke to contemporary American life. For if there is, as Jefferson insists, a connection between the kind of work we do and the character of the people we are, then Americans today, clustered in cities and suburbs, commuting long distances to jobs outside the home and away from the land, would seem to have lost one of the most basic conditions for "substantial and genuine virtue."[1]

For the most part, the scholarly response has been to dismiss Jefferson's defense of agrarianism as "archaic."[2] Compared with Hamilton, who anticipated and actively helped shape the course of modern economic development, all the while coolly accepting that, as riches increased and became concentrated in a few hands, virtue would increasingly be "considered as a graceful appendage of wealth,"[3] Jefferson's insistence that farmers are the only morally "healthy" parts of the country strikes many observers as moralistic and obsolete. Indeed, some scholars have gone even further, exposing what they see as the vicious underside of Jefferson's agrarian vision.[4] According to Harry Jaffa, Jefferson's efforts to increase the supply of uncultivated lands available to future generations inadvertently worked to encourage the spread of slavery in the territories. Moreover, Jefferson's insistence on the moral superiority of the independent farmer, who cultivated the soil by the sweat of his brow, inevitably spilled over to the plantation holder, reinforcing the latter's already considerable pride in his own distinctive way of life.[5]

In the face of these powerful objections, is there still a case, however modest, for agrarian virtue, or at least for those virtues traditionally associated with the cultivation of the soil?[6] And, if so, how does agrarian virtue fit in with Jefferson's overall conception of character and, more particularly, with the amiable social virtues recommended by the moral sense? We begin with the agrarian tradition in political philosophy and consider what precisely Jefferson means by agrarian virtue.

In insisting on the moral superiority of a republic of farmers, Jefferson is hardly breaking new ground. As far back as the *Politics*, Aristotle had elevated the life of the husbandman above all other modes of acquisition, while ranking the activities of the businessman, unrestrained by any natural limits in his pursuit of wealth, as worse than that of a pirate. The Roman poets, especially Horace and Virgil, sang the praises of the pastoral life, and Jefferson recorded their thoughts in his *Literary Commonplace Book* and elsewhere.[7] In his own time, both the French Physiocrats and the Scottish philosopher Adam Smith reaffirmed the moral superiority of agriculture as a way of life, even as the latter associated himself with the emerging commercial society that would eventually supplant it.[8]

Yet despite Jefferson's repeated insistence on the moral superiority of the agrarian life, nowhere does he elaborate on those virtues that agriculture supposedly fosters. Query XIX remains the fullest statement of his position; elsewhere he seems content merely to assert the positive influence of husbandry on morals, as, for example, when he observes that agriculture will "contribute most to real wealth, good morals, and happiness," or that Americans will remain virtuous for as long as they are "chiefly agricultural."[9]

Because Jefferson never systematically develops his notion of agrarian virtue, it is useful to begin by considering Adam Smith's extended discussion of the relationship between work and character in *The Wealth of Nations*, a text that Jefferson for much of his life regarded as "the best book extant" on political economy.[10] In keeping with the eighteenth-century tendency to regard economics as a branch of moral philosophy rather than an exact science, the author of *The Theory of Moral Sentiments* contrasts the effects of agricultural and commercial economies on individual character. Beginning with the agricultural system, Smith observes that the variety of tasks and skills required of even the most simple farmer makes him "far superior" to those urban factory workers whose jobs are organized around the division of labor.

Although elsewhere in *The Wealth of Nations* Smith praises the division of labor for vastly increasing productivity, in these passages he suggests that this specialization comes at a high price to the character of the laborer. Not only his judgment and intelligence but his capacity for exercising the martial and political virtues traditionally associated with citizenship diminishes as the range of his economic activity contracts. "The man whose whole life is spent in performing a few simple operations, of which the effects are, perhaps, always the same, or very nearly the same, has no occasion to exert his understanding, or to exercise his invention finding out expedients for removing difficulties which never occur." After a time, these habits of the mind atrophy, and the artificer becomes as "stupid and ignorant" as a human being can become. He not only loses his ability to enter into "rational conversation" but also becomes incapable of "conceiving any generous, noble, or tender sentiment," and consequently of performing any "of the ordinary duties of private life." On matters of public concern, he remains "altogether incapable of judging," and still less of fighting, because the stationary and repetitive character of his work "corrupts the courage of his mind," and even the "activity of his body."[11] In short, there is clearly a tension between the demands of increased industrial productivity and the cultivation of "intellectual, social, and martial" virtue that makes the laboring poor unfit for the responsibilities of citizenship, unless the state intervenes to correct these defects through education.[12]

Turning from the factory laborers to the more prosperous merchants and traders who fuel the commercial order, Smith observes that although they may possess greater knowledge and judgment, their capacity for civic virtue is open to question. Anticipating many of the current objections to corporate capitalism, Smith warns that the business classes, in single-minded pursuit of profits, are least likely to feel a sense of loyalty to their country or their fellow citizens.[13]

Finally, rounding out the moral arguments against the emerging commercial order and in favor of agriculture is an aesthetic dimension: "The beauty of the country besides, the pleasures of a country life, the tranquility of mind which it promises, and wherever the injustice of human laws does not disturb it, the independence it really affords, have charms that more or less attract everybody."[14] Thus, Smith predicts that in America, where land is plentiful and "the system of natural liberty" enables men to choose whatever way of life they regard as the most satisfying, the vast

majority will choose to cultivate the land rather than seek employment in manufacturing or other commercial pursuits that compromise their economic and moral independence. Summing up the
attitude of the American farmer, Smith observes, in words that Jefferson echoes in the *Notes:* "He feels that an artificer is the servant
of his customers, from whom he derives his subsistence; but that a
planter who cultivates his own land, and derives his necessary subsistence from the labour of his own family is really a master and independent of all the world."[15]

Smith's discussion of how an agricultural economy shapes the
character of its citizens provides a useful point of departure in trying to understand what Jefferson means by agrarian virtue. Like
Smith, Jefferson credits the variety of agricultural tasks with stimulating both the intellect and the imagination. With obvious pleasure,
Jefferson can point to the wide range of subjects on which the
farmer can converse: "I talk of ploughs and harrows, of seeding and
harvesting, with my neighbors, and of politics too, if they choose."[16]
What Jefferson has in mind is not the transmission of traditional arts
of cultivation from father to son, or the exchange of mere pleas-
antries among neighbors, but the discovery and dissemination of
the most up-to-date scientific knowledge of agriculture. To encourage the study of agriculture as a science, Jefferson proposes that
"every College and University" establish a "professorship of agriculture" to restore this most useful and respectable calling to its
rightful place as "the crown of all other sciences."[17] And to dissem-
inate this knowledge among farmers, he supported the establishment of a system of agricultural societies across the country and in
1817 helped found the Agricultural Society of Albemarle.

But it is not simply the knowledge of crop rotation, agricultural experiments, new machinery, and the like that Jefferson expects farmers to acquire. The spirit of scientific husbandry
invigorates all the faculties of the mind; at the same time, the
leisurely rhythms of the farm year supply opportunities to read
and learn. It is a point of considerable pride that American farmers
are not compelled, as European factory workers are, to labor sixteen hours a day merely to survive on "oatmeal and potatoes,"
with "no time to think" or to participate in politics.[18] Americans are
"the only farmers who can read Homer,"[19] for pleasure and, perhaps more important, for useful information and instruction.

Judged by the modern standard of utility, the kind of scientific agriculture Jefferson supports can plausibly be said to invigorate the faculties of imagination and understanding, and so contribute to what Smith in some very loose sense calls "intellectual virtue." The discernment and skills involved in overseeing the varied activities of farm life require a wide range of knowledge and are likely to stimulate new ideas, especially when compared with the monotonous, repetitive tasks performed by an artificer on the shop floor. Although this is not genuine intellectual virtue as Smith or Jefferson understands it (and still less as the ancients conceived it), the broad competence of the farmer in all matters relating to his own well-being provides a solid foundation for republican self-government.[20]

If Jefferson roughly follows Smith in regarding the life of the plowman as more favorable to the cultivation of the mental faculties than that of the artificer or mechanic, he makes no claim that farming promotes the martial virtues traditionally associated with republican citizenship. Neither the rigors of physical exercise nor the spirited engagement with nature disposes the American farmer to the kind of physical courage and military valor that characterize Rome and Sparta. In his most utopian moments, Jefferson seems to believe that agrarianism has a special affinity with peace. More than once he suggests that if all Americans would withdraw from the world and take up agriculture, there would be no need for martial virtue because there would be no wars. "Were I to engage my own theory, I should wish them [the states] to practice neither commerce nor navigation, but to stand with respect to Europe precisely on the footing of China. We should then avoid wars, and all our citizens would be husbandmen."[21] From this perspective, the moral superiority of agriculture might be said to consist in rendering martial virtue obsolete.

Yet whatever the theoretical merits of a nation devoted exclusively to farming, and holding itself apart from the commercial and warlike impulses that ravaged Europe, Jefferson understands that he is not free to engage in idle speculation about which way of life best contributes to human happiness and virtue. He must start with the American character as it is, not how he would like it to be. Americans have no wish to live in agrarian isolation, shut off from the rest of the world. "Our people have a decided taste for navigation and commerce,"[22] which they insist upon exercising for themselves in trade, transportation, and fishing. Realistically, this means that wars "must sometimes be our lot; and all the wise can do, will be to avoid that half of them which would be produced by our own follies, and our own acts of injustice; and to make for the other half the best preparations we can."[23]

How should America prepare for war, and how important are the classical republican virtues of patriotism and martial courage in the agrarian republic? As early as the *Notes*, Jefferson warns that the principal threat to the nation's growing international shipping and trade will come from over the waters: "The sea is the field on which we should meet a European enemy."[24] Accordingly, he supports a modest naval force sufficient to defend American coasts and harbors, as well as to repel attacks on her ships at sea.[25] At the same time, the establishment of a naval militia promises to relieve another of Jefferson's anxieties concerning the future of agrarian America: what to do with a surplus population no longer able to earn a living from the land. Jefferson worries that at some point, still "distant," agriculture will no longer be able to sustain the growing American population. Agricultural abundance, spurred by the kind of scientific advances and technological innovations Jefferson champions, will force growing numbers of Americans off their farms. Faced with the question of where to channel this surplus population, Jefferson recommends that these individuals turn "to the sea in preference to manufactures: because comparing the characters of these two classes [sailors and manufacturers] I find the sailors the most valuable citizens."[26]

Jefferson's proposal is surprising because it flies in the face of the entire republican tradition, which from the time of Plato and Aristotle up to our own day has viewed the life of the sailor as destructive of both individual and national character.[27] Constant exposure to a variety of strange and exotic practices weakens the sailor's sense of right and wrong and undermines his moderation and self-control. Meanwhile, the nation pays the cost of large naval establishments in the form of burdensome taxes and frequent wars. For these reasons, James Madison, in a newspaper essay a few years later considering the most desirable "Republican Distribution of Citizens" in terms of the "health, virtue, intelligence, and competency in the greatest number of citizens," would rank the occupation of sailing as the least eligible in every respect for republican societies, beneath both the manufacturing and mechanical occupations. Sailing not only is dangerous to the body but also deadens the mind. "Though traversing and circumnavigating the globe, he sees nothing but the same vague objects of nature, the same monotonous occurrences in ports and docks; and at home in his vessel, what new ideas can shoot from the unvaried use of the ropes and the rudder, or from the society of comrades as ignorant as himself." Moving from the intellectual to the moral domain, Madison warns that the sailor's moral "virtue, at no time aided, is occasionally exposed to every scene that can poison it."[28]

What is it, then, about the life of the sailor that leads Jefferson to conclude, against the accumulated weight of the republican tradition, that seafaring ought to be preferred over manufacturing as a valuable occupation for republican citizens? Jefferson's answer has less to do with the putative virtue of sailors than with the corrupting effects of manufacturing: "I consider the class of artificers as the panders of vice, and the instruments by which the liberties of a country are generally overturned."[29] In Jefferson's catalog of vices, exploited factory workers, eking out a bare subsistence producing useless luxury items for a decadent aristocracy, pose a far greater threat to moral virtue than a "respectable body of citizen-seamen."[30] Moreover, the kind of navy Jefferson envisions will avoid the evils historically associated with great naval powers. By focusing on a defensive naval force, aimed principally at repelling coastal attacks, Jefferson hopes to avoid the ruinous costs, both financial and moral, of maintaining a powerful navy. Although this policy would enrage New England Federalists who charged successive Republican administrations with neglect of the navy, Jefferson in his first message to Congress in 1801 commends the bravery of American sailors in Tripoli and later, during the War of 1812, takes special pleasure in celebrating "the brilliant achievements of our little navy" in rescuing the American "character" and rendering "a great moral service" to the nation.[31] Ironically, if any class of citizens can be singled out for its possession of military virtue, it is the sailors who fight to defend the agrarian republic.

What, then, of the farmers? Are they not also expected to display courage and patriotism when called upon to fight for their country? For internal defense until actual invasion, Jefferson prefers a militia composed of all eligible citizens over a standing army, which, in keeping with the republican tradition, he regards as a danger to liberty. Although they are not professional soldiers, Jefferson expects that a militia consisting mainly of farmers fighting in defense of their homeland will display the greatest *amor patriae*.[32] Yet when the test came during the War of 1812, militiamen showed little enthusiasm for protracted engagements far from their homes. Although part of the problem can be traced to a liberty-loving administration determined to "introduce the least coercion possible on the will of the citizen,"[33] there is also something about the "solid charms" of agrarian life, especially in a liberal republic, that turns farmers away from extended military service. "I think the truth must now be obvious that our people are too happy at home to be drawn into regular service"[34] without some form of government compulsion. And for the most part, Jefferson is right. Rural farmers have historically inclined toward isolationism in international affairs, preferring to channel their spiritedness into the cultivation of the earth, "and not to its destruction."[35]

That Jefferson approves of the farmers' conduct tells us much about the nature of patriotism in a liberal republic. The kind of patriotism Jefferson seeks to foster is not the unqualified love of country, the instinctive, almost religious attachment to one's ancestors and traditions, which characterizes the ancient republics. Instead, Jefferson seeks to promote what Tocqueville calls well-considered, or rational, patriotism, based on each citizen's recognition that his own freedom and happiness depend on the safety and well-being of the whole.[36] Jefferson's understanding of patriotism encourages a reasonable pride in one's country, but it does not insist, as the classical republicans did, that everything belongs to the state. Agrarian virtue is not martial valor or unconditional patriotism.

Yet, on reflection, it should not be surprising that the "substantial and genuine virtue" Jefferson expects farming to promote must be something other than the intellectual or military virtues Smith attributes to the farmer. For if farming sought primarily to encourage these virtues, the sturdy yeoman would no longer be a farmer but a philosopher or soldier.[37] Rather, the virtues that grow out of the agrarian life are concerned with the care and cultivation of the self, the family, and the land; they are forged by the peculiar interplay of physical labor and the moral imagination, stimulated by the sustained engagement with nature. These virtues include industry, moderation, patience, frugality, tranquillity of mind, love of order, and, above all, independence.

Agriculture and Character: The Moral Virtues

The first of the agrarian virtues is industry. One consequence of independence is that American farmers, freed of mercantile restrictions, now have an incentive to work harder and become more productive, since there are new markets for their crops and an increasing supply of comforts for them to buy. But it is not only the farmers who become more industrious; the latent enterprising spirit unleashed by the Revolution invigorates the efforts of all. In addition to working harder themselves, farmers put their wives and children, their hired hands and servants to work manufacturing goods for exchange in local markets.[38] Even at Monticello, where much of the household and farmwork was performed by slaves, Jefferson lectured his children and grandchildren about the evils of indolence. In his letters home, he exhorts his daughters and later his grandchildren, when not engaged in their studies, to occupy themselves with a variety of domestic chores, ranging from the cultivation of peas and strawberries to the care of bantam chickens and Algerine fowl. Through these regular tasks, Jefferson hopes to instill in his family the habits of useful occupation and industry, qualities that, next to moral rectitude, he considers essential to human happiness.[39]

If, however, modern, scientific agriculture invigorates the channels of industry, it is by no means a life of endless work and drudgery. Jefferson tacitly rejects the biblical teaching that the cultivation of the soil is the punishment Adam and his descendants must pay for having disobeyed God's commandment. In Jefferson's retelling, farmers have become "the chosen people of God, if ever he had a chosen people," while the cultivation of the soil is paradise, the Edenic life before the Fall.[40] It is this promise of comfort and plenty that Jefferson hopes will continue to stimulate the moral imagination, summoning future generations back to the land and to a life of simple virtue.

Sustained engagement with nature shapes the yeoman's character in other ways as well. The natural discipline of the life cycle teaches the virtues of patience and resourcefulness, while the regular passage of seasons reinforces a quiet love of order. Moreover, although farming was increasingly a commercial operation from which the plowman hoped to profit, the life of the cultivator is not fundamentally about making money. The small scale on which Jefferson envisions the average farmer operating naturally tempers material expectations and enforces frugality. In sum, "the moderate and sure income of husbandry" provides a comfortable subsistence, while promoting a spirit of "permanent improvement, quiet life, and orderly conduct both in public and in private."[41]

Finally, Jefferson insists that those who produce their own food are more independent than mechanics, who take orders from others, or merchants, who depend on the "caprice" of customers to support themselves and their families.[42] For Jefferson, "competency" in economic matters has important political consequences as well. As landowners with a tangible stake in the community, and enjoying the benefits of seasonal leisure, these independent yeomen can be expected to take the lead in local politics. For the farmer, local political participation is the fullest extension of his natural spiritedness, of his struggle to cultivate the land and make it bear fruit.[43] Moreover, because the farmer is his own master, he views his fellow citizens as equals, rather than as instruments of profit or sources of preferment and influence.[44] Subservience and venality, the vices of economic dependence, neither undermine his self-respect nor distort his relations with others.[45] At the same time, and no less important, the proud independence of the farmer, buttressed by habits of frugality and moderation instilled over a lifetime of sustained labor, reinforces a healthy suspicion of all government removed from the watchful eye of the people. Accordingly, Jefferson concludes that the "cultivators of the earth are the most valuable citizens. They are the most vigorous, the most independent, the most virtuous, and they are tied to their country and wedded to its liberty by the most lasting bonds."[46] The core of the American character is rooted in agrarian virtue.

Agrarian Virtue and the Moral Sense

Jefferson's insistence on the capacity of agriculture to encourage and preserve a virtuous citizen body raises three problems. In his letters discussing the foundation of morality, he maintains that virtue arises out of the innate promptings of the moral sense, reinforced from childhood by regular exercise and steady habits. But his paean to agrarianism gives the impression that virtue results exclusively from a particular kind of work, rather than from the complex interplay of the moral sense with the world around it. Second, in his discussion of the moral sense, Jefferson insists that morality rests on some foundation other than self-interest. Yet the agrarian virtues seem to be rooted in precisely a concern for the self and its possessions. Third, and closely connected with the second problem, the qualities Jefferson regards as the core of agrarian virtue seem to clash with the amiable virtues approved by the moral sense. Industry, frugality, patience, moderation, independence, and the like are virtues that perfect individual character, but, Jefferson argues, morality arises out of our social nature and has to do with our obligations toward others.

Let us begin with the process by which character is formed. When Jefferson discusses the moral sense he tends, quite properly, to focus on those moral sentiments that all human beings are innately equipped to receive. But these sentiments do not spontaneously result in virtuous actions; they require a long process of development and habituation before they produce the steady inclination to virtue that is called character. These habits include the proper dispositions toward learning, citizenship, and work. Although work by itself does not fully account for character, the particular habits and attitudes associated with different ways of life—for example, agricultural, slaveholding, commercial, or military—are among the most important cultural influences on the operation of the moral sense. The individual habits and virtues that different modes of acquisition encourage help to shape each society's particular understanding of justice and benevolence.

We turn next to the ground of moral action. How can the agrarian virtues, which seem to arise out of the selfish desire for individual happiness and well-being, be reconciled with Jefferson's assertion that morality must rest on some principle other than self-love? Here it is helpful to recall Jefferson's precise argument. When he observes that self-love is no part of morality, he is talking about morality "in strict language"[47] as involving only our obligations to others. Jefferson's point is not that we have no moral obligations to ourselves—that would be absurd—but that we can never arrive at a correct understanding of the duties we owe to others by starting with our own interests. Rather, our obligations to others are rooted in the more generous sentiments that bind us together as social beings. Yet, even then, the line between the selfish and the social passions is not always clear, since one of the reasons we cultivate the purely personal virtues is to win the approval of others.

Finally, we consider the relation between the agrarian virtues and the moral sense. What is the connection between the virtues relating to the independence and competency of the individual and the more admirable moral obligations we owe to others? Jefferson correctly assumes that the personal habits and virtues that agriculture encourages are a prerequisite for the exercise of the more generous moral virtues. Both moral excellence and civic virtue begin with the government of the self. Before we can fulfill our obligations to others we must first achieve independence and learn to exercise responsibility, moderation, patience, and self-control. Only then is it possible to consider the rightful claims of others, starting first with the family, then moving to the larger circle of neighbors and friends, and from there to the nation and beyond that, in however limited a capacity, to humanity as a whole.

The virtues the moral sense recommends are, above all, justice and benevolence. Justice, we recall, is that virtue that preserves and defends each individual's equal rights, including his right to property. Because of the close connection between justice and property, we shall consider this virtue more fully later on. For the present it is sufficient to note that Jefferson believes justice is most secure in a society where most citizens "possess property, cultivate their own lands, have families," and through their own moderate labor are able to support themselves in modest comfort.[48] Independence and self-mastery teach citizens to obey laws that they have made and simultaneously to resist all encroachments on their rights as free individuals.[49] To this end, Jefferson labored successfully to abolish the remnants of a feudal aristocracy in Virginia and proposed in his 1776 draft constitution for Virginia that every "person" who did not already own fifty acres of land be given that much, or so much as to make up the difference, out of unappropriated public land. Had this latter proposal succeeded, Jefferson would have achieved two of his most important goals with one stroke: every citizen of

Virginia would have had it in his power to take up small-scale farming, and each would have been attached by his most immediate interest to republican justice and the equal protection of rights. A decade later, observing the widespread misery occasioned by the unjust distribution of property in France, Jefferson repeats his wish for America: "It is not too soon to provide every possible means that as few as possible shall be without a little portion of land. The small landholders are the most precious part of the state."[50]

Secure in his rights and moderately prosperous, the independent yeoman can now heed his more generous impulses. In the *Notes*, Jefferson singles out those "discrete farmers" who, "impelled by motives of philanthropy, [the desire for the] approbation of their neighbors, and the distinction which this gives them,"[51] assume the responsibility for overseeing the support of the deserving poor. The tithe they collect is then distributed to "good farmers" who undertake to care for those "who have neither property, friends, nor strength to labor," while those who can help themselves a little or have friends who can assist them receive "supplementary aids," so that they can "live comfortably" either alone or with friends. Illness, too, brings out the most benevolent impulses in friends and neighbors. "When sick, in the family of a good farmer, . . . every member is emulous to do them kind offices, where they are visited by all the neighbors, who bring them the little varieties which their sickly appetites may crave, and who take by rotation the nightly watch over them."[52]

From the perspective of contemporary politics, fiscal conservatives and libertarians may be tempted to dismiss Jefferson's description of the "good farmer" as romantic sentimentality, while liberals may see it as laying the groundwork for a more active role for government in caring for the most vulnerable members of society. But both would be mistaken. Jefferson's farmers are not selfish individualists who recognize no moral obligation to those around them. The independent yeoman of the *Notes* is not an isolated frontiersman seeking to escape from moral and social responsibilities but a Virginia husbandman bound to neighbors and friends for mutual assistance and cooperation.[53] On the other hand, the "discrete farmers" who impose tithes on their fellow citizens do so only to support those unfortunates whose character and circumstances are personally known to them. Moreover, they act directly as a self-governing community, rather than rely on a more distant government unable, or unwilling, to make moral distinctions among the poor. Despite his generally sunny view of human nature, Jefferson recognizes that some people are poor because they lack character and will. Thus, his Bill for the Support of the Poor (No. 32) provides for workhouses and compulsory labor enforced by corporal punishment.[54] It is precisely this combination of benevolence and tough-mindedness that separates his understanding of the American character from many of today's liberals and conservatives.

It is, moreover, a conception of character that is in the truest sense organic. Jefferson expects that the agrarian virtues connected primarily with the care of the self, family, and land will lay the most durable foundation for the more amiable virtues directed toward the well-being of others. Kindness and benevolence to friends and neighbors grow out of the "germ" of agrarian virtue as naturally and abundantly as plants from seeds.

Agrarian Vice

Still, we may wonder, what relation does Jefferson's celebration of the agrarian life bear to reality? This question points in two different directions. First, as several scholars have argued,[55] Jefferson's insistence on the moral superiority of the husbandman ignores the actual dependence of much of American, and especially Southern, agriculture on slavery. But this is not exactly true. For in the query on "Manners" immediately preceding his praise of the virtuous yeoman, Jefferson frankly acknowledges that among Southern planters slavery undermines the very virtues he looks to farming to encourage: "With the morals of the people, their industry also is destroyed. For in a warm climate no man will labor for himself who can make another labor for him." Indeed, slavery not only encourages indolence, but also promotes overbearing pride, incompatible with respect for the equal rights of others. "The whole commerce between master and slave is a perpetual exercise of the most boisterous passions, the most unremitting despotism on the one part, and degrading submissions on the other. Our children see this, and learn to imitate it; for man is an imitating animal." And over time, this daily education in tyranny warps the moral sense. "The man must be a prodigy who can retain his manners and morals unde-praved by such circumstances."[56] In treating the planter separately from the independent farmer, Jefferson tacitly recognizes that wherever agriculture is allied with slavery, vice, and not virtue, will likely prevail.

To appreciate how distinctively modern, and ultimately dem-ocratic, Jefferson's vision of the agrarian republic is, it is useful to compare his views on slavery, agriculture, and virtue with those of the classical republican tradition. In the *Politics*, Aristotle argues that farming is the most desirable mode of acquisition in a regime where citizens are obliged to work, but he deems it even more ad-vantageous not to have to work at all. Accordingly, in his discus-sion of the best regime, he suggests that agriculture should be carried on by slaves so that those who are citizens may participate in politics and pursue moral and intellectual virtue unencumbered by the demands of work.[57] By contrast, Jefferson regards work, in particular the work of the husbandman, as the indispensable foun-dation for the most admirable virtues. The concern with leisure by no means disappears for Jefferson. This, in fact, is one reason he prefers the life of the husbandman to that of the manufacturer; the farmer has time for politics, friendship, and learning. But however satisfying, or even noble, these activities, they must now be fitted into the hours and seasons when farmers are not in the field. Jef-ferson's conception of virtue elevates industry over the full-time leisure of the slaveholder, which he views not as the prerequisite for the most complete virtue but as the breeding ground for the most contemptible vices.

There is, to be sure, something morally troubling about a cele-bration of agrarian virtue that overlooks the vices endemic to the slaveholding planter. But for Jefferson the virtuous yeoman be-comes the poetic embodiment of all that is good about the agrarian way of life. The success of this "myth" throughout much of our his-tory testifies to the power of the imagination, quite apart from ac-tual experience and sometimes even in spite of it, to inspire the distinctive vision of virtue and freedom that lies at the core of Jef-ferson's conception of character.[58]

Yet ironically, to the extent that Jefferson succeeds, not only in his own mind but also in the minds of his countrymen, in divorc-ing the vices of slavery from the virtues of agriculture, he leaves himself open to criticism from the opposite direction, namely, that the kind of scientific, profit-making farming he so actively promoted encourages the same vices as the commercial society he fought against. By encouraging ordinary farmers to grow more than they need in order to acquire articles that will make their lives more comfortable, does not Jefferson's system unleash the vices of avarice, venality, speculation, and dependence on foreign markets? As one critic has observed, "There certainly was never a commercial operation which begot such subservience upon a market, over which the producer himself had little or no control, or which begot such venality and ambition as the cotton kingdom."[59] Or, to put the question more broadly, as agriculture becomes, under Jefferson's direction, increasingly more commercial, is there still a case to be made for a distinctive agrarian way of life, or do the virtues and vices of agriculture simply mirror those of the larger liberal and commercial order?[60] Before we can answer these questions, we must first consider the moral case for commerce.

Commerce and Character

Jefferson's distrust of commerce and his fear of its "de-moralizing" effect on character stand in marked contrast to the generally favorable reassessment of this principle that takes place during the eighteenth century.[61] With the one notable exception of the French Physiocrats, who defend the primacy of agriculture for economic reasons, Enlightenment philosophers begin to consider the possibility that commerce may actually supply the moral foundation for a new kind of republic.

In *The Spirit of the Laws*, Montesquieu starts by examining the classical antipathy to commerce and shows how the pursuit of material well-being undermines the classical dedication to republican virtue and the common good. Yet ultimately Montesquieu's assessment of commerce is more complicated. Although commerce encourages "a traffic in all human activities and all moral virtues" as they had traditionally been understood, it also fosters new and different virtues. "The spirit of commerce brings with it the spirit of frugality, economy, moderation, work, wisdom, tranquility, order, and rule."[62] By the end of the work, he concludes that these virtues are actually preferable to the more austere and self-denying virtues so prized by the ancients because they are more conducive to individual liberty.

In his essay "Of Commerce," the Scottish philosopher David Hume applies this insight to those ancient republics that eschewed commerce in favor of purely agricultural economies. As long as the vast majority of the people devote themselves solely to farming, there is no incentive to work hard, since, in the absence of manufacturing and mechanical arts, there is nothing to buy. Thus, in all economies organized exclusively around agriculture, "a habit of indolence naturally prevails. The greater part of the land lies uncultivated. What is cultivated, yields not its utmost for want of skill and assiduity in the farmers."[63] Moreover, in such a society, where desires are so modest, and opportunities to work outside the land so limited, those who cannot make a living from farming are forced into military service. Fleets and armies may add to the grandeur of the state, but they do nothing to increase the happiness of the people. Thus, Hume concludes, the policy of the ancients, which deliberately suppressed commerce in order to control the acquisitive impulses, is "violent, and contrary to the more natural and usual course of things."[64] By contrast, modern commercial policy gives life and vigor to all parts of society, including the farmers. "When a nation abounds in manufacturing and mechanic arts, the proprietors of land, as well as the farmers, study agriculture as a science, and redouble their industry and attention."[65]

Nor does Hume's praise of commerce stop here. Turning his attention to the full range of human excellences, he insists that the luxury "which nourishes commerce," and in turn is nourished by it, gives rise to the highest intellectual and moral virtues. These are not, of course, the self-denying virtues so admired by the classical republicans. But in Hume's assessment, the austere virtues of Greece and Rome are violently at war with human nature. By contrast, the virtues that commerce tends to encourage, "industry, knowledge, and humanity," as well as "mildness and moderation,"[66] accord with human nature, and so are both more achievable and humane.

Perhaps the most interesting treatment of the relation between commerce and virtue is to be found in the works of Destutt de Tracy, the French philosopher whose political and economic writings eventually supplanted those of Montesquieu and Adam Smith in Jefferson's eyes. In his *Commentary and Review of Montesquieu's Spirit of the Laws* and his *Treatise on Political Economy*, both of which Jefferson translated for the American reading public, Tracy expands on Montesquieu's discussion of the relation between commerce and virtue. While acknowledging that "the moral effects of commerce" are too extensive to be examined in all their particulars, Tracy nevertheless spells out in considerable and appreciative detail the connection between the two. "Commerce, that is, exchange, being in truth society itself, it is the only bond among men; the source of all their moral sentiments; and the first and most powerful cause of the improvement of their mutual sensibility and reciprocal benevolence: we owe to it all that we are possessed of, good or amiable; . . . it is the author of all social good." Although Tracy concedes that commerce may sometimes cause legal disputes and even war, he nevertheless insists that on the whole it tends to soften these destructive impulses. As for those who see commerce as immoral, as founded essentially on selfishness and greed, Tracy dismisses their objections as "most insipid" and "insignificant." For Tracy, "avidity consists in taking the goods of others by force or deceit, as in the two noble trades of conquerors and courtiers." In language that far exceeds Smith's more measured assessments, Tracy then goes on to praise the moral character of merchants: "Merchants, like all other industrious persons, seek only for reward in their talents, by means of free agreements entered into with good faith and guaranteed by laws. Application, probity, moderation are necessary, for them to succeed: and consequently they contract the best moral habits." Pausing only briefly to consider whether merchants are too concerned with profits, Tracy concedes that perhaps we could wish them "more liberal and tender in their disposition" than they usually are. But seeing as how perfection is not to be expected from men, he concludes, "a people modelled in general on such as those we have mentioned, would be the most virtuous of all others."[67] What Tracy has done in his commentary on Montesquieu's discussion of the moral effects of commerce is for the first time to make the link between commerce and the moral sense explicit.[68] Because commerce arises out of the desire to satisfy the needs of others, rather than self-interest (as Smith had maintained), it is the source of all our moral feelings, including "reciprocal benevolence."

Although in all other respects an enthusiastic supporter of Enlightenment principles, Jefferson worried that a fully developed commercial society would encourage moral vice and political corruption. Still, the agrarian republic he defends is one that accepts the necessity, and even the desirability, of commercial exchange, albeit in "restricted" form. Even in his most poetic rendering of agrarian life, the spirit of commerce is never far from the surface.[69] As Query XIX makes clear, Jefferson's virtuous farmers are all involved in commerce. The only way a nation of cultivators can make a living without going into debt (and debt, more than acquisitiveness, is, for Jefferson, the great character flaw) is by producing a surplus of raw materials and using the profits to purchase imported manufactures unavailable in America. In a variation on Hume's theme, Jefferson seems to agree that the availability of "finer manufactures" (especially when they come from workshops in Europe) can have a positive effect on the character of farmers by stimulating them to greater industry and resourcefulness. Liberated from mercantile restrictions, Americans are as "enterprising and energetic as any nation on earth."[70]

Although elsewhere in the *Notes* Jefferson frets that Americans (these same virtuous farmers of Query XIX) might become *too* concerned with making money, the whole point of commercial agriculture is to encourage farmers to grow more than they need so they will have the money to buy goods that will make their lives more comfortable.[71] For more than a quarter of a century, Jefferson sought to expand opportunities for farmers to participate in the international market. Writing to the French political economist Jean-Baptiste Say not long after the acquisition of Louisiana, the president predicted an even brighter future for commercial agriculture. If the vast uncultivated lands of America, now greatly increased, could be farmed and made productive, food supplies could be doubled or trebled and "its surplus go to nourish the now perishing births of Europe, who in return would manufacture and send us in exchange our clothes and other comforts." In pursuing this economic policy, morality was twice served: American farmers helped feed starving Europeans, while they enjoyed a way of life that gave "just weight to the moral and physical presence of the agricultural, over the manufacturing, man."[72] Old World political economists might be correct in arguing that every nation in Europe ought to develop its own manufactures, but in America, where land was plentiful, the theory of comparative advantage made good economic and moral sense.

Jefferson's endorsement of commercial agriculture brings us back to the question raised earlier. If, as Joyce Appleby has argued,[73] the agrarian republic is not an alternative to commercial society but merely one variation on this theme, what becomes of the argument for the moral superiority of the farmer? Are there any substantial moral differences between a republic of commercial farmers and a republic where all men labor in a variety of "honest" and "honorable" callings?[74] Conversely, once the commercial principle is introduced into agriculture, can this occupation escape the vices Jefferson associates with a more fully developed commercial order? Or are there still important moral distinctions between these two competing economic models?

The question of work and character in a republic both agricultural *and* commercial is further complicated by Jefferson's shifting views on the subject. He had started out in the *Notes* asserting the absolute moral superiority of farming but was later forced by events partly of his own making to encourage the development of some occupations he had earlier dismissed as unworthy of free Americans. In backing away from his position in the *Notes*, did Jefferson himself come to accept the moral equivalence of all forms of honest labor?

Query XIX is justly famous for its celebration of the virtues of agrarian life, but the title of the essay reminds us that Jefferson's subject is the desirability of encouraging manufactures in America. In developing his answer, Jefferson focuses principally on the demoralization of European workers crowded together in great urban factories. But Query XIX also disparages those household manufactures that had sprung up to supply the most basic articles of clothing during the Revolutionary War. As soon as trade with Europe could be resumed, Jefferson expected that American farmers would abandon their "coarse, unsightly, and unpleasant" productions in favor of superior imported manufactures. So powerful was his aversion to *every* form of manufacturing that he advised: "While we have land to labor . . . let us never wish to see our citizens occupied at a work-bench or twirling a distaff."[75] Carpenters, masons, and smiths he accepted as adjuncts to the agrarian enterprise, but for all manufactured goods he preferred to "let our workshops remain in Europe."

At first sight, Jefferson's hostility to household manufactures is puzzling, as the production of clothing materials and other household necessaries would seem to add to, rather than detract from, the farmer's independence. For eighteenth-century Americans, however, independence meant not self-sufficiency but avoiding those activities and jobs that placed one person under the command of another.[76] For them, selling one's labor for a living, as factory workers were forced to do, or engaging in certain crafts such as spinning or shoemaking under the supervision of another, were occupations not befitting the dignity of independent citizens. Within the household these crafts were usually assigned to dependent sons and daughters and were held in lower esteem than the life of independent farming. By contrast, commercial exchange, such as Jefferson envisions for his farmers in Query XIX, not only did not carry with it the same connotation of dependency but was actually the means to escape from this degrading condition. There was nothing demeaning about entering into the marketplace as an independent farmer to buy and sell surplus goods because the farmer took orders from no one. He entered into these market exchanges as a free and independent agent.

The corollary to the kind of commercial agriculture Jefferson envisions is free trade.[77] If the American economy focused exclusively on agriculture, cultivators must be able to export their raw materials and in turn purchase imported manufactures. To this end, Jefferson actively sought to break down foreign trade barriers and open new European markets for American agricultural products. Again from the *Notes*: "Our interest will be to throw open the doors of commerce, and to knock off all its shackles, giving perfect freedom to all persons for the vent of whatever they may chuse to bring into our ports, and asking the same in theirs."[78] For more than twenty years, first as foreign minister, then as secretary of state, and finally as president, Jefferson sought to remove discriminatory barriers to American shipping and trade. When, despite these efforts, relations with Great Britain and France deteriorated during Jefferson's administration, the president retaliated by imposing an embargo on all foreign trade. Once again, Americans responded by setting up domestic manufactures to produce what they could no longer import, this time with Jefferson's blessing.

In the face of these developments, it was inevitable that Jefferson would be asked if his views on manufacturing in the *Notes* had changed. In response to a query from one correspondent, the president conceded that had he the time to make revisions, he would certainly "qualify" his earlier remarks. What he had in mind at the time was the plight of the laboring poor driven into large-scale manufactures in "the great cities of the old countries . . . with whom the want of food and clothing necessary to sustain life, had begotten a depravity of morals, a dependence and corruption, which renders them an undesirable accession to a country whose morals are sound."[79] But in predominantly agricultural America, manufacturing arose as the natural extension of farming and reflected the virtues of an agrarian republic. Often it was the farmer himself who established a home manufactory, setting his wife and children to the production of clothing and other household goods.[80] In its more elaborate manifestations, farmers might employ laborers (together with slaves) to produce clothing and other useful household articles. As early as the 1790s, Jefferson established a nail factory at Monticello and sought unsuccessfully to restore a gristmill at Shadwell. After the embargo, he too accepted the necessity of domestic spinners and weavers, and later could inform another correspondent that he had "thirty-five spindles agoing, a hand carding machine, and looms with the flying shuttle"[81] for the supply of his farms. In contrast to the wretched situation in Europe, Jefferson came to see that in America "manufacturers are as much at their ease, and as independent and moral as are our agricultural inhabitants, and they will continue to remain so as long as there are vacant lands for them to resort to; because whenever it shall be attempted by the other classes to reduce them to the minimum of subsistence, they will quit their trades and go to laboring the earth."[82]

Thus, by the outbreak of the War of 1812, Jefferson had become an enthusiastic convert to domestic manufactures. He welcomed news of their rapid progress in the western states and eagerly reported on advances in his own "country." Manufactures were just beginning in Virginia, but the effects were altogether "salutary" and likely therefore to continue even after the war had ended. They not only encouraged the habits of economy and thrift but also freed Americans from an undue dependence on European manufactures.[83] As Jefferson belatedly came to understand, there could be no personal independence until the nation developed its own manufactures and became economically self-sufficient. In language once used to describe the small landholder, he now declared household manufactures to be "really precious."[84]

But this is as far as he is prepared to go. Unlike some of the younger members of his party, including James Madison, who eventually supported government subsidies for infant industries,[85] Jefferson only halfheartedly accepted the development of large-scale manufacturing brought on by the War of 1812, and then with considerable misgivings. As he wrote to Charles Wilson Peale, "I concur with you in doubting whether the great establishments, by associated companies, are advantageous in this country."[86] The "country" he has in mind is, of course, Virginia. In the North, large-scale "company establishments" had already begun to develop, and Jefferson agreed with the Massachusetts Republican Benjamin Austin that they were useful in asserting American independence from English manufactures. But unless future exigencies required it, he could see no reason, once American supply equaled demand, to encourage *surplus* labor to take up manufactures rather than continue to cultivate the land. To his old friend William Short, Jefferson was far more candid: "Our enemy has indeed the consolation of Satan, on removing our first parents from Paradise: from a peaceful agricultural nation he makes us a military and manufacturing one."[87] While recognizing its necessity, Jefferson resisted the development of large-scale manufacturing because he feared that work organized along industrial principles and dedicated to the "fabrications of art" rather than "the culture of the earth" would fundamentally alter the American character. His ideal remained the domestic manufacturer who worked "by the side of the agriculturalist,"[88] thereby preserving the predominance of the agrarian way of life.

Accordingly, Jefferson sought throughout his long career to strengthen and reinforce the "essentially agricultural" character of America. The task of the republican statesman is to pursue those policies that promote the true happiness and prosperity of the people, while interfering as little as possible with individual choice and free enterprise.[89] Jefferson took it for granted that, given the opportunity, most men would prefer to make their living from the land. To encourage them to do so, he sought to maintain an "equilibrium," which in fact accorded pride of place to agriculture. As he wrote to Governor James Jay, "An equilibrium of agriculture, manufactures, and commerce is certainly become essential to our independence. Manufactures, sufficient for our consumption, of what we raise the raw material (and no more). Commerce sufficient to carry the surplus produce of agriculture, beyond our own consumption, to a market for exchanging it for articles we cannot raise (and no more). These are the true limits of manufactures and commerce."[90] To exceed these healthy limits and encourage economic growth and acquisition for their own sake was to invite a "licentious commerce" inimical to the well-being of the republic.[91]

In supporting a commerce "restricted" primarily to agriculture, Jefferson believes he has discovered a middle way between the impoverished agrarian republics of antiquity and the vices he associates with the more developed commercial societies in Europe. If, through prudent statesmanship and intelligent choice, commerce can be confined to its "true limits," it would be possible to create a republic that partakes of all of its virtues and few of its vices. For although Jefferson does not admit it, many of the virtues he associates with the agrarian life are, as Hume makes so clear, stimulated by commerce. It is commerce that invigorates the channels of industry and assiduity; commerce that promotes honesty, frugality, and self-command. Ultimately, it is commerce that makes possible the moral and economic independence of the farmer.

At the same time, Jefferson hoped that a society rooted in the soil would exercise a salutary curb on the destructive commercial passions, stifling their propensity toward avarice, speculation, exploitation, and war. There would always be vice, but its causes would lie in human nature and not in the economic system. "Corruption of morals in the mass of cultivators is a phenomenon of which no age or nation has furnished an example."[92] Jefferson expects the discipline of the life cycle to reinforce a sense of natural limitation, especially with respect to economic growth and the accumulation of wealth. The great difference between Jefferson's defense of small-scale commercial agriculture and a fully developed commercial economy lies precisely in their respective capacities to produce wealth. There is a natural limit to how rich the ordinary farmer, relying principally on his own labor and that of his family, could hope to become. Even taking advantage of the most up-to-date scientific knowledge and machinery, the enterprising yeoman could hope to live comfortably, but he would never become rich. (This, incidentally, explains how Jefferson can worry about the corrupting effects of wealth and yet defend the natural right of each to the fruits of his labor. In an agrarian republic, even one animated by commerce, the tension between these two principles is far more attenuated.) Moreover, since farming is not simply a job but a way of life, Jefferson expects the nonmaterial satisfactions of husbandry to keep the acquisitive impulses in check.[93] Thus Jefferson's support for commercial agriculture cannot be understood simply in economic terms, for Jefferson, following in the tradition of eighteenth-century political economists, understands that economic choices have moral consequences. Jefferson's support for commerical agriculture is ultimately based on his understanding of which way of life is best for free men and women.

Yet if farming remains unquestionably the best way of life, Jefferson was forced early on to back away from his position in the *Notes* and to concede that it is not the only honorable calling.[94] From the first, craftsmen were welcomed, followed by fishermen, merchant marines, and sailors. Then came domestic manufacturers and, grudgingly, Northern factory workers and merchants. The list is by no means exhaustive, but Jefferson's point is that in the agrarian republic, the husbandman sets the standard for what is honorable. Certain occupations, such as banking, speculation in markets, and patronage jobs,[95] while "honest," are still not entirely honorable because they undermine society's basic values and threaten its character.

With the benefit of hindsight, it is easy to see what Jefferson missed. He did not see, as Tocqueville clearly did, that farmers too might get caught up in the scramble for wealth, indulging in land speculation and deserting their farms for the promise of greater riches in the city.[96] Nor did he anticipate how his faith in progress and scientific technology would transform agriculture by making it difficult for family farms to compete successfully with ever larger and more mechanized enterprises. As in every area of Jefferson's thought, there are tensions. But in this instance Jefferson left no doubt how they should be resolved. Reflecting on the differences between rural and urban life, he concedes that cities "nourish some of the elegant arts," but, he insists, "the useful ones can thrive elsewhere, and less perfection in the others with more health, virtue and freedom would be my choice."[97] For the vast majority of Americans, the simple charms of agrarian life more than offset the false glitter of greater material rewards.

Finance, Industrialization, and Urbanization

There is no question that Alexander Hamilton understood the newly emerging capitalist order far better than Jefferson. On the great economic issues of the day—manufacturing, banks, debt, public securities, and finance—Hamilton is generally regarded as the superior thinker. Yet in his instinctive distrust of a more "licentious commerce," Jefferson grasped something about the moral implications of capitalism, what Daniel Bell has called its "cultural contradictions,"[98] which Hamilton failed to appreciate. It was, captured in eighteenth-century terms, the question that John Adams, the backward-looking republican, asked Jefferson toward the end of their lives: "Will you tell me how to prevent riches from being the effects of temperance and industry? Will you tell me how to prevent riches from producing luxury? Will you tell me how to prevent luxury from producing effeminacy, intoxication, extravagance, vice and folly?"[99] In other words, how can a self-governing people prevent commerce, as it expands, from devouring the very virtues it promised to promote and upon which republican government in large part depends? Determined to avoid all discussion of politics with his old political rival, Jefferson chose not to respond to Adams's query. But he could have replied that this was what the Republican Party, in its opposition to large-scale industrialization, public and private debt, banks, bankruptcy laws, stockjobbers, paper money, and urbanization, hoped to prevent. For the overall effect of these commercial developments was to centralize economic and political power, multiply government offices and dependencies, promote the growth of cities, and erode moral character. A "licentious commerce" would gradually undermine industry, frugality, self-command, and independence, while encouraging a spirit of gambling, avarice, prodigality, and dependency.

Although the financial institutions of corporate capitalism differ greatly from those of the eighteenth century, Jefferson's worries about how a fully developed commercial society might corrupt the American character continue to resonate across the political spectrum. On both the left and the right, the chief complaint against capitalism is not narrowly economic; it is generally conceded that capitalism has been wildly successful in creating wealth. Rather, the complaint against capitalism is moral: it undermines allegiance to family, community, religion, and, ironically, even work, all for the sake of greater material rewards.[100] It is on the broader question of character that Jefferson's more skeptical view of capitalism remains instructive.

Consider first the question of debt. Jefferson repeatedly denounced Hamilton's observation that "a public debt [is] a public blessing."[101] Instead, he insisted that each generation should assume no more debt than it could pay off during its lifetime. Having just come through a war that could be "paid with ease, principal and interest, within the time of our own lives," he concluded that each generation should bear the burden of its own conflicts rather than carry them on at the expense of their children.[102] Obviously a nation required to pay its own way in war must also pay its expenses in peace. Frugality was the general principle; if borrowing was necessary, it must go hand in hand with taxation. In matters of public spending, the nation was merely the household writ large: public servants were expected to "expend the public money with the same care and economy we would practise with our own, and impose on our citizens no unnecessary burden."[103] There is an unconscious irony here, since Jefferson himself failed so spectacularly in matters of household economy, incurring enormous debts that would plague him throughout his life and burden his daughter and her family after his death. Nevertheless, the point remains: both the nation and the individual were expected to live within their means and not burden future generations with debt. For Jefferson, the choice is clear: "We must make our election between *economy and liberty* or *profusion and servitude*."[104] And for much of our history, Americans did exercise admirable self-restraint in matters of spending, matched by prudence in matters of saving. But beginning with the Great Depression and World War II, Keynesian economics challenged the assumptions underlying these habits.[105] The rule of fiscal prudence was the first to go; nations were not at all like families and need not worry about deficit spending. But, in time, the analogy between the household and the nation reasserted itself in a new and more destructive form. Families too need no longer worry about debt, nor about saving for the future. Personal indebtedness soared, while the American rate of savings plunged to the lowest of any industrialized economy. The generation that, in its youth, had displayed such uncommon courage and self-command now looked to its children and grandchildren to finance the mounting costs of a comfortable retirement and an extended old age. Americans are only beginning to recognize that something must be done before the baby boomers start to retire. One recent and hopeful sign is the renewed interest in a balanced budget and limiting the growth of entitlement spending.[106] But as the equivocal outcome of this debate thus far suggests, once the virtues of frugality and self-restraint have been eroded, and a consumer mentality has grown up in its place, it will not be easy to persuade Americans, either individually or as a nation, to live within their means.

Then there is the question of banks and bankruptcy laws, speculation and paper money. Jefferson feared and hated banks because he believed they exercised an arbitrary and mysterious power over the lives of ordinary citizens. Banks had the power to expand or contract the supply of money (by issuing bank notes), tighten or loosen credit, and determine which ventures to underwrite. In making these decisions, Jefferson believed it was inevitable that bankers would be guided by their own self-interest and that of their friends. Then as now, when they fail, it is the citizens who pay, in both higher taxes and personal bankruptcy.[107]

Similarly, Jefferson warned that the mania for speculation in paper money, bank notes, stocks, and bonds was diverting capital from useful investments in commerce, buildings, agriculture, and so forth, while encouraging individuals to believe they could become rich overnight without having to work. Although the gullible would surely be ruined, no one could predict where this frenzy of speculation would end, "for the spirit of gaming, when once it has seized a subject, is incurable. The tailor who has made thousands in one day, though he has lost them the next, can never again be content with the slow and moderate earnings of his needle."[108]

Of special current interest here is the growing mania for gambling, not so much in the stock and bond markets or real estate, where investment actually does some good, but in lotteries, betting establishments, and the exploding casino gambling industry across the country, where ordinary Americans risk their life's savings in the vain hope of getting rich quick.[109] Jefferson's early warnings against a "licentious commerce" serve as a useful reminder that, however successful capitalism has been in improving the lives of ordinary men and women, it fosters its own distinctive vices as well.

On the question of large-scale manufacturing Jefferson was, happily, mistaken. Based on his experiences with manufacturing in Europe, Jefferson feared that the concentration of the working poor in grim industrial cities like Manchester would prove the Achilles' heel of republican government. Forced to work sixteen hours a day just to survive, the urban poor would be putty in the hands of demagogues and unscrupulous politicians. Despite his faith in scientific progress, he did not foresee a time when the machines that so excited him in the agricultural context would revolutionize the manufacturing process, so that skilled workers might achieve an enviable level of comfort and ease.[110] Nor did he imagine that laborers might form themselves into associations to promote their economic interests, while at the same time practicing the virtues of cooperation, responsibility, and self-rule.[111] The great worry today is not the rise of large-scale manufacturing but its decline, and with it the loss of good-paying jobs in those urban areas where much of the population is concentrated.

There is, however, much to be said today in favor of Jefferson's view that great cities, *especially in America*, are injurious to "the morals, the health, and the liberty of man."[112] For even if, as Harry Jaffa once argued, American cities have historically played an important role in safeguarding the religious and civil liberties of diverse groups of citizens, so much has happened to our cities in the thirty years since Jaffa first published his essays that a reconsideration of Jefferson's praise of the virtues of rural life seems appropriate. Starting with what George F. Will has called the "physical discontent" afflicting contemporary urban life, people in cities are cramped together in ways that strain the most elementary civilities.[113] Consider the rush hour commute on the highways and in public transportation, the floor space of an average apartment, the interminable lines and crowds at every major cultural and social event, the demands on our most basic resources, including water and air. At no time in human history have so many people lived so closely together, and the situation is likely only to get worse, exacerbating not only the physical but also the moral discontents.[114] For, as Jefferson recognized, "When we get piled upon one another in large cities, as in Europe, we shall become corrupt as in Europe, and go to eating one another as they do there."[115]

What form will this corruption take? The threat today is not, as Smith warned, from demoralized factory workers, performing monotonous tasks that suffocate the germ of intellectual, moral, and civic virtue, or, as Jefferson at one time feared, from artificers and merchants degraded by their dependence on bosses or customers. The danger to moral character arises, on the one hand, from the increased dependency of a growing "underclass" that knows none of the virtues associated with work of any kind and, on the other, from the licentiousness, and even decadence, of a growing upper middle class, itself dubious about the traditional moral virtues and celebrating instead personal liberation, self-indulgence, and vulgar imitation of the underclass.[116] While Jefferson was wrong about the details, he was surely right in the larger picture: the problem with American cities is that wealth and luxury conspire with poverty and dependency to transform rights (understood as protections against the state) into morally neutral entitlements (or claims *upon* the state irrespective of moral character), while remaining oblivious to the de-moralizing effects of dependency and nihilism upon the soul of individual and country alike.

But if Jefferson correctly predicted many of the vices that would grow up in a more advanced commercial society, what use is his praise of a way of life that is now irretrievably lost to most Americans? At the most general level, Jefferson's thought remains instructive because what interests him is the effect of different kinds of work upon character. And while we are no longer a nation of farmers, it is still the case that certain kinds of work tend to encourage greater industry, independence of spirit, and better character than others. But perhaps most important, Jefferson also believed that, for rich and poor alike, work is almost always preferable to no work at all.

Seen from this broader perspective, the challenge today is twofold: first, to continue current efforts to break the cycle of dependency that corrupts the lives of so many inner-city dwellers and to begin to reverse the more subtle but pervasive entitlement mentality that afflicts a growing number of Americans from all races and classes; second, to discover how work outside the home and away from the land, concentrated in public employment, service industries, or giant corporations, can rekindle the virtues Jefferson associates with farming, not only industry and independence of spirit but also tranquillity of mind, love of order, patience, moderation, resourcefulness, and the like.

For the modern-day Jeffersonian, the first of these two tasks is complicated by the fact that the rise in dependency disproportionately involves African-Americans, who, Jefferson believed, could never be successfully assimilated into American society.[117] Although Jefferson remained confident that once blacks were no longer compelled "to live and labor for another" and were instructed in some useful employment, their character would change for the better, he did not think this moral regeneration could succeed in America.[118] Where blacks are concerned, Jefferson's pessimistic views on racial integration overshadow his thoughts on the salutary connection between work and character.

But dependency is not exclusively a black problem. The number of whites sinking into the underclass has increased ominously in recent years.[119] Moreover, a more subtle form of dependency touches all classes and races of Americans: middle-class college students, elderly retirees, the working poor, large-scale corporations, newly arrived immigrants hoping to benefit from affirmative action or social security, even Jefferson's beloved farmers, all depend on some form of government preferment and/or assistance to insulate them from the risks of daily living. To put an end to this paternalistic despotism in which "the citizens quit their state of dependence just long enough to choose their masters and then fall back into it" (Tocqueville) will require a fundamental change in public opinion. Jefferson's insistence that republican government requires self-reliance and spirited independence provides a useful starting point in this process.

Turning to the second problem, how can we restore to work under very different conditions the virtues Jefferson associated with farming? Before proceeding, we should keep in mind that some of the virtues Jefferson attributes exclusively to the husband-man, such as industry, frugality, self-command, and independence, actually depend on the stimulation provided by commerce, albeit a "restricted" commerce that takes into account the moral and political consequences of economic decisions. Moreover, even a more "licentious" commerce produces its own particular virtues, which we should try to take advantage of, rather than extinguish. Ambition, risk taking, audacity, and cosmopolitanism all have a positive effect on the American character.[120] Nevertheless, the modern-day Jeffersonian might insist that we rethink our present enthusiasm for unlimited economic growth and a constantly rising standard of living in terms of their moral consequences. While certain industries, such as casino gambling, may bring high-paying jobs to a region, what are the long-term social and moral consequences of encouraging such behavior? Alternatively, what happens when corporate enterprises squeeze out the small businesses that have traditionally supported community and civic organizations? Nor are the moral issues confined to particular industries or the decisions of individual corporations. As Daniel Bell has argued, the full-throttle capitalism of the post–World War II era has unleashed a dynamic of its own that has eroded the very virtues commerce was expected to encourage and upon which self-government depends.[121] The necessity of stimulating ever more desires and devising ingenious means of affording them has undermined frugality, moderation, tranquillity of mind, patience, and financial independence among Americans as a people.[122] At the very least, Jefferson's insistence that we consider the larger moral and political consequences of our economic system, even as we reaffirm our general commitment to free enterprise and the right of the individual to choose his or her own occupation,[123] may help to remind Americans of those "bourgeois" virtues that capitalism in its more "licentious" stages has eroded. Indeed, at a time when marketing and consumerism have insinuated themselves into the very institutions whose task it has traditionally been to restrain the commercial impulse—the family, schools, universities, and religious organizations—Jefferson's concerns about the corrosive effects of unfettered commercial activity on the character of the people seem more farsighted than obsolete.

Finally, how might the modern-day Jeffersonian creatively ap-
proximate those virtues that flourished in a rural, agricultural society? First, Americans can use modern technology to reunite the
workplace and the home. Part of what continues to make farming
attractive is that it centers economic productivity in the home and
on the land, thereby reinforcing the primacy of the family as both
the moral and the economic social unit. The separation of the
household from the workplace has tended increasingly to elevate
work and to trivialize the activities of the home, including the
moral education of children.[124] The current technological revolution may make it possible for greater numbers of Americans to
achieve the kind of moral and economic independence that existed
before the Industrial Revolution, which, in the twentieth century,
only farmers and self-employed workers have known. It may also
help to ease the population pressures on cities by enabling more
families to relocate to less congested areas.[125] Second, even if most
workers remain in or near the city, they can cultivate some of the
virtues and more healthful habits traditionally associated with rural
life by participating in recreational, sporting, and environmental organizations. Patience, resourcefulness, tranquillity of mind, love of
order, moderation in material expectations, as well as physical and
spiritual well-being, can all be strengthened by sustained contact
with the rigors and beauty of nature. Finally, public policy can continue to encourage more Americans to become home owners and to
acquire private property, for property ownership promotes personal industry and independence, as well as responsibility to the
larger community. And these, in turn, reinforce the natural sense of
justice by teaching people to honor their agreements and to respect
the equal rights of all individuals, especially their right to property.

Property and Character

Just as different kinds of work shape the American character in
subtle but perceptible ways, so, too, do the laws bearing on the inheritance, acquisition, possession, and disposition of property.
What does Jefferson mean by property, and what is the significance
of its omission from the Declaration of Independence? What
virtues does he associate with property acquisition and ownership?

And how specifically does he seek to promote these virtues through public policy?

The Origin and Nature of Property

In 1813, Jefferson, responding to a query from Isaac McPherson whether there exists a natural right to the "exclusive property" in ideas and inventions, delivered his most complete thoughts on the nature and origin of property.[126] Jefferson made short shrift of McPherson's question: there is no natural right to inventions or ideas. If anything, nature intends the opposite: "Ideas should freely spread from one to another over the globe, for the moral and mutual instruction of man, and the improvement of his condition." More than any other form of property, ideas are "incapable of confinement or exclusive appropriation." Societies may, of course, choose to protect the property of ideas in order to encourage useful inventions, and Jefferson earlier indicated that he favored such protection;[127] there is, however, no *natural* right to a property in ideas.

But the true significance of the letter lies in Jefferson's reflection on the origin and nature of property rights in general. Jefferson's approach is historical rather than philosophical. He does not seek (as Locke did) to discover the origin of the right to property in some hypothetical state of nature but instead looks to how the first societies understood the term.[128] Following the lines laid down in Kames's tract on property, which Jefferson had entered into his *Commonplace Book* while a student nearly a half century earlier, Jefferson notes how the earliest property relations were based on the principle of first occupancy. In these primitive societies, which were composed of nomadic hunters and shepherds, property "by universal law belongs to all men equally and in common, [and] is the property for the moment of him who occupies it, but when he relinquishes the occupation, the property goes with it."[129] This is why there is no *natural* right to "a separate property in an acre of land." In the earliest societies, property, whether "fixed or movable," belongs to an individual only as long as he is in direct possession or occupancy and, it would seem, is able to defend his position. Thus, there is "property" in these primitive societies, but it does not extend to what Jefferson considers the core of private property: exclusive and stable ownership. This latter form of property comes into existence only with the emergence of agriculture, which comes relatively "late in the progress of society" and, far from being the natural or original condition, is "the gift of social law." Hence Jefferson's observation that it is "a moot question whether the origin of any kind of property [in the sense of exclusive and stable ownership] is derived from nature at all."

If property rights are not strictly speaking natural rights, we can now appreciate why Jefferson omits them from the inalienable rights listed in the Declaration. For, as we have seen, inalienable rights refer to that category of natural rights that we cannot give up or transfer to another, either because it is not possible for others to exercise these rights for us (e.g., the right of conscience) or because such a transfer runs contrary to our own good. Although all inalienable rights are natural rights, deriving their inalienability from man's inherent nature, not all natural rights are inalienable. Stable and exclusive property, being less than a natural right, cannot be inalienable.

Nevertheless, it would be a mistake to conclude that property rights are simply conventional, that they rest on no firmer foundation than the wishes of the majority. Although "stable ownership" is established by consent, it does have a certain natural foundation. As Jefferson elsewhere observes, "The right to property is founded on certain natural wants, in the means by which we are given to satisfy these wants, and the right to what we acquire by these means, without violating the similar rights of other sensible beings."[130] The implications of this statement become clearer when we compare it with Madison's famous argument in *Federalist* No. 10.[131] Whereas Madison sees the rights of property originating in men's unequal faculties alone and concludes that society's first task is to protect these unequal faculties, Jefferson holds that property is grounded in *two* natural principles that are to some extent in tension with each other: men's equal wants and their unequal talents for satisfying these needs. Through its conventions, society must somehow reconcile these two contradictory aspects of human nature that lie at the core of property relations. If, as in prerevolutionary France, society fails to do so, then existing property laws must give way to the more "fundamental right to labor." Although there is no natural right to the secure and exclusive ownership of property, particular property laws either accord with or "violate natural right."[132] Insofar as property arrangements are based on each individual's "natural wants" and natural talents, they are not simply conventional.

The Virtues of Private Property

Jefferson's understanding of the virtues connected with property is decidedly modern and democratic. Whereas classical political philosophy tends to emphasize the virtues that flow from the right use of property and possessions after they are acquired, and to deprecate those ways of life that are unduly concerned with the mere acquisition of wealth,[133] modern political philosophy, beginning with Machiavelli and continuing through the seventeenth and eighteenth centuries, looks at acquisitiveness in a more positive light. "All men," observes Machiavelli, "desire to acquire." And those who do so successfully are praised and not blamed. In this revised assessment of acquisitiveness, those passions and actions that help men to acquire and increase their possessions are now considered virtuous.[134] After Machiavelli, political philosophers like Locke continue to speak of the right use of property, but this now means encouraging greater industry and productivity, rather than liberality or hospitality, as the ancients had argued.[135] Indeed, from the perspective of an emerging commercial society, liberality and hospitality seemed to Adam Smith more like necessities than virtues. Classical gentlemen freely shared their possessions with friends and guests because, in a society that actively subdued the acquisitive instincts, they had no productive outlet for their wealth and property.[136] But the ancients were wrong: it was not necessary to suppress the acquisitive impulses in order to encourage the most admirable virtues. As the author of both *The Wealth of Nations* and *The Theory of Moral Sentiments*, Smith tries to show that the selfish and the social passions work toward the same end. The man who gives free rein to his selfish desire to acquire now has the means, and also the motive, to act on his more generous impulses. Apparently Jefferson agreed, for the only entry on property recorded in his *Commonplace Book* contains the following observation by Lord Kames: "Property gives life to industry, and enables us to gratify the most dignified natural affections." What Kames approvingly calls "a remarkable propensity for appropriation" provides the material foundation for the free and full exercise of "generosity, benevolence, [and] charity."[137]

In keeping with the modern emphasis on acquisitiveness, the first of the virtues Jefferson associates with property is industry. Jefferson's firsthand observation of the unjust property laws of prerevolutionary France, where much of the land lay idle and uncultivated, while the poor were unable to find work, leads him to reflect on the reasons society consents to private property in the first place. After all, the earth is originally given as a *common* stock for man to labor and live on. Why should society agree to protect the individual's exclusive claim to a portion of that property, for both himself and his heirs? Here, too, Kames's influence is evident. In the section from the "History of Property" that Jefferson entered into his *Commonplace Book,* Kames had argued that it is only when societies reach the agricultural stage that the question of stable ownership arises, for men would not undertake the arduous task of cultivating the earth unless they were guaranteed the enjoyment of the fruits of their labor. Like Kames, Jefferson concludes that societies agree to protect the exclusive right to own private property "for the encouragement of industry."[138] Exclusive and stable ownership can be justified only when it increases productivity so that all the members of society, including those without land, benefit from the partition. The aristocratic conception of property ownership, which permits lands to lay "idle mostly for the sake of game," promotes indolence among the nobles and wretchedness among the people. It is, moreover, manifestly unjust because it denies to those who are willing to work their "fundamental right to labor the earth" for the sake of mere sport. By contrast, Americans agreed to abolish aristocratic property laws and mercantile restrictions precisely to encourage greater industry and productivity. And where individual effort is so richly rewarded, the people are most at their "ease" when they are most busy, not only in their private pursuits but also in "opening rivers, digging navigable canals, making roads, building public schools, establishing academies, . . . [in short, in] reforming and improving our laws in general."[139]

By expanding opportunities for all individuals to acquire, increase, and freely dispose of their possessions, Jefferson, like Kames, hopes to multiply acts of liberality, generosity, charity, hospitality, and benevolence. There is not a country on earth "where strangers are better received, more hospitably treated, and worth a more sacred respect."[140] Nor is there a nation in the world where charity is more "comfortable" and more "certain." Because it is easy for most men to earn a comfortable living in America, they are more inclined to assist those who by some misfortune are thrown back upon the charity of their neighbors and friends.[141] Americans can afford to be generous to those in need among them.

The operative words here are "among them." Jefferson's efforts to promote the widespread ownership of landed property give his understanding of charity and generosity a decidedly concrete and particularistic cast. A nation of small landholders will have only modest resources with which to assist others, and these are best deployed to relieve the suffering of those "nearest around them."[142] Despite his admiration for the universal benevolence of the Gospels, Jefferson repeatedly declines to support benevolent associations that seek to practice an "expanded liberality" by doing good in "remote regions of the earth."[143] "Why," he asks another petitioner, should we "give through agents whom we know not, to persons whom we know not, and in countries from which we get no account, when we can do it at short hand, to objects under our eye, through agents we know, and to supply wants we see?"[144] Jefferson speaks for all rural landholders, attached to particular places and to particular people, when he makes it a rule to confine his own private giving to individuals and institutions "within the circle of his own inquiry and information," and over which he (and not some remote institution) can exercise control.[145] Moreover, although every man has "a duty to devote a certain portion of his income for charitable purposes,"[146] in a liberal republic this is a private matter to be determined by the prudence and moral sense of each individual.

While the modern understanding of property provides the material foundation to practice the most amiable moral virtues, the virtue most closely connected with property is justice.[147] At the most general level, justice is the virtue that binds a political community together; through its laws and institutions, each society expresses its judgment about how property and honors should be distributed among its members. Different societies do, of course, differ in their conceptions of justice; hence there are different forms of government. Oligarchies seek to protect wealth; aristocracies honor good birth and virtue; democracies elevate equality above all other considerations. Yet despite the variety of opinions respecting justice, Jefferson denies that justice is merely conventional. Nature does instruct those who will but consult her on which political arrangements are best. However unequal men may be in their talents and virtue, all are equally endowed with the same inalienable rights.[148] Justice requires that all men honor their agreements with others and respect the rights of all, including the equal right to unequal amounts of property arising from the inequality of talent. For Jefferson, natural right and natural rights coincide; true justice is republican and democratic.

Accordingly, in the same year that Jefferson penned the Declaration of Independence, he introduced into the state legislature bills to dismantle the remnants of aristocratic privilege in Virginia. And in 1779, as part of the Revisal of the Laws, Jefferson succeeded in abolishing primogeniture and entail. Speaking of A Bill Directing the Course of Descents in his *Autobiography*, Jefferson makes clear that the right of all children, male and female, to inherit equally, rather than have the entire estate descend to the eldest male, accords with natural right. To the objections of Edmund Pendleton, who supported primogeniture and proposed as a compromise measure that "we should adopt the Hebrew principle, and give a double portion to the elder son," Jefferson replied that "if the eldest son could eat twice as much, or do double work, it might be a natural evidence of his right to a double portion; but being on a par in his powers and wants, with his brothers and sisters, he should be on a par also in the partition of the patrimony."[149] More generally, the right of parents to distribute their estates equally, as their natural affections inclined them, will have a positive effect on the character of the children. For laws that privilege the firstborn son injure "the morals of youth by rendering them independent of, and disobedient to, their parents."[150] Thus, by rooting out the last vestiges of the old "Patrician order," Jefferson helps lay the foundation for his distinctively republican view of justice.

Property, Virtue, and Public Policy

Although Jefferson believes that true justice accords with the democratic and republican principle of equality, justice in America neither requires nor supports radically egalitarian or redistributionist measures. It is true that some of Jefferson's theoretical pronouncements, in particular his argument that "the earth belongs in usufruct to the living" and his observation that "legislators cannot invent too many devices for subdividing property,"[151] seem, when considered in the abstract, more radical than they are. When, however, we examine the context of these remarks and consider the specific proposals that follow from them, Jefferson's view of property and of the virtues connected with it accords with his own particular brand of liberal republicanism, and not with more radically egalitarian or communitarian philosophies.[152] Take, for example, the first of these two principles. Reflecting on the implications of this "thought experiment," Jefferson concludes that it is

> of very extensive application and consequences, in every country, and most especially in France. It enters into the resolution of the question whether the nation may change the descent of the lands holden in tail? Whether they may change the appropriation of lands given antiently to the church, to hospitals, colleges, orders of chivalry, and otherwise in perpetuity. Whether they may abolish the charges and privileges attached on lands, including the whole catalogue, ecclesiastical and feudal? It goes to hereditary offices, authorities and jurisdictions; to hereditary orders, distinctions and appellations; to perpetual monopolies in commerce, the arts and sciences; with a long train of et ceteras; and it renders the question of reimbursement a question of generosity and not of right.[153]

Note that this is obviously an extraconstitutional principle. Jefferson does not imply that people are free to act on this idea in disregard of settled law as a matter of course. Such a radical redistribution of property can take place only in a revolutionary situation, outside the established constitutional order. Yet when such a revolution occurred in America a decade earlier, Jefferson acted with far greater circumspection. Although "the earth belongs to the living" would have permitted Virginia to claim lands that the Crown had granted the Anglican Church in perpetuity, and Jefferson himself would have distinguished between public and private donations, allowing the churches to retain in perpetuity only that property that was privately given, his draft of the Bill for Saving the Property of the Church Heretofore by Law Established allowed the church to retain its ancient holdings.[154] Perhaps this was, as Jefferson would later suggest in his thought experiment, a question of "generosity and not of right," but in the event, Jefferson acceded to the legislature's wish to preserve intact the ancient property rights of the church.

Nevertheless, Madison, responding to Jefferson's proposal, objected that periodic constitutional revisions would lay the ground for a permanent revolution in which all security to property disappeared, as different parties within the rising generation jockeyed to redivide the wealth of the previous generation in their favor.[155] In principle this is true, but as Herbert Sloan has pointed out, although Jefferson continued to advocate constitutional change at regular intervals throughout his life, in later years "the practical weight of Jefferson's principle moves heavily in favor of hostility to debt"[156] and not to a radical revision of property laws. Lance Banning gets at the same point from a different direction when he emphasizes that Jefferson wished to protect not only the industry of each man but also *that of his fathers*," thereby suggesting that whatever the theoretical reach of his thought experiment, in practice Jefferson had no serious interest in redistributing the wealth of the previous generation.[157]

On closer inspection, Jefferson's remark that "legislators cannot invent too many devices for subdividing property" is also less radical than it at first appears. He is, after all, talking about the "enormous inequality" of prerevolutionary France. Yet even then, the only two devices he mentions are quite moderate: the abolition of entail and primogeniture, together with progressive taxation. Moreover, the goal is never an egalitarian redistribution of wealth: "An equal division of property is impracticable." In fact, what Jefferson objects to is not inequality per se but the inequality of aristocratic property laws that result in "so much misery to the bulk of mankind"[158] because they allow land to lay idle, thereby discouraging industry and productivity.

Turning from Europe to America, Jefferson's recommendations are even more modest. In addition to the abolition of entail and primogeniture, Jefferson urges republican legislators to "provide by every possible means that as few as possible shall be without a little portion of land." But widespread property ownership is to be achieved through the sale of public lands by Congress,[159] rather than confiscatory taxation.

Once this broad foundation is laid, the question of "equal and impartial justice to all citizens" arises most clearly in matters of taxation, the subject in which "citizens are most apt to be refractory."[160] Here, too, justice lies on the side of rewarding individual industry and effort rather than redistributing the wealth. Thus, in his Second Inaugural Address, Jefferson defends "that state of property, equal or unequal, which results to every man from his own industry or that of his father."[161] And a decade later, in the "Prospectus" introducing Tracy's *Principles of Political Economy*, a work that extends the system of economic liberty begun by Smith, Jefferson makes the point even more emphatically: "To take from one, because it is thought that his own industry and that of his fathers has acquired too much, in order to spare to others, who, or whose fathers have not exercised equal industry and skill, is to violate arbitrarily the first principle of association—the *guarantee* to every one of his industry and fruits acquired by it."[162] As long as property is "rightly used," that is, encourages individual industry and increases productivity, justice requires that unequal property rights be protected.

What, then, of Jefferson's call for "progressive taxation"? Although Jefferson would have approved a progressive property tax as a means of "silently lessening the inequality of property" in France, the only form of federal taxation he believed necessary in America was a tax on imported luxuries. Such taxes can loosely be called "progressive" because they fall "exclusively on the rich."[163] But even here there are limits to how far Jefferson is willing to go: singling out particular domestic luxuries, such as pleasure horses, is "tyranny."[164] So, too, is "double taxation"; government may tax income or consumption, but not both.[165] Jefferson's opposition to anything like what we would today call "progressive taxation" is made explicit in the "Prospectus": "If the overgrown wealth of an individual be deemed dangerous to the state, the best corrective is the law of equal inheritance to all in equal degree; the better as this enforces a law of nature, while extra-taxation violates it."[166] Although Jefferson does not deny the danger of excessive wealth, the fact that he regards a general tax on imported luxuries, together with the "equal partition of intestates' estates," as "the best agrarian law"[167] suggests that the greater injustice comes from the discouragement of individual industry and the enjoyment of the fruits of honest labor by a government overzealous in the pursuit of economic equality.[168]

At first sight, it may seem paradoxical that, although Jefferson distrusted the wealthy and ambitious, he did nothing to halt economic inequality in America. But in contrast to the social and economic inequalities in the Old World, the disparities in America result from an economic system that rewards individual effort and talent. Since this is the reason individuals enter into society in the first place, republican governments must guarantee to each the fruits of his labor. Moreover, in a largely agrarian republic, social and economic differences are far less pronounced than in Europe. Even after the War of 1812, as a commercial economy began to take hold in America, Jefferson could still observe that the rich, "who can live without labour, either manual or professional," are "few and of moderate wealth."[169] Nor was there the grinding poverty that Jefferson, when separated from his countrymen and surrounded by aristocratic luxury, had sometimes feared. In contrast to the "starved and rickety paupers and dwarves of English workshops,"[170] America has "no paupers, the old and crippled among us, who possess nothing and have no families to take care of them, being too few to merit notice as a separate section of society, or to affect the general estimate."[171] Instead, America has developed into what political philosophers from Aristotle to Jefferson's own time regarded as the rarest of social phenomena, a property-owning middle-class republic. Accordingly, Jefferson can boast: "Never was a finer canvas presented to work on than our countrymen. All of them engaged in agriculture or the pursuits of honest industry, independent in their circumstances, enlightened as to their rights, and firm in their habits of order and obedience to the laws."[172] And indeed it is this vision of a middle-class property-holding republic, spurred to industry by the abolition of feudal aristocratic property laws, and liberated from dependency and servility by honest labor

and the ownership of "real" estates, that leads Jefferson to conclude: "If ever the morals of a people could be made the basis of
their own government, it is our case."

Conclusion

Jefferson lived at a particular historical moment when the newly
emergent forces of the market seemed almost magically allied with
moral progress. He looked to a free economy to create the material
preconditions for achieving his distinctive moral vision, one that
encourages and rewards individual industry, fosters economic and
political independence, cultivates liberality and benevolence, and,
most important, secures justice by apportioning wealth and honor
according to merit and effort rather than social status or legal pre-
scription. Yet as Jefferson also recognizes, it is an unstable alliance
that operates felicitously only in the earlier stages of economic development, when small-scale agriculture and domestic manufacturing impose what seem to be natural limits on the accumulation
of wealth. Once the economy outgrows these restraints, and the full
productive powers of capitalism are unleashed, the tension between the economic and moral foundations of republicanism becomes apparent. Faced with these contradictions, most followers of
Jefferson would choose sides, either defending a libertarian economic program of low taxes and minimal government or, conversely, urging the expansion of government power to enforce a
moral vision of greater social and economic equality at odds with
market forces.[173] But in so doing, each side simplified and, to some
extent, betrayed the distinctive moral vision that underlay Jefferson's economic program.

   Although the tension between the economic and the moral requirements of liberal republicanism can never be completely resolved once capitalism reaches its more advanced stages, Jefferson's
reflections allow us to think about the problem in ways that break
out of current ideological divisions. To begin with, Jefferson never
champions the free market as an end in itself. His attack on mercantile restrictions and aristocratic hierarchies is aimed not simply
at making men richer or even freer but at securing the conditions in
which all Americans might develop their full political and moral

potential. A more advanced commercial society may generate greater wealth, but at the cost of encouraging licentiousness and vice. Accordingly, Jefferson is not prepared to permit economic development to proceed unchecked. While generally in favor of free enterprise and individual choice, he is not averse to using federal, as well as state and local, power to discourage those commercial activities that he regards as harmful to the American character.[174]

On the other hand, although Jefferson believes that republican statesmen should consider the moral consequences of particular economic policies, he does not regard economic inequality as *the* great moral evil that government must eradicate. Extravagance, luxury, folly, licentiousness, dependence, vulgarity, and single-minded preoccupation with material gratification remain for him the principal vices of an advanced commercial society. It is these evils that the republican statesman should gently seek to discourage.

Nevertheless, Jefferson recognizes that both poverty and excessive wealth may also endanger the republican experiment, and both are more likely in an advanced commercial society with a growing population concentrated in urban areas. If, in the future and through no fault of their own, large numbers of Americans fail to find employment, the government will be obliged to act in order to secure the "fundamental right" of individuals to labor for a living. Conversely, Americans must always be on guard against the ambitions of the wealthy and the wellborn, who, if left to their own devices, will try to install themselves and their heirs as a permanent aristocracy in America. Thus, although Jefferson does not shy away from using political power to avert the first of these evils (it is less clear what, beyond urging eternal vigilance, he thought could be done about the second),[175] his policies generally seek to increase opportunities for the poor, rather than use government to redistribute wealth for the sake of greater economic equality.

How does Jefferson's thought bear on our contemporary situation? At a time when the only Democratic president to be reelected since Franklin Delano Roosevelt has declared that "the era of big government is over" and has called on all Americans to take greater responsibility for their lives, to exercise greater self-restraint with respect to entitlements, and to seek financial independence through work, Jefferson's reflections on economics and character seem more relevant today than at any other period since the New Deal. For he invites us to move beyond contemporary partisan lines and to consider anew, from the perspective of an older and more restrained liberalism, how the work we do and the means by which we acquire and use property can either strengthen or diminish our capacity for republican self-government.

Chapter Four

Civic Virtue, Statesmanship, and Republican Self-Government

In thinking about the American character, Jefferson was led inevitably to reflect on the meaning and requirements of civic virtue in a modern liberal republic. In such a society, where citizens devote most of their energies to families, neighbors, social organizations, and work, participation in politics ceases to be, as it was for the ancients, the noblest activity of free men; civic virtue is no longer the crown of moral excellence.[1] Nevertheless, for Jefferson politics still possesses a certain dignity: among the natural rights that civil society is established to protect is the right of all men to self-government.[2] By self-government, Jefferson does not mean merely the right of the people to be governed by representatives of their own choosing. Alone among the Founders Jefferson came to believe that, in addition to representation, self-government requires the direct political participation of the citizens on matters within their reach and competence. Nor does he conceive of this involvement in purely instrumental terms, a means to ensure that elected representatives work faithfully to protect the private rights of their constituents. For Jefferson, the right of citizens to participate directly in government retains, however faintly, something of its ancient luster. Acting with others on matters of common concern is more than a way to protect one's own private interests; participation in public affairs also gratifies men's pride in their capacity to govern themselves as free moral agents.[3]

Yet while self-government in this broad sense would not be possible without some conception of civic virtue, it is likewise a mistake to exaggerate the "civic humanist" dimension of Jefferson's thought.[4] While civic virtue remains an indispensable element of the American character, the virtues of citizens and statesmen do not comprehend all—or even the most important dimension—of human excellence. However important republican self-government is for Jefferson, he never argues that human beings can attain their highest perfection only by participating in politics. In a liberal republic, the most important virtues, both moral and intellectual, flourish outside the political arena.

More particularly, Jefferson's understanding of civic virtue differs from that of the classical republicans in three important respects.[5] First, the ancients tended to emphasize the importance of virtuous statesmanship in promoting obedience to the law, love of country, reverence for the gods, and patriotic sacrifice among the citizens. Jefferson, by contrast, denies that good government depends first and foremost on the character of its leaders. The hope of republican government lies not with its statesmen, no matter how "great and virtuous," but in an "enlightened, peaceable and really free" people.[6] Civic virtue flows from the bottom up, not from the top down. Accordingly, Jefferson devotes much more of his efforts to forming the character of the citizens than he does to thinking about the distinctive virtues republican statesmen should possess. Indeed, even when he does reflect on the virtues appropriate to republican statesmen, he tends to view these virtues from the perspective of the people rather than from the standpoint of those who rule. How does Jefferson's lopsided concern for civic virtue over the virtues of those who must lead the people affect the American character?

Second, not only does Jefferson focus more on the virtues and activities of citizens than of statesmen, but in thinking about the qualities citizens should cultivate he hardly ever uses the word "virtue." It is true that Jefferson frequently talks about the need to cultivate virtuous dispositions in the people, but what he has in mind is moral conduct, the obligations of one individual to another. When he thinks about the qualities men (and to a lesser extent women) should cultivate as citizens, he is more likely to use the term "spirit." Whatever else civic virtue may entail, it seems fundamentally to involve a certain kind of spiritedness in the people.

What precisely does this mean? Is spiritedness identical with civic virtue, or is it rather the natural foundation of these virtues, much as the moral sense is the seat of the moral virtues? Here again, Jefferson is not always consistent. He frequently speaks as if spirited self-assertion were the same as civic virtue, though at other times, especially in his public addresses, he seems to view spiritedness as the ground of civic virtue, including those more conservative virtues, such as patriotism, love of order, obedience to the laws, and support for public authority.[7] Moreover, while spiritedness is natural to human beings, it is unclear whether the civic virtues that grow out of spiritedness are natural in the way that the moral virtues are. Jefferson's comment that the "qualifications" necessary for self-government "are not innate" but result from "habit and long training" suggests they may not be. The "spirit of order and self-respect" on which republicanism depends must be "woven into the American character" through education.[8]

If, however, we begin with our original supposition that civic virtue involves a certain kind of spiritedness in the people, the question that then arises is this: What is the character of this spiritedness? Is spiritedness essentially positive, the proud expression of men's natural desire to govern themselves (now sufficiently domesticated that it no longer includes the desire to rule over others), or negative, the first line of defense against unscrupulous politicians seeking to encroach upon the rights and liberties of the people? Here again, Jefferson seems not to be entirely sure. At times he locates this spirit in the peaceful and orderly deliberations of citizens in their social and political associations. Spiritedness is the very definition of republican self-government.[9] Yet on other occasions, spiritedness appears as something darker and more menacing. It seems to thrive on jealousy, distrust, and even armed resistance, not to hereditary monarchy or other unrepresentative regimes but to popularly elected governments. To what extent can these conflicting views of spiritedness be reconciled?

Third and finally, Jefferson does not believe that civic virtue, in the sense of spirited attachment to republican rights and liberties, requires the suppression of self-interest, at least not for citizens. In contrast to the classical republican tradition, which sought to attach citizens to the common good by strictly regulating their private lives, Jefferson argues that citizens will love their country better if it respects their rights to worship as they please, to think and speak freely, and to accumulate wealth and possessions. Jefferson seeks to cultivate in citizens a rational, or considered, attachment to the public good.

Yet while acknowledging the importance of self-interest in binding the individual to the political community, Jefferson does not go as far as some modern political philosophers who substitute appeals to interest for civic virtue. He seeks instead to carve out a middle way between the most self-denying antique virtue and the insistent claims of self-love. In Jefferson's liberal-republican "synthesis,"[10] interest can cooperate with pride in forging a new kind of republican virtue that channels each individual's selfish motives toward the larger common good.[11] But does this work for statesmen as well? Can the disinterestedness Jefferson seeks to cultivate in statesmen be reconciled with the interest and pride that lie at the heart of Jefferson's understanding of civic "virtue"?

Following Jefferson's lead, we focus first on the character of the people and on the virtues required of them as republican citizens. As we shall see, Jefferson's tendency to link civic virtue with spirited self-assertion rather than austere self-denial is more indebted to the *neo*classical republican tradition, which begins with Machiavelli, than it is to the classical tradition. From Renaissance Italy, this new brand of republicanism spread to England, where, over the next century and a half, it was domesticated and popularized by thinkers like James Harrington, Algernon Sidney, John Locke, and the radical Whigs,[12] and carried thence to the New World. The main elements of this neorepublican civic virtue include fear of corruption; the need for a frequent return to first principles to restore the republic to its original purity; an armed citizenry vigilant in protecting its liberties; and acceptance of partisan division as a positive contribution to republican government.

But Jefferson's understanding of republican virtue is never simply backward glancing.[13] He looks forward to a republican future in which an educated citizen body, actively participating in local affairs and capable of selecting the best men to represent them in state and national politics, will vindicate his confidence in the capacity of the people to govern themselves. His democratic faith argued strongly against relying too heavily on the wisdom of the past, even a republican past. Striking out on his own, Jefferson democratizes republican spiritedness still further and seeks to create, where none previously existed, practices and institutions that will keep this spirit alive. In his conception of civic virtue, as well as in his analysis of the ways in which this virtue can be both corrupted and preserved, Jefferson seems to anticipate, though never fully to attain, the insights of the great nineteenth-century student of democracy, Alexis de Tocqueville.

Corruption and Decay

Corruption was the opposite side of the republican concern with civic virtue, and Jefferson was quick to detect it everywhere. At the very moment when Americans were demonstrating their greatest virtue in throwing off British rule, Jefferson feels compelled to remind his countrymen that "every government on earth" contains "some trace of human weakness, some germ of corruption and degeneracy, which cunning will discover, and wickedness insensibly open, cultivate, and improve."[14] And America was no exception. Indeed, precisely because republican self-government requires more virtue of its citizens than do other regimes, Americans must study well the vices that corrupted earlier republics. If they fail to heed these melancholy lessons, America will degenerate, just as surely as Greece and Rome before her.

What sort of corruption does Jefferson fear? Reflecting on the ways in which the American republic might decline, Jefferson concludes that modern discoveries in the science of politics, especially the substitution of representation for direct political participation, have rendered the classical analysis of constitutional change and decay obsolete.[15] In the ancient republics, where the people exercised all political power directly and in person, minority rights were regularly sacrificed to the "plundering enterprises of the majority."[16] By contrast, in the modern representative republic, the election of the best men to political office filters and refines the public views, thereby protecting the rights of the minority, while enabling the majority to rule.

But if, by removing public affairs from the immediate reach of the people, representation offers a solution to the clash of "local egoisms"[17] that had been the downfall of the ancient republics, this great modern discovery nevertheless poses its own set of dangers. Since the people no longer directly participate in public affairs, elected representatives may be tempted to betray the public trust for their own private advantage. Thus, even as he praises the principle of representation, Jefferson continues to warn that "every government degenerates when trusted to the rulers of the people alone."[18]

Caught up in the fervor of the Revolution, Jefferson particularly feared that after the war was over and politics returned to more routine matters, the people would lose their spirited love of liberty and devote themselves exclusively to "making money."[19] Several years later, while serving as minister to France and cut off from all direct observation of his countrymen, Jefferson grew alarmed by reports of a growing desire for luxury and extravagance back home.[20] Anticipating what Tocqueville would later criticize as excessive individualism and preoccupation with material gratification,[21] he concludes that if people become too involved with their own private concerns, they will no longer pay attention to public affairs, and civic "lethargy" will set in.[22] Lethargy in turn spells "the death of public liberty," for, left unguarded, elected representatives will be emboldened to try to perpetuate wealth and power for themselves and their families without regard for the public trust.[23] Not even men of virtue and wisdom, Jefferson's cherished natural *aristoi*, can safely be trusted with political power unless they are vigilantly held to account. The lessons of European politics, in which nations are divided between devouring wolves and defenseless sheep, stand as a warning to America. If his countrymen should ever become "inattentive to the public affairs," he warned Edward Carrington, "you and I, and Congress and Assemblies, Judges and Governors, shall all become wolves."[24] Human nature is the same on both sides of the Atlantic.

Returning to America in 1789 to serve as secretary of state in the first Washington administration, Jefferson was relieved to discover that his fears were exaggerated. What had seemed to be extravagance turned out in most instances to be nothing more than the desire for modest comforts and improvements. The vast majority of the American people still possessed the virtues necessary for republican self-government. But within two years, Jefferson became convinced that corruption had taken a new and more ominous form, striking at the heart of republicanism from within the government itself and threatening to spread its evil to the body of the people.[25]

In Alexander Hamilton's financial program, Jefferson detected a deliberate and systematic plan by the Treasury to undermine the independence of the legislature and to slide the constitutional balance away from its republican foundation not just toward monarchy but toward a monarchy "bottomed on corruption."[26]

The origin of the crisis was innocent enough. As Jefferson recounted it many years later, in April 1791 he had invited Vice President John Adams and Secretary of the Treasury Alexander Hamilton to dine with him in Philadelphia while the president was out of town on his Southern tour. After dinner, conversation turned to the British constitution and Adams confided, "Purge that constitution of it's [sic] corruption, and give to it's [sic] popular branch equality of representation, and it would be the most perfect constitution ever devised by the wit of man." Hamilton, raising the stakes, replied provocatively, "purge it of it's [sic] corruption and give to it's [sic] popular branch equality of representation and it would be an *impracticable* government: as it stands at present with all it's [sic] supposed defects, it is the most perfect government which ever existed."[27]

Taking Hamilton's remark at face value, Jefferson became convinced that the Treasury secretary deliberately sought to corrupt the legislature along the English model and pave the way for a restoration of monarchy in America. Twice he sought in writing to warn the president privately of Hamilton's machinations, and toward the end of his life compiled the *Anas,* his own highly partisan account of these years. Echoing the charges of Walpole's critics six decades earlier, Jefferson accused Hamilton of constructing a vast engine aimed at corrupting the legislature. Jefferson began with the debt. Hamilton's proposal for managing the public debt rewarded speculators, including members of Congress who benefited personally from their support of funding and assumption, and bound them to Hamilton's schemes. While Jefferson was quick to concede that the majority in Congress remained untainted by this corruption, this "mercenary phalanx" gave Federalists in Congress a majority in both houses and ensured the success of Hamilton's measures. From here, Jefferson moved on to the Bank. At issue was not its constitutionality, for Jefferson conceded that on this point there existed a difference of opinion that must be tolerated. Instead, he charged that Hamilton had named members of both houses of

Congress to the Board of Directors of the National Bank, thereby ensuring support for his bank policies by this "corrupt squadron" within the legislature. With these two pieces of the puzzle in place, Jefferson returned to the debt. He now accused Hamilton of providing friendly legislators with advance notice of his plan to finance the debt by introducing paper money in place of gold and silver. Armed with this knowledge, particular members of the legislature had "feathered their nests" with paper and then voted for the laws that would enrich them. In condemning Hamilton's attempts to rule by appealing to men's interests, Jefferson insisted that he was not trying to banish interest altogether from politics. But he drew a bright line between "the little accidental schemes of self interest" that always influence individual legislators and "a regular system for forming a corps of interested persons who should steadily be at the orders of the Treasury."[28] Hamilton had crossed the line.

More ominously, this was only the beginning. Corruption of the legislature was the first but most fatal step because it laid the foundation for all that would follow. Having secured the cooperation of the legislature, the next step was to expand the powers of the federal government through a broad interpretation of the general welfare and necessary and proper clauses of the Constitution. Hamilton's liberal construction of these powers to fund domestic manufactures would undermine the very idea of limited government, dangerously expand the powers of the national government, and lay the foundation for a return to monarchy on the corrupt English model. By removing public affairs from the watchful eye of the people, consolidation would make it easier for legislators to pursue their private interests at the expense of the public good. As Jefferson later observed, "Our country is too large to have all its affairs directed by a single government. Public servants at such a distance and from under the eye of their constituents, must, from circumstances of distance, be unable to administer and overlook all the details necessary for the good government of the citizens, and the same circumstances by rendering detection impossible to their constituents, will invite the public agents to corruption, plunder, and waste."[29]

For Jefferson, it is neither the natural resistance to energetic government characteristic of free peoples nor the ambitious designs of politicians seeking popular favor that pose the greatest threats to republicanism. What Jefferson fears are the venal and ordinary desires of nearly all elected officials to increase their power and advance their private interests at the expense of a complacent and distracted majority. Consolidation is a useful tool for ambitious politicians; it creates an "immense patronage" that helps build support for an ever-expanding government, but at the price of corrupting the American character. The proliferation of patronage positions poisons "the very source of industry, by presenting an easier resource for a livelihood and . . . corrupting the principles of the great mass of those who passed a wishful eye on office."[30] Thus, in his First Annual Message, Jefferson signals his intention to reduce the number of government offices and dependencies, and by the time of his Second Inaugural, he can point with pride to "the suppression of unnecessary offices, of useless establishments and expenses."[31] By cutting government spending, eliminating unnecessary patronage jobs, creating a "sinking fund" to retire the debt in a timely fashion, ending the Treasury's influence over the legislature, and restoring the constitutional balance between the states and the federal government, Jefferson believes that, at least for the time being, he has rooted out the sources of corruption that threaten the republican experiment in self-government.

Although Jefferson was wrong to accuse Hamilton of deliberately plotting to destroy republican government, he was right to point out that some of Hamilton's policies, however inadvertently and against his best efforts, did encourage a frenzy of speculation and corrupt practices inside the legislature and without, and even among republicans.[32] Moreover, he was right to warn that a consolidated government would expand the number of government jobs to be funded by the taxpayers, and that these officials, operating largely out of the public eye, would work less industriously than citizens employed in more useful occupations. Finally, he was also right to warn that as the objects of national legislation grew more complex and confusing, citizens would find themselves alienated from the workings of their own government, inviting representatives once again to "feather their nests" at the expense of their constituents. Judging from the general apathy and cynicism surrounding investigations into recent political scandals, corruption of both the citizens and their representatives along the lines sketched by Jefferson remains a danger in our ever more centralized and bureaucratic government.

But corruption can come in a variety of other ways as well, some of which, like slavery, degrading work and living conditions, and extravagant preoccupation with money and material goods, Jefferson, at different times and in varying degrees, acknowledged. Still, he did not fully appreciate the most seductive way in which the citizens of a democratic republic, nourished in the love of equality and ill informed about the meaning and extent of their rights, could become corrupt. Although he did anticipate important elements of Tocqueville's analysis of the democratic character, especially the danger of excessive individualism and the love of physical gratification, he failed to see that a democratic people might actually come to prefer a consolidated paternalistic government that left them free to pursue their private interests and relieved them of the risks and responsibilities of self-government. That the majority might grow excessively dependent on government and acquiesce in the expansion of governmental power and services, to be paid for by future generations who never consented to these arrangements, were dangers to the American character that he did not foresee. While he rightly feared a people grown too lethargic to care about their rights, he did not envision Americans becoming too self-indulgent to restrain their expectations of what government should do for them. Indeed, Jefferson may even have inadvertently contributed to this development: his singular focus on equal rights may have raised popular expectations of what government could do to promote material well-being, and his growing insistence that all political institutions be made more immediately responsive to the people may have suggested how this could be done.

Still, to leave the matter here would seriously distort Jefferson's intention. For his principal aim is to make it possible for Americans to govern themselves as far as possible, not to be governed by others no matter how well intentioned. And the rights he seeks to protect are claims that free citizens can assert as members of self-governing communities, individual rights such as free speech and conscience, or to labor for a livelihood, as well as the rights of communities to determine how to educate their children, maintain law and order, care for their poor, and in general manage their collective concerns.[33]

Moreover, by decentralizing political power and expanding opportunities for self-government, Jefferson correctly anticipates Tocqueville's solution to the more subtle problems of dependency and paternalism. For however incomplete his understanding of the problem of political corruption, Jefferson, like Tocqueville, recognizes that "it is the manners and spirit of a people which preserve a republic in vigor."[34] And if this spirit declines, the entire constitutional order will decay. Accordingly, he turns his attention to a variety of proposals for how this spirit can be perpetuated and corruption avoided.

Return to First Principles I: Rebellion

It was Machiavelli who, writing in the *Discourses*, first counseled the need for a frequent return to first principles in order to restore republican governments to their original purity. Since all human things eventually become corrupt, wise leaders must take advantage of foreign threats and domestic emergencies (or create them) to renew the original spirit of the constitution. Machiavelli did not shrink from the implications of this thought. As the *Discourses* make clear, this was not to be a symbolic return, a periodic celebration of once-vigorous principles, but an actual attempt to rekindle the spirit and power of the Founding. Public accusations, followed by ferocious punishments and spectacular executions, would strike fear and awe into a dissolute people and their leaders.[35]

Although Machiavelli believes that republics that build on the people are more powerful and more durable than those that rule with the support of the great, he has no illusions that the people are morally superior to the few. It is true that, unlike the great, the people want only not to be oppressed, but they can be both fickle and ungrateful toward their rulers. The return to first principles can restore the people, as well as the great, to their original virtue.

Late in life, Jefferson acquired a copy of the *Discourses*,[36] but it is likely that he came to know the Florentine's work much earlier through the seventeenth- and eighteenth-century English thinkers whose works he already owned. In Algernon Sidney and James Burgh, as well as the authors of the more popular *Cato's Letters*, Thomas Gordon and John Trenchard, Jefferson could find admiring references to Machiavelli's call for a return to first principles. Nearer to home, the Virginia Declaration of Rights, by George Mason, enshrined Machiavelli's call for a "frequent recurrence to fundamental principles" as an essential element in preserving free government.

Perhaps more than any other Founder, Jefferson endorsed Machiavelli's call for a return to first principles as he learned it from the English republicans. When a government grows corrupt and assumes powers that exceed its legitimate scope, nothing but armed resistance can correct the abuses. To ensure that the citizens are able to defend themselves and their communities against such encroachments, Jefferson insists on the anciently established "right and duty [of the people] to be at all times armed."[37] A people lacking the spirit to resist such threats, by actual force if necessary, cannot long preserve its freedom.[38] The great example of a return to first principles was, of course, the American Revolution,[39] but Jefferson continued to look favorably upon armed resistance long after other revolutionary leaders had renounced violence and turned their attention to erecting new constitutions that would achieve a measure of stability and order. Nowhere is this more evident than in his reaction to Shays's Rebellion, the armed uprising by farmers in western Massachusetts protesting against the imposition of new taxes and calling for debtor relief. Whereas most republican leaders condemned the rebellion and used it as the occasion to call for a Constitutional Convention that would strengthen the powers of government to suppress such violent demonstrations, Jefferson remained unperturbed. Although he, too, acknowledged that the insurrection produced acts that were "absolutely unjustifiable," he nevertheless insists that "a little rebellion, now and then, is a good thing, and as necessary in the political world as storms are in the physical."[40] What explains this anomaly?

Let us give Jefferson the benefit of the doubt by recalling that at the time he was serving as ambassador to France, and so was at some remove from the agitated mood of his countrymen.[41] Moreover, as he reported to one correspondent, he had expected that the uprising would have led Europeans to form an unfavorable opinion of the newly independent state governments, and it had not. What impressed the Europeans, however, was "the interposition of the people themselves on the side of government."[42] While Jefferson, too, praised the "good sense of the people" in suppressing the rebels, he nevertheless continued to insist that "the spirit of resistance to government is so valuable on certain occasions, that I wish it to be always kept alive."[43]

Jefferson's singular enthusiasm for Shays's Rebellion takes us to the heart of what he, in his early attempts to think through the question of preserving republican government, understands public-spiritedness to consist of. Spiritedness here manifests itself in a jealous insistence on one's rights, suspicion of all political power, and a willingness to resist, by arms when necessary, every encroachment, real or imagined, on these rights.[44] Although the people may sometimes err out of ignorance or "misconceptions," it is always better that they assert themselves rather than sink into lethargy. "Turbulence," Jefferson concedes, is an evil, but it is a small one, and "productive of good." Here especially, Jefferson may be closer to Machiavelli than he realizes, since he regards this "evil" as the spring of civic virtue. Turbulence "prevents the degeneracy of government, and nourishes a general attention to the public affairs."[45] It is a way of returning the republic to its first principles, by warning its rulers from time to time "that the people preserve the spirit of resistance" to their government.[46]

Since it is the people who, by their spirited opposition, correct the abuses of their rulers, Jefferson advises "honest republican governors" to be "mild in their punishment of rebellions, [so] as not to discourage them too much."[47] Moreover, compared with the bloody uprisings in Europe and elsewhere, the Massachusetts rebels were a model of moderation and mildness.[48] Thus reassured, Jefferson arrived at the happy calculation: "One rebellion in every thirteen states in the course of eleven years, is but one for each state in a century and a half. No country should be so long without one."[49] To Colonel William Smith, the Adamses' son-in-law, he indulged his tendency to push his thoughts to their logical conclusion: "What signify a few lives lost in a century or two? The tree of liberty must be refreshed from time to time with the blood of patriots and tyrants. It is its natural manure."[50]

Here we come to the paradox in Jefferson's early understanding of civic spirit. For while he despises the military virtues, which the ancient republicans honored and Machiavelli regarded as the foundation of republican government, indeed of all good government, Jefferson continues to celebrate the virtues of an armed citizenry, animated by "the jealous spirit of liberty."[51] Only now, this suspicion and jealousy are to be directed not only against foreign enemies but also against their own popularly elected governments. The willingness of a people to rise up even against their own representatives whenever they exceed their legitimate powers is both the mark of civic virtue and the means of restoring the republic to its original principles.

While much has been made of Jefferson's provocative call for a return to first principles and his equation of civic spirit with armed resistance, critics fail to place these remarks in context. Insurrection is not the only means by which Jefferson seeks to return to first principles, nor is armed rebellion the whole, or even the greatest part, of civic virtue.[52] After the rash of letters approving Shays's Rebellion, Jefferson never again embraced such uprisings with quite the same enthusiasm. The Whiskey Rebellion of 1794 elicited a tepid response,[53] and even the Kentucky Resolutions, especially in the form in which they were anonymously published, did not call upon the states to take up arms against federal encroachments. As the principal draftsman of the resolutions, Jefferson warned that the hated Alien and Sedition Acts, "unless arrested at the threshold, may tend to drive these States into revolution and blood,"[54] but he stopped short of calling for armed rebellion. As Douglas L. Wilson has pointed out, if, eleven years after Shays's Rebellion, Jefferson still believed that armed resistance was a desirable way of returning the republic to first principles, the Kentucky Resolutions presented the perfect opportunity for him to say so.[55] He did not.

It is true that Jefferson's preferred solution, nullification, would have, if the states had attempted it, prompted the federal government to respond with force, but the Kentucky legislature wisely deleted this provision from the final published version, and Jefferson never made his support for nullification public.[56] Moreover, despite his argument in the unpublished draft of the resolutions that nullification is the only rightful remedy for the assumption of powers not delegated to the federal government, two years later, Jefferson silently retracted his position and accepted electoral change as a remedy for governmental overreaching.

The "revolution of 1800" confirmed Jefferson's suspicion that the "spirit of 1776" was not dead but only "slumbering."[57] More important, it demonstrated that this spirit could be awakened without resorting to violence, "but by the rational and peaceable instrument of reform." In a properly ordered republic, where all power derives from the people, citizens can in fact assert their spiritedness through a "jealous care of the right of election," the "mild and safe" alternative to violent revolution. Paradoxically, once this "spirit" has been awakened, Jefferson recognizes the need to cultivate other, more conservative, aspects of civic virtue. Critics who focus exclusively on his defense of Shays's Rebellion ignore this side of his thought. But letters from this period praise Americans for their "habit of implicit obedience" to the laws,[58] and the First Inaugural Address holds up before the nation a radically different conception of civic virtue, one that envisions every man "at the call of the law" rushing to defend "invasions of the public order as his own personal concern."[59] And later, when New England Federalists threatened to rise up in rebellion against *his* administration to protest the Embargo Acts that were ruining Northern commerce, Jefferson condemned these "embodied expressions of discontent, and open outrages of law and patriotism," as both "dishonorable" and "injurious" to the well-being of America.[60]

Thus, while spiritedness remains the most distinctive aspect of Jefferson's understanding of the American civic character, it is a mistake to reduce all of civic virtue to spiritedness alone or to view spiritedness simply in terms of political jealousy and armed resistance to government. Once he was confident that the original republican principles were secure, Jefferson increasingly came to appreciate the more conservative and law-abiding qualities necessary for republican citizenship.[61] And what is perhaps most important, these were the qualities that Jefferson sought *publicly* to cultivate. In his carefully crafted public addresses, Jefferson never urged armed resistance to government. On the contrary, he identified the "sincere spirit of republicanism" with "love of country, devotion to its liberties, its rights, and its honor," and he sought to instill in citizens moderation, love of order, obedience to the laws, and respect for public authority.[62] And later, after he retired from public office, Jefferson would turn his attention to more constructive means of nourishing and perpetuating the spirit of the people.

It is true that privately he continued until the end of his life to hold out the possibility of armed resistance as a last desperate resort against "usurpation" and "degeneracy,"[63] and he remained maddeningly sympathetic to violent uprisings around the world.[64] But after Shays's Rebellion he never again, not even privately, urged armed resistance as a *periodic* remedy for preventing "degeneracy" in the body politic. Indeed, even before the Massachusetts uprising, he had begun to think about other, more orderly (though hardly less controversial) ways of periodically returning the republic to its first principles.[65]

Return to First Principles II: Constitutional Revision

As early as the *Notes*, Jefferson suggested that constitutional amendment might offer a desirable alternative to armed uprisings. Salutary corrections to rein in the tendency of government to expand beyond its proper scope would "render unnecessary an appeal to the people, or in other words a rebellion, on every infraction of their rights."[66] Acting on this insight, Jefferson sought in his own draft for a Virginia Constitution in 1783 to facilitate the process of calling a convention to alter the Constitution or to correct breaches of it.[67]

A few years later, reflecting on the work of the Constitutional Convention from his post in Paris, Jefferson reiterates his conviction that some form of revision, in the form of amendments or a second convention, is the preferred means of corrrecting the document's flaws and keeping the Constitution in harmony with the spirit of the American people.[68] From the outset, he looked to frequent revisions to correct "what is amiss," and in this way advance "towards perfection, step by step."[69] But it was not until 1789 that Jefferson applied his penchant for calculation to the issue of constitutional revision. In a letter to Madison on the eve of his departure from Paris, Jefferson attempted to think through the literal consequences of the idea that "the earth belongs in usufruct to the living." He took this to mean that one generation has no right to bind another with constitutions, laws, or debts. Jefferson was not content merely to draw out the obvious implication of this thought, namely, that future generations are free to revise or even overthrow their historic conventions and agreements if they desire, but even recommends that they do so at regular intervals. Again, applying the same calculating mind that led him to endorse rebellions every eleven years in each of the sixteen states, he now estimates that the length of a generation is thirty-four years. From this he concludes, "Every constitution . . . and every law naturally expires at the end of thirty-four years."[70] Later on, as Jefferson became acquainted with the "European tables of mortality," he revised the length of a generation downward to "nineteen or twenty years," but he continued to insist that each "new majority" be given "a solemn opportunity" of revising the Constitution, "so that it may be handed on, with periodic repairs, from generation to generation to the end of time."[71]

For the most part, scholars have been noticeably unsympathetic to Jefferson's call for constitutional conventions every generation[72] and have tended to side with Madison's respectful but firm dissent. In the *Federalist Papers*, Madison had already felt it necessary publicly to refute Jefferson's first and more mild attempt to make it easier to alter the Virginia Constitution or to correct breaches of it. Even before Jefferson tried out the idea of a constitutional convention every generation, Madison sensed trouble. Writing in Number 49, Madison pointed out that frequent revisions would undermine the reverence for the law on which just and stable government depended. While according "enlightened reason" its due, Madison insisted that even "the most rational government will not find it a superfluous advantage to have the prejudices of the community on its side." Moreover, having actively participated in the Federal Convention, he knew from experience how difficult the art of constitution making was, and how "ticklish" it would be to try to repeat the process once the dangers that "repressed the passions most unfriendly to order and concord" and united the people in the cause of liberty had subsided. Finally, he worried that frequent appeals to the people would invite partisan divisions over proposed amendments, thereby strengthening the forces of passion and interest over those of reason and deliberation.[73] In his response to Jefferson's "earth belongs to the living" letter, Madison reiterated these arguments and then addressed himself to the theoretical question of whether constitutional revision by majority rule would in fact achieve Jefferson's goal of making each generation as independent as the founding generation had been. He ended by repeating his belief that, however useful these reflections might be to a "philosophical Legislator," the great practical problem facing the United States was the "weakness in Government, and licentiousness in the people,"[74] evils that, if he was correct, would only be exacerbated by Jefferson's efforts to free the living generation from its ties to the past.

These are serious objections that need to be addressed. There is no doubt that Jefferson tended to denigrate the importance of veneration where laws and constitutions were concerned, dismissing as "sanctimonious reverence"[75] the notion that the Constitution embodied superhuman wisdom and should therefore never be changed. Yet while conceding the overall force of Madison's insistence that even the most rational government has need of a kind of nonrational veneration to preserve it, at least part of Jefferson's argument in favor of constitutional revision deserves attention. For while both agreed in principle that every Constitution would have to be amended over time, Jefferson was more inclined than Madison to stress the inevitability of constitutional change. If, when the need for alteration arises, the people piously refrain from revising their Constitution, changes nevertheless slip in through broad construction and judicial interpretation. In this case, the people pay false homage to a permanent Constitution, unaware that their sovereign power has been usurped and that their federal republic shifts imperceptibly toward consolidation and rule by the judiciary.

Madison's second objection that periodic appeals to the people to restore the proper distribution of constitutional powers would divide Americans along partisan lines and inflame the passions on matters where reason ought to rule involves two separate questions. The first is whether constitutional revision ought to be institutionalized and made available to each generation on principle; the other is whether constitutional amendment is the preferred means of adjusting the inevitable shifts in the separation of powers and federalism or enlarging the powers of government. With respect to the first question, Madison is right on both practical and theoretical grounds. Far from providing a "solemn opportunity" for each generation to repair the errors of its ancestors, periodic revision would trivialize the amendment process and undermine respect for the Constitution as fundamental law. Since the people already have the right to amend the Constitution whenever they see fit, there is no need to invite them to revise it every generation, especially if there is nothing seriously wrong with the government. Despite his sensible opposition to "frequent and untried changes" and his counsel that "moderate imperfections had better be borne with,"[76] Jefferson's proposal for regular revision would encourage innovation for its own sake and invite frivolous change.

On a more theoretical level, Madison employed his "perspicuity and cogent logic" to strike at the heart of Jefferson's proposal. In arguing for periodic constitutional revision, Jefferson believed he had discovered a way to return each generation to first principles and so to keep alive the spirit of the Founding. But, as Madison pointed out, if each generation were required to give its express consent by remaking the Constitution, that consent would have to be unanimous, as it was at the moment civil society was formed. Unanimity, and not majority rule, was the law of nature.[77] (What Madison did not add is that Jefferson's proposal would render the Constitution, the Declaration, and even the American Revolution invalid. The requirement of unanimity makes sense only with respect to the will of the people to be a people. And even then, unanimous consent is largely implicit or unconscious.)

If, however, Madison successfully refuted Jefferson's arguments for periodic constitutional revision as a peaceable way of returning each generation to first principles, he was less persuasive in arguing against the occasional use of the amendment process to adjust the constitutional distribution and scope of powers. For Jefferson was surely right when he warned that time and fortune tend to warp the original constitutional order by offering up new and unforeseen circumstances that encourage the enlargement of political power. These alterations, in turn, embolden the government to continue its expansion while simultaneously sapping the spirit of the people to resist them. Should experience suggest that institutions are not working the way they were intended, as Jefferson came to believe was true of the judiciary, or that more power is necessary than the Constitution originally granted, as was the case with internal improvements and a national establishment for higher education,[78] the way to correct these flaws is not by a broad construction of the Constitution, carried out by judicial interpretation or executive decree, but by returning to the source of all political power, the people.[79]

It is true that such appeals may inflame partisan passions, but so, too, does the alternative of interpreting the powers of the Constitution broadly. Court decisions and executive orders expanding federal powers and restricting the powers of the states and localities to govern themselves in accordance with their distinct political cultures have done nothing to remove the most highly contested issues from the field of partisan debate. Indeed, they have heightened it.[80] For implicit in these actions is the suggestion that the majority, and *especially* the local or state majorities Jefferson supports, are incapable of governing wisely or justly through the democratic process. Increasingly, judges and bureaucrats substitute their own notions of justice, rights, and power, in place of the will of local majorities and without their consent. Thus does the Constitution become a "thing of wax,"[81] and the "peculiar security" of a written Constitution with limited and enumerated powers is eroded.

Consequently, Madison's warnings about partisan division and "licentiousness" have to be weighed against what for Jefferson are the more insidious dangers of consolidation, with its "necessary consequence, corruption,"[82] in its many manifestations. Jefferson's understanding of self-government requires that the people—and not the judges—have the last say on the meaning of the Constitution. Thus, he views the amendment process as one important way to educate each generation in the principles and practices of free government (though on most matters he prefers that disagreements be settled in the public arena, through the rough-and-tumble of political debate). Not only does he not fear partisan division, but, following Machiavelli, he believes that party differences are good for the health of the republic.[83] Parties induce a spirit of watchfulness in government, while providing the organization and structure for preserving spirited involvement in politics. Political parties are another means of preventing civic lethargy.[84] Accordingly, Jefferson welcomes the "party division of Whig and Tory [as] the most wholesome which can exist in any government, and *well worthy of being nourished* to keep out those of a more dangerous character."[85]

Moving beyond Madison's objections, we now consider a more general question: What is the point of periodic constitutional revisions? Is it, as Jefferson sometimes suggests, to restore the republic to its original purity, which time and fortune inevitably corrupt,[86] or is it, as he elsewhere opines, to keep pace with "progressive advances of the human mind or changes in human affairs"?[87] If the former, does this not imply that the original principles are good and therefore worthy of veneration? And if the latter, what is the connection between a Constitution that changes every twenty years and the first principles to which he invites citizens to return? In other words, how can Jefferson advocate returning to first principles if the earth belongs to the living and the future is better than the past?

Here it is necessary to distinguish between the "spirit" of the people, which Jefferson regards as the soul of republicanism, and the actual Constitution, or constitutions, which are at best the embodiment of this spirit. When Jefferson calls for a return to first principles, he means reviving the vigilant, freedom-loving spirit of the people, which manifests itself most fully at the Founding but tends inevitably to slacken without regular opportunities for renewal. He emphatically does not mean a return to the original constitution, either of his native Virginia or of the federal government. Although the "revolution of 1800" did attempt to return the country to its first principles, by restoring the original ideas of limited government, a proper separation of powers, and federalism, increasingly Jefferson came to believe that both the federal Constitution and the Virginia Constitution were still seriously flawed. Speaking of the Virginia Constitution in 1816, he asked, "Where is our republicanism to be found?" And he answered, "Not in our constitution certainly, but merely in the spirit of our people." So faulty is this charter that the spirit of the people "is not the fruit of our constitution, but has prevailed in spite of it."[88] Turning to the federal Constitution, Jefferson now finds the formal institutions inadequately republican as well: "In the General Government, the House of Representatives is mainly republican; the Senate scarcely so at all, as not elected by the people directly, and so long secured even against those who do elect them; the Executive more republican than the Senate, from its shorter term, its election by the people in practice," through an informal rotation; the judiciary is the least republican because it is "independent of the nation."[89]

It is to remedy these defects of the Founding, by applying the lessons of the American experience, that Jefferson would amend the Constitution every generation. As he later confessed, at the time of the Founding Jefferson mistakenly believed that any government that was not monarchical was republican. Moreover, he, too, had been under the spell of European philosophers who defended the mixed regime because they doubted the capacity of the people for self-government. At that time, the great desideratum was to avoid making the offices "a mere creation by and dependance [sic] on the people."[90] Accordingly, his 1776 draft of the Virginia Constitution proposed that both the upper house of the legislature and the executive be appointed by the lower house, and the judiciary appointed jointly by the executive and the Privy Council.[91] But forty years of experience corrected these errors. Thus, by 1816, Jefferson has almost reversed himself; he now insists that "the further the departure from direct and constant control by the citizens, the less has the government of the ingredient of republicanism."[92]

Accordingly, he now proposes the following amendments to the Virginia Constitution: "1. General suffrage. 2. Equal representation in the legislature. 3. An executive chosen by the people. 4. Judges elective or amovable. 5. Justices, jurors, and sheriffs elective. 6. Ward divisions. And 7. Periodical amendments of the Constitution."[93] Similarly, he favors amendments to the federal Constitution to make the executive and the judiciary more responsive to the will of the people. In particular, he endorses constitutional changes to restrict the "term of Presidential service" and to place "the choice of President effectually in the hands of the people."[94] Elsewhere, he supports restricting judicial appointments "to four or six years" and making them "renewable by the President and the Senate."[95] And, once, he floats the idea of removing the power of borrowing from Congress.[96] Thus, in answer to the question raised earlier, Jefferson proposes to use the amendment process *both* to return to first principles *and* to "keep pace with the advance of the age in science and experience."[97] By removing the original obstacles to self-government and majority rule, Jefferson hopes to preserve for successive generations of Americans the liberty-loving spirit of the people as it manifested itself at the Founding.

At first sight, Jefferson's mature conclusion that the institutions of government must be made more accessible and immediately accountable to the people seems to accord with contemporary populist criticisms on both the Left and the Right of the Constitution as too formal and unresponsive.[98] But, in fact, Jefferson's understanding of the relation between the spirit of the people and the spirit of their constitutions is more complex. For even when he becomes more critical of the state and federal constitutions for creating offices not directly elected by and responsible to the people, he still defends the constitutional division of legislative power,[99] as well as the distribution of power among the different branches of government and between the federal government and the states. In contrast to today's populists, who have little patience with the "gridlock" that so frequently results from bicameralism and the separation of powers, and still less appreciation for the diversity of legislation engendered by federalism, Jefferson believes that genuine responsiveness can be achieved only by dividing and subdividing political power, distributing to each government, down to the local wards, responsibility for those matters within their range and competence.[100] Accordingly, he insists on maintaining "that wholesome distribution of powers established by the Constitution for the limitation of both; and never to see all offices transferred to Washington, where, further withdrawn from the eyes of the people, they may be more secretly bought and sold as at market."[101] For Jefferson, the great enemy of liberty and the rights of man is the "generalizing and centralizing of all cares and powers in one body"[102] far removed from the watchful eye of the people. Genuine responsiveness requires a separation of powers, federalism, and decentralization; it begins with the wards at the base of the federal pyramid and flows up.

But while Jefferson is right to link self-government with the broad diffusion of political power, he fails to see how his calls for periodic constitutional change to promote greater responsiveness in the long run undermine the very forms and institutions on which self-government depends. Once again, it was left to Tocqueville to explore this tension more fully. Speaking of the complex institutional arrangements that moderate and subdue the will of the majority, Tocqueville observes: "Forms arouse their disdain and often their hatred. As they usually aspire to none but facile and immediate enjoyments, they rush impetuously toward the object of each of their desires, and the least delays exasperate them. This temperament, which they transport into political life, disposes them against the forms which daily hold them up or prevent them in one or another of their designs."[103] This is not to say that the people are never justified in reexamining how their institutions are actually working, for ultimately they are the final judges of these matters. But in general democracies should approach constitutional revision with more caution than Jefferson believed necessary or desirable. As Tocqueville recognized, it is precisely in democratic societies that the forms and formalities of constitutional government are most needed and least understood. The task of the republican statesman is to resist the populist temptation.

Nor is this the only problem with Jefferson's calls for periodic constitutional reform. As Hannah Arendt has argued, there is a larger conceptual difficulty in Jefferson's attempts to return to first principles, either through armed rebellion or through regular constitutional revision. While both proposals have the admirable goal of preserving the spirit of the people, they do so by trying to repeat the activities of the Founding, that is, the violent tearing down of the old order and constitution of the new.[104] In this, too, it is possible to discern the indirect influence of Machiavelli, again in a more benign form: the experience of the Founding becomes the paradigm for all later political activity. Only later does Jefferson recognize that the virtues connected with preserving the republic must be cultivated in ways that are different from how they were exercised at the Founding. This insight gives rise to his most constructive recommendation for how to keep alive republican spirit in the people.

Education and the Cultivation of Civic Spirit

While Jefferson's defense of armed uprisings as a means of preventing corruption in the body politic and keeping alive the spirit of republicanism has lately received much attention, in fact, even before Shays's Rebellion, Jefferson recognized that there are better and more constructive ways to achieve these ends. In the opening section of the Bill for the More General Diffusion of Knowledge (1779), Jefferson begins by observing that the "most effectual means" of warding off "degeneracy" is to "illuminate, as far as is practicable, the minds of the people."[105] The aims of universal education are distinctly political: first, to supply the people with the knowledge of those subjects that will ensure their future "freedom and happiness," and second, to select from each of these local school districts or wards the most virtuous and talented boys to be sent on for further study at public expense. In return, these natural *aristoi* were expected to secure the rights and liberties of their fellow citizens or to use their scientific knowledge to improve the health, subsistence, and comforts of human life.

The elementary school curriculum Jefferson devised was heavily weighted in favor of history, especially the histories of Greece, Rome, England, and America. If his countrymen would only study the ways by which other nations had risen to greatness, and by what errors and vices they had declined, they would be able to secure their future happiness. It is not that Jefferson expects history to provide positive examples. "History, in general, only informs us what bad government is."[106] But these lessons will be instructive for republicans: studying the past will "enable them to know ambition under every guise it may assume; and knowing it, to defeat its views."[107]

If history can provide few examples of good government, still less can it supply moral instruction. "Considering history as a moral exercise, her lessons would be too infrequent if confined to real life. Of those recorded by historians few incidents have been attended with such circumstances as to excite in any high degree this sympathetic emotion of virtue."[108] Nor does he believe that religion, at least orthodox Christianity, can provide children with a solid moral grounding. Indeed, in the *Notes*, Jefferson explicitly rules out "the Bible and Testament," observing that at this early age the judgments of children are "not sufficiently matured for religious inquiries."[109] While accepting the role of the primary schools in "instilling the first elements of morality" into the minds of the students, the moral principles Jefferson has in mind are decidedly secular: children are to be taught the virtues of independence, industry, and self-reliance. As befits the future citizens of a self-governing republic, they are to learn that their "greatest happiness" is not a matter of chance but is always the result of their own actions.[110] Much later, Jefferson would identify the particular virtues he expected public education to instill. Every citizen should understand his duties to his neighbors and his country, exercise his rights with "order and justice," show "discretion" in the selection of public officials, and display "diligence, . . . candor, and judgment" in assessing their performance. In all their social relations, children should be taught to act with "intelligence and faithfulness." Finally, to ensure the independence of each individual in his personal and business affairs, all children should be instructed in "common arithmetic" and the "elements of mensuration." The object here is to enable each to "express and preserve his ideas, his contracts and accounts, in writing"[111] without having to rely on others.

After three years of schooling, most children would possess the necessary skills and moral character to ensure their future freedom and happiness. Jefferson fully expected that as adults Americans would continue to acquire useful knowledge through newspapers,[112] libraries, and the purchase of books. He obligingly drew up suggested reading lists for several correspondents and for members of his family.[113] So important was literacy to a free, self-governing society that Jefferson, in his 1817 Act for Establishing Elementary Schools, inserted a provision disenfranchising future citizens who, after the age of fifteen, "cannot read readily in some tongue, native or acquired."[114] For Jefferson the first task of universal public education is not job training or the encouragement of the artistic imagination and creativity, but the formation of citizens who understand their rights and duties to themselves, their neighbors, and their country.[115]

In his bill for universal public education, Jefferson explicitly provides that the local primary schools admit "all free children, male and female." But unlike his friend Dr. Benjamin Rush, who published a tract on the aims of female education in republican America, Jefferson did not, in this bill or in subsequent reports on education, discuss the matter in any detail. Indeed, in the one letter where a correspondent asked him for his views on the subject, he confessed that "a plan of female education has never been a subject of systematic contemplation with me."[116]

In light of Jefferson's remark, it is tempting to conclude that he has nothing to contribute to this important debate. But while he does not offer elaborate theories about the role of female education in republican government to support his proposals, the proposals themselves do not differ in any significant respects from what men like Benjamin Rush and Noah Webster, who did think systematically about the subject, have to say.[117] Jefferson's bills for universal public education in Virginia would have enabled girls and boys to enroll in elementary school for three years at public expense; held them both to the same standards of literacy; and offered the same basic curriculum to both sexes. The aim of universal public education, about which Jefferson *had* thought systematically, was to impart to boys and girls alike the skills and knowledge that would make them responsible citizens and productive members of society.

Yet despite his insistence that universal public education was more important than institutions of higher learning to the long-term prospects of republican government, none of his proposals for elementary education was enacted during his lifetime. And the private education well-born Virginia ladies continued to receive was a far cry from what Jefferson envisioned. As Christopher Lasch has pointed out, more than in any other section of the country, Southern education reflected the dominant European and aristocratic notions that girls should be segregated from boys and educated in the feminine arts of pleasing men.[118] The task of education was to prepare young ladies for a fashionable life of frivolous amusement and ornamentation. This was still another remnant of the old "patrician order" that Jefferson's educational proposals sought unsuccessfully to extirpate.

Only once, in response to a query by Nathaniel Burwell, does Jefferson directly take up the question of female education. In the absence of any public system of education, Jefferson focuses on the private education young ladies receive at home. He regards the current "inordinate passion . . . for novels" as the chief obstacle to a "solid education." Novels are not only a waste of time but also a "poison" that turns the mind against more "wholesome reading": "The result is a bloated imagination, sickly judgment, and disgust towards all the real businesses of life." Still, even in this "mass of trash," Jefferson discovers a few writers whose narratives "make them interesting and useful vehicles of a sound morality." In particular, he singles out the new moral tales of Marmontel, along with a few other writers whose works have now fallen into obscurity. For the same reasons, he warns against indulging in too much poetry, though he concedes that some "is useful for forming style and taste." In particular, "Pope, Dryden, Thomson, Shakespeare, and of the French, Molière, Racine, and Corneilles, may be read with pleasure and improvement." In a more subdued way, Jefferson returns to the theme of his letter to Robert Skipwith, nearly fifty years earlier: the main purpose of literature and poetry is to edify and instruct, not merely to amuse.[119]

Not surprisingly, given his diplomatic service and political in-clinations, Jefferson considers instruction in the French language "an indispensable part of the education of both sexes," both be-cause French has become the language of general intercourse among nations and because France has made the most rapid ad-vances in all branches of science. Apparently there was no reason to prevent girls from acquiring the most up-to-date useful knowledge.

And on a more practical level, Jefferson believes that all girls should be trained by their mothers in the household arts. Here, too, he quietly dissents from the opinion that Southern ladies should be educated for a life of leisure and amusement. The well-being of the household requires that both men and women be instructed in their respective domestic duties. "The order and economy of a house are as honorable to the mistress as those of the farm to the master, and if either be neglected, ruin follows, and children destitute of the means of living."[120]

At the same time, however, Jefferson does not entirely over-look the ornamental arts and amusements. It is entirely appropri-ate for girls to study dance, drawing, and music, and he saw to it that both his daughters received instruction in these subjects. But in republican America these graceful arts merely adorn an education whose overall aim for both sexes is utility. Accordingly, Jefferson recommends dancing for the social graces it develops, drawing be-cause it is "an innocent and engaging amusement" but also "use-ful" for "one who is to become a mother and an instructor," and music because it is a "delightful recreation," which most conforms to "the taste of this country."[121]

In his response to Burwell, Jefferson remains curiously silent about the study of history. But in his proposals for universal public education, as well as in the private education of his daughters, he insists on the importance of both ancient and modern history.[122] In recommending the study of history for girls, Jefferson's first object is to educate them in the ways in which past republics had become corrupt and lost their liberties, so that they might in turn instruct their own children in these matters. But perhaps he also had in mind the lessons of David Hume's essay "Of the Study of History." In this charming piece, Hume speaks directly to female readers, ar-guing that history can teach them two important truths about the human condition that novels and romances tend to obscure. First,

that "our sex, as well as theirs, are far from being the perfect creatures they [women] are apt to imagine." And, second, that "love is
not the only passion which governs the male world, but is often
overcome by avarice, ambition, vanity, and a thousand other passions."[123] It is difficult to know for certain whether Jefferson had
these particular lessons in mind, but he certainly agrees with Hume
on the larger issue that girls should spend their time reading history rather than trashy novels.

If, however, Jefferson sought to provide essentially the same
elementary education for girls and boys, and educated his own
daughters privately for a life of active utility, to what end was this
education directed? Although citizens, women were not permitted
to vote, even on the local level, where public affairs are supposedly
within the reach and competence of every citizen. Indeed, Jefferson
seemed to fear that the mere attendance of women at public meetings would lead to a decline in public morals. If women were permitted to mix "promiscuously in the public meetings of men," the
likely result would be "depravation of morals and ambiguity of
issue."[124] As for their holding political office, he dismissed the idea
curtly: "The appointment of a woman to office is an innovation for
which the public is not prepared, nor am I."[125] What, then, was the
purpose of their education?

Using his own daughters' "solid education" as a model, Jefferson explains that his principal aim is to prepare them for the duties
of domestic life, including the education of their own daughters and
even that of their sons "should their fathers be lost, incapable, or
inattentive."[126] Good manners prevent him from acknowledging to
his correspondent that this in fact had become the case with his only
surviving daughter, Martha Jefferson Randolph. But he clearly
thought her prepared for the task and willingly deferred to her judgment. Here again, from what is known of the early education of the
Randolph children, the boys and girls received a similar education.
The list of eighty-three works that Martha Jefferson Randolph drew
up for the education of her children differs little for the boys and
girls, except for certain technologically oriented works.[127] For Jefferson, the purpose of female education is precisely to make women
"republican wives" and "mothers,"[128] who take pride in the political
accomplishments of their husbands and sons, while at the same time
leading useful and active lives at home. Although this will no doubt

strike contemporary readers as old-fashioned, it represents a considerable advance over the still popular aristocratic idea that women should be educated for a life of idle fashion and amusement.[129]

Moreover, Jefferson's thoughts on female education accord with his particular understanding of women's rights. Although feminists today often question whether Jefferson meant to include women when he asserted in the Declaration that "all men" are "created equal" and are endowed with "certain unalienable rights," it is more accurate to say that although women possess the same natural rights as men,[130] Jefferson believes that the pursuit of happiness means something fundamentally different for the two sexes. For women, happiness is to be found above all in the domestic sphere, especially in the quiet satisfactions and moral obligations of family life; benevolence does not extend beyond the circle of their closest connections. As a result, Jefferson sees nothing contradictory in declaring that women are endowed with equal *natural* rights, while at the same time denying them equal *political* rights. A world in which women concern themselves with public affairs is a world gone "mad," if not worse. Observing the enthusiasm for politics among French women, Jefferson concludes that American women are far happier because they sensibly confine themselves to the "tender and tranquil amusements of domestic life." The proper role of women is to "soothe and calm the minds of their husbands returning ruffled from political debate."[131] The study of history will help them to understand the political passions the better to know how to soothe them.

Although Jefferson, to the frustration of his more prudent friends, often delighted in pushing ideas to their logical conclusions, he declined to do so on matters of sexual equality. Yet had he chosen to do so, the issue of women's rights presented a perfect opportunity to indulge in another of his famous thought experiments. According to the liberal political theory Jefferson espouses in the Declaration, whatever differences separate one individual from another, no individual is so superior that he can rule over another without her consent. Each individual is the best judge of what protects her interests. How, then, can Jefferson deny women who refuse their consent the right to participate in politics, and so to safeguard their most vital concerns? Although Jefferson would famously argue that each generation must be free to remake its laws and Constitution in order to ensure that "the earth belongs to the living," it never occurred to him that the only way women could ensure their equal natural rights was to grant them equal civil rights.

Instead of pushing this idea to its logical conclusion, as the nineteenth-century feminists did when they redrafted the Declaration of Independence at Seneca Falls, Jefferson takes what for him is an uncharacteristically equivocal turn, one that anticipates Tocqueville's nuanced but not altogether convincing examination of sexual equality in *Democracy in America*.[132] Like Tocqueville, Jefferson suggests that the superiority of the American republic derives in part from the moral superiority of its women. When women confine themselves to the domestic sphere, that is, to the society of their husbands, the care of their children, the arrangements of their homes, and the company of their close friends, they preserve their virtue and that of their husbands. By contrast, in aristocratic France, where women regularly dispense their sexual favors to gain political advantages for husbands and lovers, morals have sunk to a desperate state.[133] The spirit of female intrigue in politics has destroyed chastity, fidelity, and simplicity, rendering virtue and happiness all but impossible.

Thus, although Jefferson is correct when he admits that he has "not thought much" about the formal education of girls, his comparisons of American and French women suggest that he has thought about the larger role of women in shaping the spirit of republican manners and morals. He believes that republican families are essential to the formation of republican citizens and that women are the pillars of the republican family. The aim of female education is to create republican wives and mothers whose own virtue will help to preserve the virtue of their husbands and children. When the political rights of women clashed as they seemed to do with the requirements of virtue and the needs of the family, Jefferson had no desire to engage in radical thought experiments that pushed ideas to their logical conclusions.

Civic Spirit and Political Participation

Although the wards first emerge in Jefferson's thought in connection with his plan for universal public education, they later acquire greater prominence as a means of bringing public affairs within the direct reach of the citizens and thereby keeping alive the civic spirit that lies at the heart of his mature understanding of republicanism. As Jefferson writes to Joseph C. Cabell in 1816, "Begin them [the wards] for a single purpose [education], they will soon show for what others they are the best instruments."[134] Indeed, the germ of this broader vision is already present as early as the *Notes*, where Jefferson observes that although the minds of the people must be improved to a certain degree if they are to govern themselves, this "is not all that is necessary, though it is essentially necessary."[135] He then proceeds to sketch what will later become the hallmark of his republicanism, namely, participation of the people in those political decisions that fall within their competence and directly affect them. Taken together, general education and the division of counties into wards are the two "hooks" on which republicanism depends.[136]

Ironically, Jefferson first seems to have realized how effective the organization of the people in their local governments could be in keeping alive the spirit of resistance to governmental encroachments when as president he felt the combined force of the New England townships in opposing the Embargo Act. "How powerfully did we feel the energy of this organization in the case of the embargo? I felt the foundations of the government shaken under my feet by the New England townships."[137] Although Jefferson regarded the New England opposition as nothing more than a "selfish minority" whose organization "enabled it to overrule the Union," his fear of lethargy as the greatest danger to republican government led him to approve of these associations even when they used their power to protest against his administration. Moreover, because he was confident that the people did not willingly err and would not long persist in their errors once they understood them as such, he never opposed these grassroots organizations, even when they acted against him.[138]

Although the ward theory of political participation did not fully crystallize until after Jefferson left the presidency, it became increasingly central to his understanding of republicanism. Always fearful of the corruption that might result when public affairs were determined entirely by the representatives of the people, while the citizens attended to their private business, Jefferson eventually came to equate republican government with participation in political affairs.

"Purely and simply," a republic means "a government by its citizens in mass, acting directly and personally, according to the rules established by the majority; and that every other government is more or less republican in proportion as it has in its composition more or less of this ingredient of the direct action of its citizens."[139]

While a republic in its purest form is clearly not possible, or even desirable (Jefferson was no admirer of ancient Greece), some space has to be reserved for the people to manage those affairs that are within their range and competence. The New England towns had historically provided such opportunities; the rest of the country would have to take deliberate steps to encourage what Tocqueville would later call "the art of association."[140] Accordingly, Jefferson proposes that the Virginia Constitution be amended to create the ward system of local governments out of the larger and less responsible county divisions: "Each ward would thus be a small republic within itself, and each man in the State would thus become an acting member of the common government, transacting in person a great portion of its rights and duties, subordinate indeed, yet important, and entirely within his competence."[141]

Jefferson envisages a variety of tasks that citizens might manage for themselves: caring for the poor of the community, maintaining roads, supervising the police, overseeing elections, selecting jurors, administering justice in small matters, organizing the militia, and, of course, superintending the schools.[142] On this last point, Jefferson is emphatic: elementary schools should be managed "by the parents within each ward." Just as citizens do not entrust the governor or other state officials with the operation of their farms, mills, and stores, so neither should they deliver to any governmental authority responsibility for the education of their children.[143] To believe that any public official can administer the ward schools better than the parents is "a belief against all experience." What Jefferson fears is that the county governments might appoint religious fanatics as teachers,[144] but his larger point is that parents working together in their communities, and not politicians or advocates, are the best judges of what their children should learn.

As the preceding catalog of activities suggests, the wards cast Jefferson's opposition to energetic government in a new light. For although Jefferson wishes to limit the powers of the federal government, he believes that the states are primarily responsible for protecting the lives, property, and morals of their citizens,[145] and that many of these tasks can best be performed locally by the people themselves. Taken as a whole, Jefferson's political philosophy is not antigovernment; what he seeks to secure, as far as is practicable in a large republic, is self-government by citizens acting together in their local communities. For Jefferson, "making every citizen an active member of the government and in the offices nearest and most interesting to him" is an essential part of the life of free men and now, also, women.[146]

For this reason, the constitutional protection of the wards is Jefferson's most original suggestion for how to combat lethargy and preserve the spirit vital to republicanism. In a liberal republic, which removes so many of the most important human activities, including child rearing, religious worship, and work, from the public realm, Jefferson worries that citizens may find sufficient inducements in a merely private life to turn them away from their shared public responsibilities. Along with resisting the development of speculative commerce, which he fears will turn the people's attention exclusively to "making money," the cure for this evil is to strengthen and nourish the spirit of self-government.[147] "Where every man is a sharer in the direction of his ward-republic, or of some higher ones, and feels that he is a participator in the Government of affairs, not merely at an election one day in the year, but everyday; where there shall not be a man in the State who will not be a member of some one of its councils, great or small, he will let the heart be torn out of his body sooner than his power wrested from him by a Caesar or a Bonaparte."[148]

Again anticipating Tocqueville, Jefferson understands that the preservation of republicanism does not depend primarily on the laws or mere institutional arrangements but on the spirit of a people nourished in the habits of self-government.[149] By bringing public affairs within the reach of each citizen and showing him how his interests intersect with the interests of the community, Jefferson hopes to keep this spirit alive. More than once he observes that the wards are "the wisest invention ever devised by the wit of man for the perfect exercise of self-government, and for its preservation."[150]

But in seeking to keep alive the spirit of the people, does Jefferson perhaps underestimate the dangers of majority tyranny, especially in small, relatively homogeneous communities? What security can he offer to racial, religious, and intellectual minorities, not merely from oppressive legislation but also from more informal social coercion?[151] This question gains force when we consider that Jefferson himself believes that blacks are naturally inferior to whites in intelligence and that such prejudice is "deeply rooted."[152] Similarly, Jefferson's opinion that the Jewish conception of God is "degrading and injurious"[153] can scarcely guarantee that a Christian majority, however divided into competing sects, will always exercise toleration. Finally, his likening the congressional measures of 1798 to a "reign of witches"[154] and his frequent references to Federalists as "heretics" and "apostates" afford scant assurance that local majorities will respect the rights of racial, religious, and political minorities.[155]

There is no doubt that Jefferson tends to minimize the danger of majority faction. His abiding faith in a moderately enlightened people living under republican institutions, where power is widely diffused, leads him to dismiss the possibility that citizens can long remain under the sway of destructive passions or interests. Yet although Jefferson is too optimistic about majority rule, today we tend to err in the opposite direction. Concern for minority rights has been taken too far and extended to too many minorities, fracturing the power of a community to govern itself.[156] The threat of majority tyranny has been used as a battering ram to prevent localities from making popular decisions with which elite opinion, especially at the national level, disagrees. The result has been to deprive the states and municipalities of power and thereby to sap their spirit. What is required is finding some balance that will hedge against majority tyranny but at the same time allow localities sufficient scope to govern themselves as they see fit on a whole host of controversial social and political issues.[157] For when spiritedness declines, the people become simple objects of governance. The trick is to steer between the Scylla of local majority tyranny and the Charybdis of dispiriting centralization.[158] If Jefferson is too sanguine about the former, elite opinion today has become notably unconcerned about the latter.

Beyond this most obvious objection, that the majority can never be trusted to govern themselves without tyrannizing over some minority, there are other, more subtle, questions that arise in connection with Jefferson's ward theory. The first question is this:

What is the relationship of the people to the natural aristocracy who will be their political leaders? Jefferson is not always consistent. On the one hand, when he discusses the wards as educational units, he sees no tension between ordinary citizens and those selected on the basis of merit to go on. Jefferson's discussion of the role of the wards in filtering out the most talented envisions a spirited, reasonably enlightened people frankly recognizing their limitations and willing to defer to their natural superiors in all matters beyond their competence. It is a view unclouded by even the suggestion of resentment or democratic envy on the part of ordinary citizens, as Jefferson's candid description of the process by which the best are to be chosen as one of raking the geniuses from the "rubbish" unwittingly reveals.[159] Whatever "jealousy" citizens might be encouraged to display is directed toward the protection of their liberties, and not against those who are their natural superiors. In contrast to Tocqueville, Jefferson never imagines that the "debased" passion for equality may lead the people to try to tear down those who are naturally better.[160] Conversely, Jefferson assumes that the natural aristocracy is well disposed toward the people. He takes for granted that the interests of the best are not, in principle, at odds with those whom they are elected to serve, partly because each citizen shares in public power and partly because natural aristocrats who are elected will not magnify their differences into qualitative distinctions.[161]

On the other hand, when Jefferson shifts from his original view of the wards as school districts and considers them as the building blocks of republican self-government, the relationship between the people and their elected leaders becomes more problematic. It is not that Jefferson ever doubts the capacity of a moderately enlightened people to choose those who are really best.[162] Nor does he doubt that the best men will continue to offer their services to the public. What worries Jefferson is that if the people do not remain vigilant, if the link between the people and their representatives becomes too tenuous, not even the most wise and virtuous can be trusted to remain faithful to their duty. The best may very well develop interests apart from and contrary to the interests of those they are supposed to serve. Thus, the first question is: Can these conflicting views of the relationship between the people and their leaders be reconciled?

Closely connected with this question is a second: Do the wards play a positive or a negative role in shaping the republican character of the people? While at times Jefferson suggests that the wards bring republican self-government within the reach of the people by allowing them directly to exercise political power and responsibility, at other times he views them as purely defensive associations. The wards enable the people collectively to resist governmental encroachments and to root out and crush corruption among their elected representatives.[163]

Yet, upon reflection, these different perspectives are not as contradictory as they have sometimes been made out to be. The problem is that scholars have tended either to view the wards as modern incarnations of the Greek polis, and so invest them with a nobility of purpose beyond anything Jefferson intended,[164] or to reduce them to the liberal paradigm, where all politics is utilitarian, narrowly self-interested, and purely defensive. In fact, however, the wards are best understood as a kind of modern hybrid, in which political participation is no longer the highest human activity, but neither is it simply instrumental. The wards play a positive role in forming and preserving the character of a free people by drawing them out of their merely private concerns and into the larger common world in which they are most immediately involved. As Jefferson puts it, "By making each citizen an active member of the government, and in the offices nearest and most interesting to him, [the wards] will attach him by his strongest feelings to the independence of his country, and its republican Constitution."[165] It is easy to dismiss the mundane tasks of overseeing the schools, maintaining order, or caring for the poor as essentially uninteresting, but Jefferson warns us that a people who decline to exercise responsibility for those affairs that immediately concern them cannot be counted on to preserve a republican way of life. Here again, Jefferson anticipates Tocqueville's observation that local self-government helps to mitigate the corrosive effects of commerce and radical individualism, as well as defeat the ever-present democratic tropism toward paternalistic despotism.[166]

Nor are political jealousy and distrust of public power as destructive as they have sometimes been portrayed.[167] Jefferson may exaggerate, but he is not wrong to remind people that many representatives, including the natural *aristoi* educated at public expense, will be tempted to betray the public trust if their actions are not regularly subjected to public scrutiny. And with considerable justification, he fears that the expansion and centralization of political power will lead inevitably to corruption and abuses that are harder to detect and more difficult to dismantle. Seen from this perspective, political jealousy seems less like hostility to all political power than a reasonable insistence on political accountability, preferably by governments closer to the people.

To be sure, the tension between the so-called positive and negative functions of the wards can never be completely resolved. There is always a danger, as the growth of secret militias testifies, that Jefferson's rhetoric of distrust and resistance to government may be taken out of context and employed by those hostile to all political power to derail the full range of public tasks he sought to encourage localities to assume. But the tension can also be minimized by sustained political participation, the dissemination of information, and civic education, so that the healthy distrust of political power contributes to responsible government.

Finally, even if political jealousy can be cast in a more favorable light, there is still the third question: In what sense is civic spirit as Jefferson understands it a virtue at all? Certainly, it is not a virtue in the way the ancients understood the term. Jefferson's spiritedness demands none of the austere self-sacrifice and disregard of one's private interests that are the hallmarks of classical republican virtue. On the contrary, it begins with the assumption that citizens enter public affairs precisely to protect and advance their private interests. In this sense, spiritedness is indeed a kind of "enlightened and vigilant selfishness."[168]

But again, as Tocqueville points out, far from being a vice, the kind of enlightened selfishness practiced in communities throughout America encourages the habits and traits that lay the foundation for a new kind of democratic virtue.[169] Although each citizen starts out by asserting his own personal interest, he is compelled by the nature of public discourse to put himself in the place of his fellow citizens and to consider their interests as well. When the decision is finally taken, he is more likely to grasp the connection between his private interest and the good of the community. And even if the decision goes against his interests (here it is important to distinguish between interests and rights), the process of deliberation teaches him to submit proudly to the will of the majority. In these ways, the spirited assertion of individual interests and liberties binds citizens to their communities and cements the habits that bring the full range of civic virtues—including obedience to the law, defense of public order, rational patriotism, and love of country—within reach of ordinary citizens. This new form of civic virtue is, to be sure, a modest virtue, but this is precisely what makes it appropriate to a democratic republic. The alternative for Americans was never the heroic virtue of antiquity but the debilitating complacency Jefferson so rightly feared.

Statesmanship and Political Virtue

Although Jefferson relies principally on the manners and spirit of ordinary citizens to preserve republican government, he also recognizes the need for virtuous statesmen. Indeed, statesmen of the type he envisions are part of nature's design: a benevolent nature has created men of superior talent and virtue precisely so that they may devote themselves to the well-being of others.[170] It is this presumed harmony between the people and their natural superiors that leads Jefferson to suggest that "that form of government is best which provides most effectually for a pure selection of these natural *aristoi* into the offices of government."[171]

Yet Jefferson's own experience in public life suggests that the relation between republican citizens and statesmen is considerably more complex. If nature intends the best to find their fulfillment in advancing the interests of others, why does she seem to withhold the rewards of happiness and pleasure from the life devoted to public service? If, as Jefferson repeatedly complained, politics brings nothing but "torment" and "misery," why should good men devote themselves to serving others? Is it really in their interest to do so? On the other hand, how can these remarks, which so denigrate political life, be reconciled with Jefferson's enthusiastic endorsement of civic participation, or with his view that human beings receive pleasure and happiness when they pursue the good of others? For if private individuals derive satisfaction from such acts, how much greater must be the rewards of the statesman, whose deeds contribute on a much larger scale to the good of others?

Before taking up these and other questions, we begin by considering what the proposition that nature intends for the best to
work for the well-being of others does *not* mean. First, it does not
mean that the interests of the best are automatically or spontaneously allied with the interests of the people. As Jefferson never
tires of warning, men of virtue may have their judgment corrupted by passion and interest; natural aristocrats can, if they are
not scrupulously watched, degenerate into "wolves." Such was
the case with Aaron Burr.[172] Nor does it mean that the best do not
err. Some, like Alexander Hamilton, might be personally upright
but fundamentally misguided, so that they mistake the true
springs of human nature. Again from the *Anas*: "Hamilton was indeed a singular character of acute understanding, disinterested,
honest, and honorable in all private transactions, amiable in society, and duly valuing virtue in private life, yet so bewitched and
perverted by the British example, as to be under the thoro' conviction that corruption was essential to the government of a nation."[173] Most important, it does not mean that nature is of one
mind on the relation of the best to society. Nature sometimes
works against herself by dividing individuals temperamentally
into Whigs and Tories, democrats and aristocrats. "The sickly,
weakly, timid man, fears the people, and is a Tory by nature. The
healthy, strong and bold, cherishes them, and is formed a Whig by
nature."[174] Some natural aristocrats, like George Washington, are
temperamentally Tories; while possessing the talent and virtue to
serve the people, they nevertheless distrust them and are fearful
of the future.[175]

Yet none of these considerations altered Jefferson's conviction
that republican government could inspire the best to dedicate
themselves to the well-being of society. His faith lay in the trans-
formative powers of education to elevate morally and intellectually
citizens and statesmen alike. Nature, presumably even the sickly
Tory nature, is not so fixed that it cannot be altered or improved.
"Education generates habits of application, of order, and the love of
virtue; and controls by force of habit, any innate obliquities in our
moral organization." With a proper republican education, it is possible to engraft "a new man on the native stock" and to improve
"what in his nature was vicious and perverse into qualities of
virtue and social worth."[176] Education thus appears to complete

nature's intention by bringing into harmony the interests of the best and those whom they serve.

The kind of education Jefferson has in mind can best be seen in his discussion of the aims of education at the University of Virginia. Before everything else, the purpose of the university is "to form the statesmen, legislators, and judges" of the Old Dominion by "develop[ing] the reasoning faculties of our youth, enlarg[ing] their minds, cultivat[ing] their morals, and instill[ing] into them the precepts of virtue and order."[177] To this end, Jefferson proposes the most up-to-date curriculum, stressing classical and modern languages, as well as instruction in moral, political, scientific, mathematical, and economic matters. Noticeably absent from the curriculum are the "foggy" disciplines of metaphysics and theology. In their place, Jefferson substitutes "Ideology," which he defines as "the doctrine of thought."

The guiding principle of Jefferson's curricular reform is utility in the broadest sense of "doing good for others," rather than pursuing beauty, truth, or wisdom for their own sake. Or, to be more precise, Jefferson apparently believes that what is useful to the republican cause and what is true are largely the same. Thus, he sees no difficulty in proposing that those appointed to the faculty to teach law and government hold acceptable republican views. And as a further precaution, he recommends that in this course alone the trustees prescribe the texts to be assigned. The list includes only sound Whig and republican principles, distilled from Locke, Sidney, the Declaration of Independence, the *Federalist*, the Virginia Resolutions (though apparently not his own more radical Kentucky Resolutions), and Washington's Farewell Address.[178] No principles that are "incompatible with those on which the Constitutions of this State, and of the United States were 'genuinely' based, in the common opinion" are to be taught or even discussed. Fearing that Americans no longer "know what Whiggism or republicanism means," Jefferson hopes that the University of Virginia will keep alive "the vestal flame of republicanism" from whence it will "spread anew over our own and the sister states."[179]

It is ironic that at the same time Jefferson waged war against religious intolerance he sought to impose a rigid political orthodoxy on future republican statesmen,[180] one that not only omits all discussion of metaphysics and theology but also rejects even divisions within the modern liberal democratic camp. Locke is acceptable, but the "Tory" Hume presumably is not. Nor is there any mention of Hobbes, Rousseau, or Blackstone. How, moreover, can one understand republicanism without also studying Plato and Aristotle, Machiavelli and Montesquieu?[181] Such intellectual intolerance does no honor to the cause Jefferson purports to defend. For if the interests of the best can be reconciled with those of the people they serve only by withholding from them the opportunity to consider competing views about human nature and the best form of government, we are forced to wonder just how compatible their interests really are. It is one thing to seek to inculcate in future statesmen a love of the principles on which their country is based; it is quite another to censor alternative views. For it is only by taking seriously whether self-government is worth defending that the natural aristocracy may be persuaded that their true glory lies in defending the republican experiment, rather than pursuing their own ambitions.[182] Jefferson's attempt to impose a narrow partisan curriculum on future statesmen contradicts his own proud claim that, at the University of Virginia, "we are not afraid to follow truth wherever it may lead, nor to tolerate any error so long as reason is left free to combat it."[183]

Jefferson's enumeration of the virtues republican statesmen should possess reveals a similar, albeit more subtle, partisan bias. Above everything else, statesmen must display patriotism and a disinterested love of country. But on closer analysis, "disinterestedness" turns out to mean having no interests apart from the interests of the people.[184] Jefferson makes it clear that no one who does not fully embrace the cause of the people can be "disinterested." He is quick to detect the callow motives of the Federalists that lurk beneath their spurious patriotism: those who decline to take the side of the people are only interested in their own political power or building up their private fortunes.[185] Their motives and actions lack honor and integrity. By contrast, Jefferson assumes that the interest of the people automatically coincides with the common good, and that those who serve the people have no selfish reasons for doing so. Their only motive for public service seems to be their desire to advance the rights and liberties of others.[186]

Jefferson's conception of disinterestedness not only is colored by partisanship but also raises more general questions about his understanding of the virtues required of republican statesmen. First, is disinterestedness, as Jefferson understands it, the only, or even the most important, virtue required of those who would lead the people, or are there other virtues, at least equally compelling, that are also necessary? And, second, is his treatment of the statesman's virtues psychologically compelling? Can Jefferson explain why the most virtuous and talented should seek a life of public service? What motives and rewards does nature provide to encourage such a choice?

One virtue Jefferson seems conspicuously silent about is moral courage. Although the statesman may on occasion be compelled to stretch or even exceed the limits of the law,[187] Jefferson does not believe that he will have to challenge the long-established opinions of the people. True, the people might momentarily be mistaken, but given access to reliable information, they will not long remain deluded. When the people err, they do so innocently; the task of the statesman is to give them the facts they need to correct their errors.[188] Jefferson's faith in the capacity of the people to govern themselves prevents him from recognizing that there will always be occasions when the statesman must resist popular opinion. Perhaps nowhere is this clearer than on the question of slavery. In the *Notes*, Jefferson expects that the statesman who does nothing to advance the cause of emancipation will be loaded with "execration," but when it turns out that those who publicly champion abolition are the ones who are criticized, Jefferson is only too eager to pass the responsibility to the next generation.[189]

Jefferson's silence about the need for moral courage further assumes that the people have a single interest. They are united in their opposition to the monarchical and aristocratic interest of the Federalists. In contrast to the pluralistic conception of society sketched by Madison in *Federalist* Number 10, Jefferson does not have as clearly in focus the division of "the people" into a multiplicity of competing interests and sects.[190] The one seeming exception is the great geographic "division of interest and sentiment," which Jefferson recognized early on, but which he understands to be another manifestation of the more fundamental division between monarchical Northern urban federalists and genuine, mostly Southern, agricultural republicans.[191] Such a contest, rightly decided, requires no great fund of moral courage.

Moreover, just as Jefferson too readily assumes a harmony between both the interest and opinion of the people and the common good, so, too, does he take for granted the alliance between republican spiritedness and rational liberty, once again obviating the need for moral courage. With the exception of slavery, where Jefferson does admit that Southerners are "zealous for their own liberties, but trampl[ing] on those of others," he seems reluctant to acknowledge that the same men who love liberty may also love dominion over others.[192] Thus, the task of the republican statesman is not simply to encourage popular displays of spirited self-assertion but to resist those demagogues and fanatics who would direct the people's pride toward the exercise of those spurious liberties that would destroy republican self-government.

Jefferson also has surprisingly little to say about prudence, or the need for practical wisdom in political affairs.[193] This is not to say that statesmen do not require superior knowledge and training, but the application of this knowledge to public affairs is relatively straightforward. Here again, Jefferson's tendency to think in terms of one great popular interest arrayed against the monocrats tends to minimize the need for prudent leadership in resolving genuine conflicts of interest or opinion among different segments of "the people." So, too, do his confidence in the "steady and rational character of the American people"[194] and his inability to recognize that, even in republics, statesmen may have need of virtues not commonly found in the people.

Closely related to this last point, Jefferson seems to underestimate the moral duty of statesmen not simply to inform but also to educate the people about their rights and responsibilities as citizens. Perhaps no one understood better than the author of the Declaration how complex are the principles of political morality on which the American republic was founded. How should Americans seek to reconcile the twin principles of equality and liberty? Where do our rights come from, what do they mean, and how should we resolve the tensions that arise among these different rights? Jefferson seems to rely far too much on the spontaneous resolution of these questions by a moral sense brought to full flowering under republican institutions, an agrarian economy, and universal education. Yet preserving our rights requires more than a reliance on the innate decency of the American people and their vigilant, but (for Jefferson) benign, spirit; it requires statesmen who will instruct citizens in the true meaning and ground of their rights. The statesman is not simply the people's advocate; he is, more important, their educator. For it is only when citizens understand these principles correctly, and especially in all their limitations, that republican self-government is truly possible.[195]

We turn now to the second question raised by Jefferson's singular focus on disinterestedness as *the* virtue of the republican statesman: Is it psychologically compelling? Does Jefferson adequately understand the motives that impel the best men to seek public service? Can it plausibly be maintained that the republican statesman has no interest or ambition apart from serving the people, that he acts simply out of the unselfish desire to promote the good of others?

Jefferson's comments about his own motives for seeking public office display a curious lack of self-knowledge. He seems blind to the extent to which political ambition, however "laudable," motivates him to seek political office. When Jefferson observes in 1782 that he has "examined well my heart, to know whether it were thoroughly cured of political ambition," and declares himself "satisfied that every fibre of that passion has been eradicated,"[196] we can only wonder at his powers of introspection. And Jefferson's protest to Adams in 1796—"I have no ambition to govern men. It is a painful and thankless office"—understandably struck Adams as disingenuous.[197] By refusing to admit, even to himself, his own ambition and desire for honor, Jefferson unwittingly testifies to the self-deception of the idealist who claims only to be acting on behalf of others.[198]

Like so many idealists who deny the full range of motives for their actions, Jefferson turns out to be astonishingly thin-skinned. Having persuaded himself that he acted from purely disinterested motives, he found himself unable to bear criticism of any kind. In a revealing comment to Francis Hopkinson, Jefferson confesses, "I find the pain of little censure, even when it is unfounded, is more acute than the pleasure of much praise."[199] Not surprisingly, when Jefferson encounters criticism, he allows himself the luxury of self-pity. Not once but twice before 1800, Jefferson retired from the "torment" and "misery" of public office in pursuit of the happiness he expected to find only in his return to domestic life.[200]

But there is a problem here: How can Jefferson maintain that nature intends the best to devote themselves to the interests of others, and yet insist that politics brings nothing but "wretchedness"? Jefferson seems to be asking us to believe that we should choose to serve others for its own sake and not for the sake of any rewards that it may bring, indeed, even if the life of the statesman brings only misery and oppression.[201] But if this is so, why should the best men seek political office? Jefferson's answer is duty. Writing to George Washington to urge him to reconsider his decision to retire from the presidency at the end of his first term, Jefferson observes that Providence has imposed a law "on you in forming your character and fashioning the events on which it was to operate." The president has an obligation to put aside his predilection for "a particular walk of happiness" and to labor on behalf of the public.[202] And to the Massachusetts politician Elbridge Gerry, who was hesitant for family reasons to accept the post of envoy extraordinary to France at a critical moment in the relations between the two countries, Jefferson insists, "The man who loves his country on its own account, and not merely for its trappings of interest or power, can never be divorced from it, can never refuse to come forward in dangers which he has the means of warding off." However great the blessings of domestic life, they cannot be purchased by the refusal to serve. "Reflect that to be a good husband and father at this moment, you must also be a good citizen."[203] And Jefferson himself, returning to public office as secretary of state in the Washington administration, believes his actions are motivated solely by the disinterested call to duty.[204]

Yet this still does not answer the more fundamental question of why citizens should answer the call of duty if nature rewards only the life of the private individual. The answer is that nature does provide statesmen with both the motives and the rewards for public service, though as a political idealist, Jefferson is loath to admit that his motives are not entirely selfless. Still, his correspondence occasionally hints at the motives and rewards for entering political life. One motive for ruling, reminiscent of Socrates' argument in the *Republic*, is the desire to avoid being ruled by worse men, in this case "monocrats" and "Anglomen," who will sabotage the experiment in republican self-government.[205] But there are positive incentives as well. Nature does not ask anyone to dedicate himself to the interests of others merely out of a sense of duty. Rather, she has arranged it that in working for the good of others, the statesman gratifies his own passions and interests. Laudable ambition, pride in eminence of character, desire for the esteem and approbation of one's countrymen, and hope of "everlasting remembrance" are reasons that statesmen answer the call of duty.[206]

Just as nature makes it in the interest of the best men to serve others, so, too, does she reward their labors. Jefferson's complaints about the misery of politics, like his comments on Shays's Rebellion, have been taken out of context and blown out of proportion. Take, for example, the letter to James Monroe, written in 1782, to explain Jefferson's decision to retire as governor of Virginia. As the correspondence makes clear, the issue is not whether the natural *aristoi* should ever serve their fellow countrymen but whether the public has a perpetual right to the services of its leading citizens. As Jefferson reminds Monroe, he had already been engaged in public service for the last thirteen years, to the total neglect of his family and private affairs. It is in this context that Jefferson remarks that "if we are made in some degree for others, yet in greater are we made for ourselves," and that to force someone like him, in many ways temperamentally unsuited to the demands of public life, to continue in office would be "to annihilate the blessing of existence, and to contradict the giver of life, who gave it for happiness and not for wretchedness."[207]

Apart from the letter to Monroe, most of Jefferson's complaints about politics occur in letters written to his daughter Martha Jefferson Randolph. Understandably, these letters emphasize the blessings of domestic life and his unhappiness at being separated from his family, his farm, and his books. To her he had written, "Politics are such a torment that I would advise everyone I love not to mix with them."[208] Yet to his nephew Thomas Mann Randolph, Jr. (who would later become Martha's husband and Jefferson's son-in-law), Jefferson had in fact advised just the opposite: "I am glad you have fixed on politics as your principal pursuit. Your country will derive a more immediate and sensible benefit."[209] In recommending the life of politics to his own family members, Jefferson seems tacitly to recognize that public service is not all duty and pain. Indeed, occasionally Jefferson admits that nature actually rewards the statesman's efforts. Perhaps wisely, nature does not reward the life of the statesman with the greatest happiness, since delight in ruling others might suffocate the spirit of self-government. But statesmen do derive considerable happiness and pleasure from the gratitude and approval of their fellow citizens. As Jefferson observes in his inaugural speech as wartime governor of Virginia, "In a virtuous and free State, no rewards can be so pleasing to sensible minds, as those which include the approbation of our fellow citizens."[210]

Still, as Jefferson was shortly to learn, nature parcels out her rewards only indirectly and by no means efficiently. For she makes the happiness of the most talented and virtuous depend on the approval of those who by definition lack the judgment and wisdom of the natural *aristoi*. Although Jefferson had entered the governor's office confident that in pursuing his duty as he understood it he would win the approbation of his countrymen, popular disapproval of his actions caused him to refine the thrust of his inaugural remarks. By the end of his unhappy term, he had learned to distinguish between the "well-meaning but uninformed" opinions of the people and the judgment of those "men of worth, of reflection, and pure attachment to republican government."[211] It was, Jefferson now insisted, praise from this more select group that was truly gratifying.[212] If this approval still did not produce the unalloyed happiness of domestic life, the approbation of the "good and just"[213] could nevertheless produce "great happiness" for those who dutifully served their country.

But as the cause of republicanism gathered strength and Jefferson became its undisputed leader, his confidence in the people steadily rebounded. The "revolution of 1800" more than restored his earlier conviction that the statesman could find his reward and satisfaction in the approbation of his fellow countrymen.[214] And, indeed, as time went on, Jefferson discovered that the rewards were far greater than he at first believed. For in pursuing the interests of the people, Jefferson could take both pleasure and pride in knowing that he would win not only the approbation of the present generation but also the love and gratitude of posterity. Immortal fame is the reward nature holds out for the greatest of the republican statesmen.[215] And, for his part in defending the people against the pretensions of the few, Jefferson became increasingly confident he had earned it, although he was reluctant to admit this even to himself.

One final point is worth noting. Although public service is not without its considerable rewards, especially for those men who are by nature "born for the public,"[216] Jefferson was willing to exempt certain men from the obligations of political life. This was not because their genius excuses them from fulfilling their responsibilities to others but, on the contrary, because nature has marked them for a higher social purpose. Thus, writing to the Pennsylvania philosopher David Rittenhouse, Jefferson asks, "Are those powers then, which being intended for the erudition of the world, like air and light, the world's common property, to be taken from their proper pursuit to do the common place drudgery of governing a single state, a work which may be executed by men of an ordinary stature, such as always and every where are to be found?"[217]

Unlike others in his generation, Jefferson did not regard legislators and statesmen as the highest order of human genius. Jefferson's greatest heroes were not the classical lawgivers but the modern philosopher-scientists Bacon, Newton, and Locke.[218] These men have rendered the fullest service to humanity, since their discoveries promise to improve the lot of all mankind without regard to political boundaries or partisan considerations. Here is philanthropy in its most complete form.

Nevertheless, Jefferson's refusal to rank the life of the statesman at the pinnacle of human activity does not strip public service of all dignity and satisfaction. Even Aristotle, who made the greatest claims on behalf of political life, ultimately conceded that for those who are so endowed the *vita contemplativa* is superior to the *vita activa*. That a few geniuses should be left alone "to fulfill the highest purposes" of their creation does not mean that a life devoted to the republican cause is unworthy of those great men whose talents incline them toward the political. For despite Jefferson's complaints, nature intends, and in the long run usually ensures, that those who serve their country nobly receive their just rewards.

Conclusion

Alone among the Founders, Jefferson located the heart of republicanism in the liberty-loving spirit of the people. Then as now, it is a spirit that resists easy classification. In its most radical moments, it does not shrink from violent measures, but most of the time it reflects the natural conservatism of a people both comfortable and secure. As long as this spirit survived, republicanism would continue. But if it succumbed to excessive materialism, democratic centralization, and political lethargy, republicanism, in the sense of genuine self-government, would effectively die. True, the formal constitutional arrangements might continue for a considerable period, creating the illusion that all was well, but once the people lost the desire to govern themselves or had their power wrested from them by politicians, bureaucrats, and judges, republicanism would begin to rot from the bottom up.

To keep this spirit alive, Jefferson rightly started with the education of children. For he understood, as contemporary educators often do not, that republicanism cannot survive indefinitely if citizens are both ignorant of, and indifferent to, the history, institutions, and manners that collectively shape their distinctive American way of life. Above all, education must instruct children in their rights, interests, and duties, both as human beings and as citizens. It must cultivate in them the moral and civic virtues that are the foundation of self-government: independence, self-reliance, personal responsibility, discretion, and judgment. Moreover, as Jefferson later discovered, it was not enough for the people merely to know what civic virtue required; they had to be given the opportunity to exercise these qualities on a regular basis. A constitutional order bottomed on federalism and decentralization would allow citizens to perfect the full range of civic virtues through the exercise of their natural right to self-government. Participation in politics would encourage proud self-assertion, rational deliberation, and reasonable accommodation to the interests and opinions of others.

But as Jefferson also understood, to draw people out of their own private worlds and into the public arena, they must be given power over those matters that most directly interest them: the education of their children, the security of their persons and property, and the provision of essential public services. It is not enough to leave to them the implementation of administrative details. Spiritedness thrives only by the exercise of genuine power and responsibility; it involves risk. The decisions of local majorities may sometimes be unwise; they will often offend elite opinion. But republicanism rests on the proposition that, with civic education and the proper distribution and diffusion of political power, people are capable of governing themselves.

If, however, self-government is not to deteriorate into a general populist assault on all institutions beyond the immediate reach and control of the people, it must be restrained by prudent and courageous statesmen. Although Jefferson was not so radical as to deny altogether the need for virtuous leadership in a democratic republic, his highly charged, ideological approach to politics tends to minimize the statesman's role in preserving the proper spirit of republicanism. Left unchecked, Jefferson's lopsided emphasis on civic virtue, and his tendency to think of this virtue in terms of a certain kind of spiritedness, may encourage a libertarian disdain for all government action even at the local level, as individuals, taking undue pride in their self-sufficiency, come to question any sense of collective purpose.[219] Or, the absence of prudent leadership may embolden community activists, funded by private foundations and government grants,[220] to seize control of local political structures, making genuine self-government more difficult, if not impossible. What is needed to perfect Jefferson's spirited citizenship is an enlarged and less partisan conception of the virtues required of statesmen. For only then will Jefferson's pride in republican self-government be fully vindicated.

Chapter Five

The Liberal Ideal: Duties to Self, Friendship, and Duties to God

It is a paradox, often noted, that although Jefferson regards morality chiefly in terms of the duties we owe to others, rather than the perfection of the individual character, he also insists that we are made in a greater degree for ourselves than for others.[1] Throughout his long years of public service, he frequently expressed the wish to return to private life, where he could enjoy the supreme pleasures of his family, farm, books, and friends.[2] In the serenity of Monticello, Jefferson found the leisure to pursue these activities and, in so doing, completed his portrait of the virtues that perfect the American character. In this chapter, we consider the moral duties we owe to ourselves, the role of the intellectual virtues in developing the American character, friendship, and the duties we owe to God. We close with a consideration of that most Jeffersonian and, indeed, American of virtues, hope.

Duties to Self

Although Jefferson gradually came to believe that the morality recommended by Christ in the Gospels was the best guide to the duties we owe to others, he continued to insist that the ancient Greek and Roman moralists were "really great" in that branch of morality that deals with the government of the self, especially those passions that, when uncontrolled, "disturb our tranquillity of mind."[3] As a young man, Jefferson seemed especially taken with the teachings of the Stoics, particularly Seneca and Epictetus, as

153

well as Cicero, whom he mistakenly classed as a Stoic. The excerpts from the *Tusculan Disputations* in the *Literary Commonplace Book* stress, among other things, indifference to bodily pleasure and pain, and the withdrawal of the soul from all the cares of the body in order to prepare for death.[4] But as he returned to these ancient moralists in his retirement he became convinced that Stoicism was too gloomy and unnatural a philosophy for Americans to follow. "The perfection of the moral character is, not in a Stoical apathy, so hypocritically vaunted, and so untruly too, because impossible, but in a just equilibrium of all the passions."[5] He is willing to grant that Seneca and Epictetus still offer a few good practical maxims, but beyond these, Stoic dogma is all "hypocrisy and grimace." What is more, he now accused Cicero and the Stoics of deliberately distorting the views of the Epicureans, casting them as vulgar hedonists in pursuit of bodily pleasures. But, as Jefferson read them, the doctrines of Epicurus are as "frugal of vicious indulgence, and fruitful of virtue as the hyperbolical extravagances of his rival sects."[6] Accordingly, he now declared himself an Epicurean: "I consider the genuine (not the imputed) doctrines of Epicurus as containing everything rational in moral philosophy which Greece and Rome have left us."[7] Jefferson's project, never completed, was to combine the moral teaching of the Gospels as revealed through the moral sense regarding our duties to others with the moral philosophy of Epicureanism made known through prudence and "sober reasoning" regarding the duties we owe to ourselves. Taken together, these two moral systems would provide a comprehensive guide for the perfection of the American character and lay the foundation for true happiness.[8]

In the "Syllabus of the doctrines of Epicurus," Jefferson sets forth in "lapidary style" the scientific and moral tenets of this philosophy. Under the moral heading, Jefferson notes that happiness is the aim of life and that virtue is the foundation of happiness. Although ultimately Jefferson will part company with Epicurus precisely on this issue, insisting that the greatest human happiness comes principally from the practice of the social virtues and not the perfection of the individual character, he regards the Epicurean understanding of happiness as superior to the classical alternatives. In contrast to Plato, who identifies happiness with the abstract contemplation of the idea of the good, while minimizing all worldly concerns, or the Stoics, whose notion of happiness even more radically overlooks the importance of bodily well-being, Epicurus insists that happiness consists of both bodily and mental pleasures. For Epicurus, happiness is not being pained in body or troubled in mind; accordingly, the enjoyment of pleasure becomes the summum bonum, and whatever contributes to "in-do-lence of body" and "tranquillity of mind" is good. The four cardinal virtues—prudence, temperance, fortitude, and justice—are all praiseworthy because they are useful in directing the passions toward the greatest pleasure, thereby ensuring happiness; hence Jefferson's observation that for the Epicureans "utility [is] the test of virtue."[9]

But, while genuine Epicureanism does not disdain the desire for moderate bodily pleasure, it is not, as commonly supposed, a philosophy dedicated to the vulgar gratification of sensual desires. For Epicurus, there is a natural hierarchy of pleasure and pain. Epicurus explicitly rules out "the pleasures of profligates and those that consist in sensuality." It is not in "continuous drinkings and revellings, nor the satisfaction of lusts," nor in "the luxuries of the wealthy table," that we find true pleasure, but from "sober reasoning" either alone or together with friends about those matters that are most likely to disturb our peace of mind.[10]

Properly understood, Epicurean philosophy teaches humans to govern their bodily desires through the use of right reason, by calculating the consequences of their actions in terms of true pleasure and pain. Thus, in contrast to the duties we have to others, which are knowable by the generous impulses of the moral sense, the duties we owe to ourselves are knowable through reason. Prudence, or the ability to consider consequences with a view to pleasure and pain, is, therefore, the first of the virtues connected with individual excellence and the spring of all the others. For prudence teaches that it is not possible to live pleasantly without also exercising temperance, fortitude, and justice.[11] Jefferson echoes this thought in his "Syllabus": prudence helps us "to procure tranquillity of mind" by avoiding desire and fear, "the two principal diseases of the mind."[12] It also counsels us to avoid deceit, the other great evil that threatens our tranquillity.

Temperance, or the regulation of the bodily desires, is the second of the Epicurean virtues. Within limits, it is altogether natural to seek bodily pleasure, but most individuals fail to recognize that beyond a certain point, the indulgence of bodily desires produces pain rather than pleasure. Such excesses could assume a variety of forms, and while living abroad, Jefferson took note of the different ways in which the Americans and the French fell wide of the mark. In the pleasures of the table, Americans would do well to imitate the French because "with good taste they unite temperance. They do not terminate the most sociable meals by transforming themselves into brutes." On the other hand, the French would increase their stock of felicity by following the rational and healthy example of the Americans on sexual matters. But, instead, they indulge all of their worst passions for momentary ecstasy, followed inevitably by "days and months of restlessness and torment."[13] Far from leading to pleasure, such indulgences bring only bodily pain and mental anguish. Accordingly, Jefferson believes (not altogether correctly, as we shall see) that the hedonism he embraces is at one with that of Epicurus, since it elevates tranquillity of mind over the gratification of bodily desires.[14]

If temperance is the virtue connected with desire, then fortitude is the virtue that helps to overcome fear. It differs from courage in that it is not primarily concerned with overcoming fear in battle.[15] To be sure, the willingness to risk one's life for one's country remains a virtue for Jefferson, but in his peaceful agrarian republic, the kind of raw courage so prized by the Greeks and Romans now becomes suspect. For when courage in battle becomes the highest moral virtue, the ends of political life are distorted; the ancient republics are defective because they honor conquest and domination, rather than the "equal rights of man and the happiness of each individual."[16] Thus, while Jefferson's conception of fortitude does not preclude military valor, it seeks to direct the natural pride and spiritedness of Americans toward other less sanguinary, and more reasonable, ends.

Fortitude also does not mean political courage, or the willingness to stand up for one's convictions in public. On the contrary, Jefferson advises his grandson, the first rule of prudence is never to enter into a political argument with another, and especially not to feel obliged to defend his grandfather's character and honor. "In the fevered state of our country," political disagreements excite all the dangerous passions and can never be settled by rational argument.

"Get by them, therefore as you would by an angry bull: it is not for a man of sense to dispute the road with such an animal." Instead he urges the lad to follow the advice of the "most amiable" Dr. Franklin and "never to contradict anybody." For good humor is "one of the best preservatives of our peace and tranquillity."[17] Similarly, he goes out of his way to avoid disagreeing with his opponents in public, preferring always to take things by "the smooth handle" and, when necessary, to have surrogates conduct his battles for him. The only time that something akin to political courage is a virtue is when citizens stand up to rulers who seek to encroach upon their rights; civic virtue requires "jealousy" and vigilance.[18] But in political disputes among private citizens or between the leaders of warring political parties, the virtue to strive for is civility; when acting as individuals, Americans should cultivate the virtues of "prudence and good humor," or at least the appearance of accommodation, and avoid confrontation.

Neither primarily courage in battle nor in the political arena, fortitude is rather a firmness of mind that helps us to overcome the mundane obstacles of daily life that may, if indulged, bring about greater pain or prevent the enjoyment of greater pleasure in the future. Fortitude, Jefferson avers as he tries to coax an old friend to more exercise and exertion, is the virtue that "teaches us to meet and surmount difficulties; not to fly from them, like cowards, and to fly, too, in vain, for they will meet and arrest us at every turn of our road." Thus, the momentary pleasures of repose must be balanced against the inevitable "debility of body, and hebetude of mind, the farthest of all things from the happiness which the well-regulated indulgences of Epicurus ensure."[19] In Jefferson's lexicon, fortitude is closely allied to resolution and self-reliance, which he considers distinctively American virtues. As he writes to his daughter when she complains of the difficulty of reading Livy in Latin without her tutor, "It is part of the American character to consider nothing as desperate, to surmount every difficulty by resolution and contrivance." As Jefferson knows from experience, this "habit of surmounting difficulties" by finding the "means within ourselves" rather than leaning on others, will enable his young daughter to persevere in learning Latin in order to enjoy as an adult the "sublime luxury" of reading these ancient authors in their original language. But because she is a child, Jefferson shrewdly focuses on more immediate consequences, reminding her that without such strength of character, "you will be thought a very helpless animal, and less esteemed."[20] Thus conceived, fortitude is a supremely rational virtue, in which pride and reason combine forces to overcome the natural aversion to what is immediately painful, for the sake of the greater pleasures of approbation and self-mastery.

The last of the Epicurean virtues is justice. Although justice is the preeminent political virtue, enforcing by law and punishment the duties we owe to others rather than to ourselves, it nevertheless presupposes that individuals have already mastered the virtue of self-control. For if they are unable to restrain their passions and desires within reasonable bounds, they will lay claim to what is not rightfully theirs, denying others what properly belongs to them. Anger, pride, avarice, resentment, and envy all lead men to try to take more than their share. Injustice is a kind of "deceit."[21] Jefferson is not so naive as to believe that self-control by itself is sufficient to guarantee justice: "The human character . . . requires in general constant and immediate control, to prevent its being biased from right by the seductions of self-love." But more than any other form of government, the kind of liberal republicanism Jefferson envisions presupposes that Americans are not "infants," but "adults" who have first learned to govern themselves.[22]

To this end, Jefferson drew up "A Decalogue of Canons for observation in practical life," setting forth, again in lapidary form, the maxims that, if made habitual, would help his countrymen to achieve that "just equilibrium" of the passions so necessary to physical well-being and tranquillity of mind.

1. Never put off till to-morrow what you can do to-day.
2. Never trouble another for what you can do yourself.
3. Never spend your money before you have it.
4. Never buy what you do not want, because it is cheap; it will be dear to you.
5. Pride costs us more than hunger, thirst and cold.
6. We never repent of having eaten too little.
7. Nothing is troublesome that we do willingly.
8. How much pain have cost us all the evils which have never happened.
9. Take things always by their smooth handle.

10. When angry, count ten, before you speak; if very angry, an hundred.[23]

Although Jefferson himself never mastered the third or even the fourth canons, the decalogue points to those moral virtues he wished to see Americans cultivate: industry, self-reliance, frugality, self-restraint, modesty, temperance, fortitude, cheerfulness, civility, and self-control. In turn, the regular exercise of these virtues lays the foundation both for the more estimable social virtues recommended by the Gospels and for the Epicurean cultivation of wisdom and friendship.

The Intellectual Virtues

Jefferson not only ranks the moral virtues that relate to others higher than those that perfect the individual character but also ranks these social virtues higher than the intellectual virtues. The virtues that perfect us in our social relations are accessible to all through the innate promptings of the moral sense, made habitual through regular practice, and reinforced by the imagination and rules of ordinary prudence. Wisdom, on the other hand, is the preserve of the natural *aristoi*, and while for men like Jefferson, the tranquil pursuit of knowledge does indeed bring "supreme delight,"[24] he nevertheless insists that our moral obligations to others stand higher than wisdom in the hierarchy of natural goods. For those few who are capable of both wisdom and virtue, "the possession of science" takes second place to "an honest heart."[25] The wise man must possess the same moral virtues, and exercise them in the same way, as everyone else.[26] In addition, he must use his wisdom for the benefit of all humankind. Wisdom may not be available to all, but it can be placed in the service of all. "The field of knowledge is the common property of mankind," and any discoveries benefit "every other nation, as well as our own."[27] Nor does the search for wisdom divide the few from the many because Jefferson assumes that what is true is also useful. Consequently, there is no tension between doing good for others and doing good for ourselves, or between the moral virtues and the intellectual virtues.

In reflecting on the role of wisdom and the place of knowledge or "science" in American life, Jefferson finds Epicurean philosophy superior to both Stoicism and Platonism. The most distinctive Stoic doctrines, especially its grim endurance of physical pain and its willful detachment from what Jefferson regards as natural and healthy human desires, provide no model for how Americans should live. But it is Platonic philosophy that Jefferson judges most harshly, blaming Plato's foggy mysticisms for the development of orthodox Christianity and its incomprehensible doctrine of the Three in One. "Platonic Christianity" is nothing more than a conspiracy between priests and kings to mystify and oppress the people for their own worldly advantage.[28] By contrast, Jefferson the scientist cannot help but be drawn to the materialist philosophy of the Epicureans, since it seems most to accord with the modern scientific account of the world as consisting solely of matter in motion. But even then, he rejects their more austere conclusions regarding the role of philosophy and the potential of the human mind for solving practical problems and increasing the stock of human happiness.

In his "Syllabus," Jefferson outlines the physical doctrines of the Epicureans: "The Universe eternal. Its parts, great and small, interchangeable. Matter and Void alone. Motion inherent in matter which is weighty and declining." As the last item under the physical, Jefferson includes, without comment, a brief statement about the gods. Although the classical Epicureans do not flatly deny the existence of God, they do not believe that the universe was created by him. As Jefferson summarizes their doctrine, the gods are "an order of beings next superior to man, enjoying in their sphere, their own felicities; but not meddling with the concerns of the scale of beings below them."[29]

The great moral question that both Epicurus and his disciple Lucretius[30] explore is: How should we live in a world where nature is understood in mechanistic, materialistic terms and where the gods have no care for humans? According to the classical Epicureans, the purpose of philosophy is to help men overcome their fear of death and of divine punishment by scientifically investigating the nature of the universe rather than relying on mythical stories about the gods. Epicureanism seeks to dispel this "fear about the most important matters" by showing that the gods, if in fact they exist at all, take no interest in human affairs. Either the universe is eternal as Epicurus believed or, according to Lucretius, it came into being by accident, when atoms collided in a particular way, and it will go out of existence in a similar fashion. Knowledge of this bitter truth can release us from the pain that comes from fear of the gods and of death, since by studying the nature of things we come to understand that, as purely material beings, nothing will happen to us after we die.[31]

Turning to the world of human affairs, both Epicurus and Lucretius argue that the wise man should withdraw from public life.[32] In the Epicurean calculus of pleasure and pain, politics is a necessary evil and justice a utilitarian compact not to harm one another. There is nothing either natural or noble about political life or service to one's country. Thus, the wise man will pursue a life of self-sufficiency in the company of like-minded friends and avoid the complications and pain of public affairs.

Finally, classical Epicureanism counsels not only withdrawal from political affairs but an attitude of resignation toward the natural world. Although nature, conceived as matter in motion, is indifferent to human life, neither Epicurus nor Lucretius believes that men should use their power to bend nature to their purposes. The attempt to conquer nature through science and technology would only inflame the desires for bodily pleasures, creating new fears that pull men further away from genuine happiness and tranquillity of mind. The best life is to retire from the world and, with the company of a few friends, free oneself through philosophy from the false opinions, baseless fears, and useless desires that make life so painful for most people. Only the wise few can really be happy.[33]

At this point, we may well wonder how Jefferson can reconcile Epicureanism with the Christian social ethics that lay at the heart of his moral philosophy, since one believes that happiness depends on the withdrawal from politics and a passive investigation of nature, while the other makes the duties we owe to others central to the good life and actively seeks to conquer nature to improve the human condition.[34] But the main pieces of this puzzle had already been put in place by the seventeenth-century Catholic priest and philosopher Pierre Gassendi, who revived and "corrected" Epicureanism to make it square with Christian teaching. It is

Gassendi's version of Epicureanism that Jefferson regards as defin-
itive. In the *Syntagma Philosophicam*, Gassendi first attacked the
atheistic assumptions of classical Epicureanism. While accepting
Epicurean atomism, Gassendi argues that the world is neither eternal nor accidental but was created and is maintained by God. He
then moves on to the more difficult task of recasting the moral and
political implications of Epicureanism to make them more compatible with Christian morality. In the "Ethica" portion of the *Syntagma*, Gassendi begins with the central Epicurean doctrine that
pleasure is the highest good and the end of human life. But, he
insists, the natural desire for pleasure and aversion to pain in
human beings is part of God's design to get human beings to carry
out his plans using their own free will. Through the use of right reason, men come to see that they cannot achieve the most pleasurable
state without being virtuous, for only virtue can bring tranquillity
of mind and absence of bodily pain. For Gassendi, the most pleasurable state is the social state, and justice, being *the* social virtue,
is not only useful but natural. Thus, in contrast to the radically individualistic and apolitical implications of classical Epicureanism,
Gassendi's revised calculus of pleasure and pain recasts human
beings as naturally social animals providentially directed toward
living well together, rather than withdrawing from public life in
order to find what private pleasure they can from a universe indifferent to human pain and suffering.[35]

After his retirement from the "prison" of public affairs, Jefferson increasingly found himself drawn to Epicurean philosophy
and, in a series of letters to old friends, declared ease of body and
tranquillity of mind to be the summum bonum.[36] And, like the Epicureans, Jefferson delighted in speculating about the nature of the
universe, the existence of God, and the right way for human beings
to live. But his letters make clear that, while he was familiar with
the classical sources in their original languages, his own understanding of Epicureanism was based on "the genuine doctrines of
Epicurus from the *Syntagma* of Gassendi."[37]

Consider, first, Jefferson's views on the nature of the universe. In thinking about the physical world, Jefferson accepted
the atomism of the ancient Epicureans, whose scientific theory
now seemed to be supported by the materialism of the best modern philosophers, Locke, Tracy, and Stewart.[38] Placing himself

firmly on the side of the most thoroughgoing materialism, he rejects outright any form of dualism that divides the world into matter and spirit, appearances and ideas. Everything that is, is matter and can be known, not (as Descartes had argued) by abstract intuitive reason but by the experience of the senses. "On the basis of sensation, of matter and motion, we may erect the fabric of all the certainties we have or need."[39] At the same time, however, Jefferson concedes that there are certain "speculations and subtleties," such as how matter could come to be endowed with thought, which are beyond the realm of concrete experience. And this is where Gassendi proves most useful. For however much such propositions may exceed "finite comprehension," Jefferson can now insist that it is not beyond the power of the Creator to endow matter with the mode of action called thinking. And with this cheering thought, he is prepared to rest his head on the soft pillow of ignorance.[40]

Or, consider next the related question of the origin of the universe. In his "Syllabus," Jefferson acknowledges that the ancient Epicureans believed the world was eternal and uncreated. Without ever mentioning Epicurus by name, Jefferson considers and rejects this argument. Citing instead the views of other atheists, both ancient and modern, Jefferson takes exception to their argument that they are merely following a "rule of sound philosophy" when they refuse to employ "two principles to solve a difficulty when one will suffice." In this view, it is "more simple to believe" that the world has always existed, and will continue to exist forever through reproduction, than to "believe in the eternal pre-existence of an ulterior cause, or Creator of the world, a being whom we see not, and know not," and whose qualities "no power of mind enables us to delineate or comprehend." But Jefferson, siding with Gassendi, argues otherwise. Considering the universe in general as well as in its more particular movements, on the basis of reason alone, and without recourse to revelation, it is impossible "for the human mind not to percieve [sic] and feel a conviction of design, consummate skill, and indefinite power in every atom of it's [sic] composition." And in striking contrast to Lucretius, who explicitly states that the world could not have been created by God because there is too much wrong with it,[41] Jefferson, reflecting on the evidence, comes to the exact opposite conclusion:

The movements of the heavenly bodies, so exactly held in their course by the balance of centrifugal and centripetal forces, the structure of our earth itself, with it's [sic] distribution of lands, waters, and atmosphere, animal and vegetable bodies, examined in all their minutest particles, insects mere atoms of life, yet as perfectly organized as man or mammoth, the mineral substances, their generation and uses, it is impossible, I say, for the human mind not to believe that there is, in all this, design, cause and effect, up to an ultimate cause, a fabricator of all things from matter and motion, their preserver and regulator while permitted to exist in their present forms, and their regenerator into new and other forms.[42]

By starting with Gassendi's belief in a Benevolent Creator, rather than from the classical Epicurean position that the gods neither created the universe nor concern themselves with human affairs, Jefferson concludes that the world is not as fearful or alien to man as the ancients believed. "I think," he confides to Adams, "that it is a good world on the whole, that it has been framed on the principle of benevolence, and more pleasure than pain dealt out to us."[43] And the same superintending providence that oversees the physical world has equipped humankind with the moral faculties and intelligence to live together in society to promote their happiness and mutual good. Thus, wisdom, like the moral virtues, now aims at social utility. Perhaps nowhere is this clearer than in Jefferson's candid admission that he is "not fond of reading what is merely abstract, and unapplied immediately to some useful science."[44]

The political implications of Jefferson's Epicureanism are twofold. First, while Jefferson insists that he personally derives greater pleasure from the pursuit of science and knowledge than from public service, he nevertheless takes a more positive view of political life than the classical Epicureans. For he not only believes that nature has created an aristocracy precisely so that the best can devote themselves to their fellow men, something Jefferson actively encourages, but also seeks to create spaces for ordinary citizens to exercise their natural right of self-government. Jefferson could not have done either if he had been convinced that politics is simply a necessary evil and, in the end, more likely to produce pain than pleasure.

Second, Jefferson does not, like the ancient Epicureans, hesitate to use the discoveries of modern science and technology to improve the lives and promote the material well-being of ordinary men and women. In fact, he pointedly declines to place a limit on how far these improvements may be carried. It is "cowardly" to believe that the "human mind is incapable of further advances" when so much knowledge in "every branch of science remains to be discovered."[45] And, again in contrast to Epicurus and Lucretius, Jefferson does not worry that such innovations may actually multiply men's desires for bodily pleasure beyond their natural limits and so increase their pain; nor does he view the redeployment of philosophy toward the satisfaction of democratic desires as a betrayal of its highest purpose. Although he himself is drawn to "the consolations of a sound philosophy, equally indifferent to hope and fear,"[46] the task of philosophy is not primarily to console the few who are able to free themselves from the religious superstitions, unnatural desires, and false opinions that bring pain to most men.[47] The wisdom Jefferson seeks is not, like classical Epicureanism, too sad and difficult for the many to comprehend. Nor, like the Platonic dialogues, is it paradoxical or mysterious; Jefferson neither recognizes nor appreciates philosophical irony.[48] Finally, wisdom is not contemplative or theoretical knowledge, good simply for its own sake, but is always engaged in some practical project. Thus, the first task of reason is to debunk those false philosophical and theological systems that have hitherto enslaved the mind and spirit of man, and then to discover new sources of knowledge that can be used to improve the human condition. As Tocqueville would later observe, this sunny materialism and unbounded faith in reason to supply the most important answers to how we should live exemplify a certain approach to philosophy that is distinctively American.[49] The democratization of the American mind and the reorientation of philosophy toward more hedonistic and utilitarian ends are as much a part of the American character as its moral dispositions.

Friendship

Although ancient moral philosophy devotes considerable attention to friendship,[50] strictly speaking, friendship is not a moral virtue.

For the moral virtues grow out of habits and dispositions that can be exercised in varying degrees toward everyone, while genuine friendship entails a degree of intimacy and affection that can be shared only with a few. Indeed, the best sort of friendship tends to render many, if not all, of the moral virtues superfluous, since it goes beyond giving friends what they deserve or need and seeks what is truly good for them. Thus, although friendship is not a moral virtue, the most noble friendships help individuals to perfect their moral and intellectual characters by enabling them to participate together in the search for what is good.

If, strictly speaking, friendship is not a moral virtue, still less is it a political virtue. Citizens and comrades are not the same as friends. Citizens, especially citizens in a continental heterogeneous republic, are united by a rational love of country and a desire for justice, understood as the equal protection of rights. Realistically, they cannot be expected to feel affectionate bonds of friendship for millions of their fellow citizens or to wish unselfishly for their happiness and good.[51] Thus, friendship is necessarily more limited and private, while justice, the virtue that unites citizens, is comprehensive and public. This is true even when, as in the case of political friendships, what binds the friends together is a common commitment to justice and the public good. We can never be friends with all those who share our political views.

In contrast to ancient moral philosophy, which has much to say about friendship and its place in the perfection of individual character, modern liberal theory is largely silent on the subject.[52] At first sight, this is surprising because liberalism is essentially concerned with enlarging the private and social domains, where friendship is supposed to flourish.[53] Yet at the same time, the liberal view of human nature as set forth by Hobbes and Locke makes friendship much more problematic.[54] For if human beings are inclined to quarrel and fight or to focus exclusively on their own selfish interests, then friendship is not simply natural but can only come about after they have subdued a part of their natures. Even then, it is not clear how important friendship is to the perfection of the moral and intellectual character; liberalism is, after all, a philosophy of individualism. Perhaps it is only business associates, whose relations are spelled out by contract, and families, bound together by ties of affection and utility, that can thrive in liberal democracy.

Yet however true this may be of liberalism in the abstract, it is not true of Jefferson or, for that matter, most of the Framers. In contrast to Hobbes, and less obviously to Locke, Jefferson insists that human beings are social animals who are endowed by a Benevolent Creator with appropriate moral sentiments, including "feelings of sympathy, of benevolence, of gratitude, of justice, of love, of friendship."[55] Friendship, Jefferson believes, echoing the sentiments of Francis Bacon's essay on the subject, adds to our felicity by doubling our joys and halving our sorrows.[56] As he grew older, he looked to his friends for consolation from life's inevitable pains and disappointments and, what is more important, to explore a vast range of political, religious, scientific, and philosophical interests. Thus, at the age of sixty-eight, he could write to his old revolutionary companion Dr. Benjamin Rush, who at that very moment was laboring to bring about a rapprochement between Jefferson and John Adams, "I find friendship to be like wine, raw when new, ripened with age, the true old man's milk and restorative cordial."[57] Jefferson would drink deeply.

Retirement from active public life provided Jefferson with the leisure to resume his many friendships, both in person and in writing. While at first sight it might seem that friendship can really flourish only in close physical proximity, letter writing enabled Jefferson to reach beyond his local society and cultivate intellectual and political bonds with like-minded men and women throughout the United States and Europe. As Andrew Burstein has written, the eighteenth century was the great age of the epistolary friendship, and Jefferson one of its most avid practitioners.[58] It is, therefore, from Jefferson's correspondence that we can best understand what he means by friendship and the role it plays in perfecting the moral and intellectual character in a liberal republic. By focusing on his letters to select correspondents, while both a public servant and a private citizen, it is possible to discern at least three different models of friendship.[59]

First is the sentimental or compassionate friendship, employed most frequently (though not exclusively) with his female correspondents and friends and best exemplified in the head-heart dialogue to Maria Cosway, Jefferson's great infatuation during the Paris years.[60] The letter is important not so much for the friendship between the two but because it discusses friendship at greater length than anywhere else in Jefferson's writings. Friendship is here treated in exclusively sentimental terms, with an emphasis on the "sublime delights" of shared grief and even more the doubling of pleasure that is shared, for "thanks to a benevolent arrangement of things," life offers more joy than sorrow. Since Maria Cosway was a landscape artist and musician, the pleasures Jefferson wishes to share are mostly aesthetic. He imagines her delight in the natural beauty of America: "the Falling Spring, the Cascade of Niagara, the Passage of the Potowmac through the Blue Mountain, the Natural Bridge," and finally, "our own dear Monticello, where nature has spread so rich a mantle under the eye. . . . How sublime to look down into the workhouse of nature, to see her clouds, hail, snow, rain, thunder, all fabricated at our feet! And the glorious sun when rising as if out of a distant water, just gliding the tops of the mountains, & giving life to all nature!" In subsequent letters, unsigned to protect his identity, Jefferson hints at other more intimate pleasures the two might share,[61] though his head surely understands that an affair with a married woman can bring neither lasting pleasure nor tranquillity of mind. (It goes without saying that such a relationship would not have perfected his character.) Ironically, Jefferson's most famous remarks on the pleasures of friendship may have been occasioned by something other than the desire for pure friendship.

In any case, the head-heart dialogue is certainly not a comprehensive reflection on the subject, since it ignores or criticizes more traditional forms of friendship, especially the friendships between men. Jefferson's letter to Maria Cosway says nothing about political friendship and, more important, goes out if its way to denigrate the kind of philosophical friendship that Epicurus, and indeed the entire classical tradition, regarded as most noble. The search for wisdom is here caricatured as the solitary activity of "the sublimated philosopher" and "the gloomy monk," sequestered in their cells, rather than a common effort among friends to attain happiness and tranquillity.

Yet Jefferson experienced firsthand the pleasures that came from both of these sorts of friendships. With James Madison, he shared a fifty year friendship that was fundamentally political: what bound these two together was their lifelong devotion to the republican cause.[62] Although it is not surprising that the letters to Madison are more restrained and businesslike than his passionate correspondence with Maria Cosway, there is also much less of the warmth and affection so evident in the late correspondence with Adams. Nowhere in the more than 1,250 letters they exchanged over half a century do we find Jefferson exclaiming to his Virginia colleague-in-arms, as he confessed to Adams, "I am sure that I really know many, many things, and none more surely than that I love you with all my heart."[63] Indeed, until the last year of Jefferson's life, the correspondence between the two remained remarkably formal and reserved, even by the standards of the eighteenth century. As students of this literary form have observed, theirs was an epistolary friendship dominated by the head. Advancing the republican cause was serious business, and there were enemies on all sides. Although partisanship can sometimes destroy private friendships,[64] in this case it served as the glue that bound the two men together. At the same time, it is perhaps the very partisan character of their friendship that may help to explain the relative lack of affection or intimacy; Jefferson and Madison are fighters, not erotic seekers after pleasure or truth.

From their earliest meeting in 1776, the two worked hand in glove to secure republican self-government, first in Virginia and later in the nation as a whole. Without Madison's assistance in the Virginia legislature in the 1780s, many of Jefferson's proposed revisions of colonial law, and especially his Bill for Establishing Religious Freedom, would never have been enacted. While serving as minister to France, Jefferson counted on Madison to supply him with news of the political situation back home, while he kept Madison abreast of developments in Europe. So solid was their partnership that even before he left for France, and again after he had settled in Paris, Jefferson proposed to Madison that he consider purchasing land "in the neighborhood of Monticello." Jefferson had already extended the same invitation to two other like-minded Virginians, James Monroe and William Short, and, at the time, both were planning to do so. If Madison would agree to make it a "partie quarree," the young widower believed he could find happiness again. For "life is of no value but as it brings us gratifications. Among the most valuable of these is rational society. It informs the mind, sweetens the temper, chears [sic] our spirits, and promotes health."[65]

But such an "agreeable society" was never to be. Of the four, only Monroe would settle in "the neighborhood," and not for another decade. In the meantime, Jefferson remained in Paris and cultivated his friendships with the Virginians through letters. The correspondence between Jefferson and Madison is notable for its exclusive attention to party politics, diplomacy, and political personalities. Sometimes the questions are theoretical, as when Jefferson asks Madison to consider the social and political implications of the idea that "the earth belongs to the living," or when he discourses on the origin and nature of private property. But Madison, generally regarded as the more practical of the two, could also think big. In a remarkable seventeen-page letter to Jefferson in Paris, Madison explores what for him is the central problem of republican government— majority tyranny in the newly independent state governments—and outlines his "republican" solution to this evil.

For the most part, however, their correspondence illuminates the practical struggles and political intrigues that engaged the energy and attention of these two great republican statesmen: the Revolutionary War, the establishment of republican government in Virginia and then for the United States, the Bill of Rights, support for France, opposition to Hamilton's plan for a National Bank and domestic manufactures, the formation of the first political party in the 1790s, resistance to the Alien and Sedition Acts, the "revolution of 1800," and the Republican ascendancy. As the letters make clear, even after their retirement from public life, the two maintained a lively interest in politics and political personalities. To the end of their lives, they continued to resist, albeit in varying degrees, the centralizing tendencies of the Marshall Court. Their last great project was the establishment of the University of Virginia, which Jefferson hoped would keep alive "the vestal flame" of republicanism until it could be spread anew throughout the states.[66] Although Jefferson periodically complained that he hated politics, the cumulative effect of these letters is to reveal how profoundly interested in all things political he was. And it was this interest that lay at the heart of his friendship with Madison.

Yet given that theirs is essentially a political friendship, it is worth noting that the two disagree on a number of fundamental political issues.[67] For example, as a delegate to the Federal Convention, Madison held that the biggest problem with the existing political order is not the weaknesses of the Confederacy, considerable as they are, but the injustices and instability in the states. To remedy these defects, he proposed extending the sphere of the republic and a federal veto over state acts. Jefferson seems not to have understood the significance of the first proposal, and he actively opposes the second. Nevertheless, his reply to Madison characteristically ends on a note of agreement.[68] In a remarkable postscript, Jefferson agrees with Madison that "the instability of our laws is really an immense evil"[69] and calls for a twelve-month waiting period on all newly enacted laws. But then, two years later, he experimented with the idea of having all laws, debts, and constitutions expire with each generation, on the theory that "the earth belongs to the living." This time it was Madison who objected. Nor did they see eye to eye on Shays's Rebellion. While Jefferson worries that the greatest danger facing republican government is "lethargy," Madison fears a too lively spirit bent on tyrannizing the minority. A decade later, Jefferson and Madison would join forces to oppose the Alien and Sedition Acts, but Jefferson's more radical language in the Kentucky Resolutions would pose problems for Madison for the rest of his life as he tried without success to put out the political fires Jefferson had started. Finally, they reacted with different degrees of alarm to the nationalizing tendencies of the Marshall Court and the administration of John Quincy Adams. Always the more radical, Jefferson denies the authority of the Court to determine conflicts between the states and the federal government. Such disputes can be decided only by recurring to the people in their sovereign capacity. Madison disagreed. In a similar vein and at roughly the same time, Jefferson was prepared to pull out all the stops in opposing congressional spending for internal improvements. A year before his death, he drafted a "Solemn Declaration and Protest" to rally the citizens of Virginia against these "usurpations" of state power, which in "point of right" (if not of law) Jefferson, repeating the incendiary language of the Kentucky Resolutions, pronounces "null and void." Madison did not view the question of internal improvements as part of a conspiracy to undermine limited government, and he certainly did not wish to raise again the specter of nullification, so he prevailed upon his friend not to go public with his protest. Thus was a reprise of 1798 narrowly averted during the administration of John Adams's son.

Not only do the two disagree on some fairly fundamental issues, but, just as surprising for a friendship based so exclusively on their common devotion to republican principles, there are a number of important political matters they never discussed. Their exchanges are noticeably silent on the different views of the Union expressed in the Kentucky and Virginia Resolutions, and especially Jefferson's doctrine of nullification. Nor do the two ever spell out their differences concerning the relationship of the few and the many in republican governments, as Jefferson does with Adams. When Madison suggests that in a republic, it is the few who need protection from the many, Jefferson ignores him. And when Jefferson concludes that republicanism requires the division of the counties into self-governing wards, he develops his ideas at great length with several correspondents, but not with Madison. Finally, although both opposed the Missouri Compromise because it thwarted their misguided strategy of diffusion, the two never exchanged letters on the subject or, still more amazing, on the larger question of slavery and what to do about it, again preferring to develop their ideas in letters to others.

What this suggests is that even the most political of friendships can survive considerable differences of opinion, *especially if they are united in a common view of the enemy.* Jefferson and Madison stood firmly against monarchy and England; they resisted the nationalizing policies of Hamilton and the Federalists; they fought against Adams and the detestable Alien and Sedition Acts. Compared with these "monocrats" and "anglomen," their differences must have appeared minor and easy to overlook. At any rate, this was how they saw it. In a letter to Madison, written only months before his death, Jefferson spoke with uncharacteristic warmth: "The friendship which has subsisted between us, now half a century, and the harmony of our political principles and pursuits, have been sources of constant happiness to me through that long period." Nearing the end of his life, Jefferson could take solace from his belief that Madison would continue to vindicate to posterity the great cause to which their lives had been devoted: preserving "to them, *in all their purity,* the blessings of self-government, which we had assisted too in acquiring for them."[70] In response, Madison could with equal sincerity declare that theirs was a friendship based on "pure devotion to the public good."

What these two great partisans failed to see was that neither their motives nor their cause was quite as pure as they thought. But perhaps, as Epicurus suggested, that is the limitation of all political friendships; in their single-minded devotion to justice and the rights of man, Jefferson and Madison mistake the nature of the good. Still, on this point, Jefferson would have dissented from his master; without going so far as to argue that political friendship is the highest form of friendship, Jefferson clearly believes that it is not without its considerable pleasures. Flawed in some respects though it was, the fifty-year collaboration between Jefferson and Madison goes a long way toward illuminating how a friendship dedicated to promoting the freedom and happiness of others rather than, as is more commonly the case, to mere amusement or self-advancement can engage the moral and intellectual energies and, in so doing, ennoble the lives of those who cultivate it.

As with Madison, the friendship with John Adams grew out of the "perfect harmony" of their political principles during the contest for American liberty and independence.[71] The two had met for the first time in 1775 while serving as delegates to the Second Continental Congress in Philadelphia and, along with Benjamin Franklin, served on the committee charged with drafting the Declaration of Independence. It was Adams who, noting Jefferson's "happy talent of composition," pressed him to write the document. The two were later reunited in Paris in 1784, when Jefferson was commissioned by Congress to join Adams and Franklin in negotiating treaties of friendship and commerce for the newly independent United States. When Adams was posted to London the following year, Jefferson corresponded with both John Adams and his wife, Abigail, who had also become Jefferson's friend. It was Abigail who, upon arriving in London, confided to Jefferson that she was "still more loth [sic] on account of the increasing pleasure, and intimacy which a longer acquaintance with a respected Friend promised, to leave behind me the only person with whom my Companion could associate with perfect freedom, and unreserve."[72] Unlike with so many of Jefferson's other female friends, the friendship with Abigail Adams was an affair of the head as well as the heart. While Jefferson appreciated her maternal qualities, especially her tender regard for his motherless young daughter, who lived with the Adamses for several months in London before

joining her father in Paris, the two also exchanged views on political events, most notably Shays's Rebellion. Later, after the two men
had fallen out, Abigail could offer her condolences to Jefferson on
the death of the daughter she had once cared for and then, in a
series of bitter letters, set forth her husband's political grievances
against him. Finally, after the two men had reconciled and turned
their attention away from politics, Jefferson sent a copy of his syllabus of the doctrines of Jesus, whose unorthodox views he had
previously confided only to Dr. Priestley and Dr. Rush, to Adams,
with instructions that it could be "perused by Mrs. Adams, but by
no one else, and to be returned to me."[73] But the peace offering was
not sufficient to rekindle their earlier affection, and the two carried
on only a limited correspondence after 1812. Unlike her husband,
Mrs. Adams could never forgive the injury and humiliation Jefferson had caused her family.

Still, the friendship with Mrs. Adams, while unusual in combining sentimental attachment with political and intellectual
engagement, was incidental to the friendship between the two
men, and, at least in the early years, it followed the same trajectory.
The New Englander and the Virginian had begun as fellow laborers in the common cause of American independence and then had
seen their friendship weakened by the partisan struggles of the
1790s. With the "revolution of 1800" the rupture was complete. As
long as Jefferson was in the White House, as the head of the victo-
rious Republican Party, there was no possibility of a reconciliation.
But once he retired from politics, their mutual friend and revolutionary compatriot, Dr. Benjamin Rush, set himself the task of
bringing the two old friends back together again. Ironically, while
partisan divisions had severed their friendship, the memory of
their earlier political collaboration helped to renew it. Recalling
their efforts on behalf of independence, Jefferson confided to Rush,
"You know the perfect coincidence of principle and action in the
early part of the Revolution, which produced a high degree of
mutual respect and admiration between Mr. Adams and myself."[74]
Later that year, when Jefferson learned from a neighbor who had
visited Adams in Massachusetts that Adams had confessed, "I
always loved Jefferson, and still love him,"[75] the stage was set for
their eventual reconciliation. "This is enough for me," Jefferson
wrote to Rush when he heard of Adams's declaration. "I only

needed this knowledge to revive towards him all the affections of the most cordial moments of our lives. . . . I knew him to be always an honest man, often a great one, but sometimes incorrect and precipitate in his judgments; and it is known to those who have ever heard me speak of Mr. Adams, that I have ever done him justice myself, and defended him when assailed by others, *with the single exception as to political opinions.*"[76]

Yet it was not mere political opinions that ruptured their friendship. Relations may have been strained by Adams's publication of his "Discourses on Davila" (the sequel to his earlier three volume *Defence of the American Constitutions*) and Jefferson's subsequent endorsement of Paine's *Rights of Man* as a much needed antidote "against the political heresies which have sprung up among us,"[77] but the friendship survived. Jefferson assured Adams that he had never meant for his remarks to be made public and that, in any case, it was possible to differ in their political opinions and still remain friends: "That you and I differ in our ideas of the best form of government is well known to us both: but we have differed as friends should do, respecting the purity of each other's motives, and confining our difference of opinion to private conversation."[78] In a remark that would echo through their later correspondence, Adams protested that their differences were *not* well known to them both, as they had "never had a serious conversation together that I can recollect concerning the nature of Government." Their comments about politics had so far been "jocular and superficial"; it was now "high time" for them to "come to an explanation with each other." Still, he ended the letter on a hopeful note, reassuring Jefferson that "the friendship that has subsisted for fifteen Years between Us . . . ever has been, and still is, very dear to my heart."[79]

What ultimately derailed the friendship was not the clash of political opinions but political ambition. When the two were rival candidates for the presidency in 1796, their political views were no longer subjects of merely private interest but would affect the future of the country. Although Vice President Jefferson at first tried to work with Adams to contain the Hamiltonian wing of the Federalist Party, by 1798 Jefferson had become persuaded that the entire Federalist Party posed a threat to the republic. With Madison, he secretly conspired against the administration to rally opposition to the Alien and Sedition Acts and began to organize the

Republican Party to challenge Adams in the next election. Jefferson's victory in 1800 signaled the end of the Federalist Party in American politics, as well as the end of his political friendship with Adams. The New Englander retired to Massachusetts, broken and bitter, but not before he enjoyed the small satisfaction of appointing a series of Federalist judges to the bench, including Jefferson's real political enemy, John Marshall.

After their reconciliation in 1812, Jefferson was determined to avoid any discussion of the political issues that had divided them. He deftly sidestepped most of Adams's invitations to revisit political questions, insisting that "renewal of these old discussions, my friend, would be useless and tiresome."[80] Undeterred, Adams returned to a theme of their earlier correspondence and once again challenged Jefferson to give an acccount of himself: "You and I ought not to die, before We have explained ourselves to each other."[81] This time Jefferson responded, taking aim at Adams's defense of a balanced constitution and his supposed infatuation with the English model of government. At first, Jefferson suggested that their differences could be understood in terms of the age-old tendency of individuals and parties to side with the many over the few or the few over the many. But when Adams pressed him, Jefferson acknowledged that republics, too, had need of an aristocracy, albeit a natural aristocracy based on wisdom and virtue. The question was then the more interesting one of whether a natural aristocracy could withstand the inevitable challenge from the more conventional aristocracy of wealth and birth. Elsewhere, Adams succeeded in extracting from Jefferson the long-sought concession that, at least so far, he was right about the French Revolution; in return, Jefferson got Adams to admit that progress in politics and morals was still possible. Nevertheless, having patched up their friendship, Jefferson was not much inclined to dwell on their political differences, arguing that "we are both too old to change opinions which are the result of a long life of inquiry and reflection."[82] Jefferson now valued tranquillity of mind too much to risk opening old political wounds.

Nor was it necessary to do so. The great beauty of a liberal republic is that it does not elevate politics over all other concerns but instead leaves space for individuals to pursue other equally, if not more important, private interests. Having "taken final leave" of politics,[83] the two could cultivate the kind of affectionate relations that most closely approximated the classical ideal, philosophic friendship. Of course, Jefferson and Adams did not aspire to become genuine philosophers and to devote themselves primarily to the pursuit of wisdom, but this is precisely what makes their friendship so attractive and accessible. For it testifies to the ever-present human desire to explore in private, with those they love and trust, those moral and intellectual questions that give meaning to life and enrich the characters of those who pursue them. With Adams, Jefferson could continue the conversations he had initiated with Priestley and Rush on religion and comparative moral systems, as well as pursue other questions bearing on the attributes of God, death and the existence of a future state, the nature of the universe, and the controversy between materialism and spiritualism. In old age, spiritedness at last yields to intellectual eros.

Early in their renewed correspondence, Jefferson was gratified by Adams's approval of his syllabus comparing the doctrines of Jesus with those of the ancient moralists. Although the two did not see eye to eye on political questions, Jefferson nevertheless suspected that "if thinking men would have the courage to think for themselves, and to speak what they think," they would not much differ in religious opinions. Jefferson's optimism derived from his conviction that true religion is not a matter of revelation, mystery, or prophecy, but can be known by reason alone. Religious belief, like all other forms of belief, is nothing more than "the assent of the mind to an intelligible proposition." Accordingly, he looked forward to the not so distant future, when all thinking men would abandon orthodox Christianity, with its "Platonic mysticisms that three are one, and one is three," and embrace Unitarianism as the "religion of all."[84]

Adams agrees that knowledge of God does not depend on prophecies or miracles. He does not, however, deny revelation as much as try to make it compatible with reason. Revelation is not the special communication of God to his chosen few but the universal gift of a Benevolent Creator to all humankind. God's first and most important revelation is Reason.[85] By means of intuition and necessary induction, individuals can discover their duties to one another, as well as investigate the first and final causes of the universe. Still, coming out of the Puritan tradition, Adams is more inclined to stress the vanity and futility of trying to understand more than it is given to human beings to know. Despite the "eager impatience of the human Mind to search into Eternity and Infinity, the first Cause and last End of all Things," there is not now and never will be anyone but God who can fully understand the universe. "And it is not only vain but wicked for insects to pretend to comprehend it."[86]

If, from an epistemological point of view, both men judge religion by its conformity to reason, then from an ethical point of view, both tend to equate religion with morality. The great superiority of Christianity, as Jefferson understands it, lies precisely in "the sublime doctrines of philanthropism, and deism taught us by Jesus of Nazareth." True religion is nothing more than "the moral precepts, innate in man and made a part of his physical constitution, as necessary for a social being."[87] Judged from a purely moral perspective, there is nothing wrong with orthodox Christianity. However irrational their sectarian dogmas, Trinitarians can be as moral as Unitarians: both religions make honest men, and that is all that matters.[88] Instead, Jefferson reserves his moral outrage for the religion of the Old Testament. Whereas the pagan moralists are deficient because they focus on the perfection of the individual while stinting his obligations to others, the religion of the Jews has very little to say about morals but "consisted in a minute enumeration of duties," the majority of them negative and very few binding upon women. Although Jefferson does not come out and say it, what he really objects to is the Old Testament's emphasis on the duties men owe to God. The third book of Moses, called Leviticus, explicitly describes itself as a manual for priests, setting forth in great detail the religious rituals and rules that priests are required to observe and enforce in order to honor their covenant with God. Jefferson shows what he thinks of this third branch of morality when he dismisses the Jewish religion as a "wretched depravity" of morals, in which priests have paraded their "artificial vestments" for the sole purpose of aggrandizing themselves.[89]

Adams, too, is dismayed by the harm that organized religions have done, but he is more inclined to see religion as a positive force for the moral government of man: "Without Religion this World would be Something not fit to be mentioned in polite Company, I mean Hell." And again like Jefferson, he, too, tends to think of religion primarily in moral terms, but he is also more respectful of the different ways in which each seeks to worship God: "The great Principle of the Hebrews was the *Fear* of God; that of the Gentiles, *Honour* the Gods, that of Christians, the *Love* of God."[90] Moreover, underneath these differences, Adams detects important similarities. Each acknowledges the existence of a supreme being who governs the universe by his providence, and who has created man in his image. In response, Jefferson agrees that this is a "just outline" of the differences, but he is clearly less inclined to emphasize the similarities or find the good in each. For this is the same letter in which he calls the morality of the Old Testament depraved.[91]

Coming to Unitarianism out of Calvinism, Adams is most critical of the religion he knows best. In particular, he refuses to believe that the Benevolent Creator he worships and adores has predestined some men for eternal damnation for his own glory. "What is his Glory? Is he ambitious? Does he want promotion? Is he vain? Tickled with Adulation? Exulting and tryumphing [*sic*] in his Power and the Sweetness of his Vengeance?"[92] Jefferson, too, rejects the Calvinist doctrines of election and predestination, as well as the idea of original sin.[93] To accept Calvinism is to deny that men are free moral agents. Equally important, the doctrine that human beings are completely depraved leads men to hate themselves and their fellow men, and this both Jefferson and Adams refuse to do.[94]

What Adams feels for his fellow men is not hatred but pity. He recognizes that most men can never escape from fear and terror. "Fears of Calamities in Life and punishments after death, seem to have possessed the Souls of all Men." What is worse, "fear of Pain and death, here, do not seem to have been so unconquerable as fear of what is to come hereafter."[95] Indeed, even those who believe that death is nothing but annihilation are terrified of dying.[96] In this respect, Adams is more of an Epicurean than Jefferson, for, while he believes that rational religion may alleviate some of these fears, he is by no means as confident that it will have widespread appeal or that it will usher in a more benevolent and philanthropic age of man.[97] If human nature is not completely depraved, neither is it susceptible of indefinite moral improvement.

Although the late correspondence deals with the most serious subjects, it is often remarkably playful in tone. Thus, Adams begins one letter: "I cannot be serious! I am about to write You, the most frivolous letter, you ever read." The question Adams asks Jefferson to ponder is: "Would you go back to your Cradle and live over again Your 70 Years?"[98] Jefferson interprets the question to mean: Is life good? and, not surprisingly, answers yes. But Adams is after bigger game, and in his next, even "sillier," letter, he draws out the full metaphysical, theological and moral implications of the question. For the decision to live again, either once or forever, presupposes an answer to the question of what happens to us after we die. Adams would choose to live life over again only if he believed that death is annihilation, or that he would suffer a worse fate after death. But if there is a better state awaiting him, or even if he cannot be certain what will happen to him, then he "certainly" would not choose to live life again.[99] Although Adams cannot prove that there is a future state, his religious and moral beliefs persuade him that it must be so. For why else would a Benevolent Creator have made man to live and die upon this earth? In the end, it is not the predominance of pleasure over pain here and now but the promise of a future state that gives moral meaning to life.[100] By contrast, Jefferson seems much more inclined to accept the view of death as annihilation[101] and, consequently, is more willing to live life over again forever, especially if he can limit his life to the ages of twenty-five and sixty. But since that is impossible, he neither fears death nor views it as an evil.[102] If Jefferson's is a philosophy indifferent to fear, so, too, is it a philosophy radically removed from Christian hope.

In still another charming exchange, prompted this time by Jefferson's casual remark that of all the passions, only grief seems to have no good purpose, Adams explores first the uses and then the abuses of grief. By far the more tough-minded of the two, Adams understands that the pain occasioned by grief can contribute, as pleasure cannot, to moral growth and the improvement of individual character. Grief compels us to think, to take stock; it "drives Men into habits of serious Reflection, sharpens the Understanding and softens the heart; it compells [sic] them to arrouse [sic] their Reason, to assert its Empire over their Passions Propensities and Prejudices; to elevate them to a Superiority over all human Events; to give them the *Felicic Annimi immotan tranquilitatem* ['the imperturbable tranquillity of a happy heart']; in short, to make them Stoicks and Christians." While agreeing with Jefferson that stoic apathy is "impossible," the New Englander suggests that the antique virtues of patience and resignation are never out of fashion.

Not content, however, to leave the matter there, Adams later "tease[s]" Jefferson with another question: "What have been the *Abuses* of Grief?" Not waiting for Jefferson's reply, Adams suggests that the greatest abuse of grief is its manipulation by scheming politicians and priests to further their own ill-conceived plans. But this evenhanded treatment fails to satisfy his pleasure-seeking friend. Considering that even the uses of grief cause great "afflictions of the soul," Jefferson concludes that its "value in the economy of the human being" is "equivocal at least."[103] However important character is to Jefferson, he is unwilling to concede that some of its most important lessons can be learned only by grievous pain and suffering.[104]

Finally, although Jefferson throws his lot in with the materialists, going so far as to accuse the spiritualists of atheism, since the argument that God is spirit is in effect an argument that there is no God, Adams can never be sure. And he sees no utility in reviving the controversy. However men define the terms, they can never satisfactorily explain how matter by itself can think or spirit alone can act. Some things are beyond the power of human understanding; it is best not to waste time in idle amusement. "Vain man! Mind your own Business! Do no wrong! Do all the good You can! Eat your Canvas back ducks, drink Your burgundy, sleep Your S[i]esta, when necessary, And *Trust in God.!*"[105]

In comparing these different kinds of friendship, the question inevitably arises: Which is nobler? There is no doubt that for the ancient moralists, and especially Epicurus, philosophical friendship is the highest because it brings the greatest pleasure and perfects that part of the soul that is most nearly divine. But with Jefferson the matter is more ambiguous. On the one hand, Jefferson, too, believes that philosophy ranks higher in the order of genius and is more pleasurable than politics.[106] And in its playful treatment of the most serious things, the correspondence between Jefferson and Adams testifies to the enduring power of philosophy to charm the most active minds. On the other hand, Jefferson's view that human beings are social animals who derive their greatest pleasure and happiness from doing good to others suggests that political and sentimental friendships are also not without their

considerable rewards. Thus, the great advantage of a liberal republic is that it provides space for, and nurtures, all kinds of friendships. It does not, like the Epicureans, elevate philosophical
friendship at the expense of politics and political friendship; nor,
like the classical republicans of Greece and Rome, does it rank citizenship and civic virtue above all other human relationships.
Finally, it does not depreciate, as both tended to do, the purely sentimental or compassionate friendship. Jefferson's liberal republic
recognizes the distinctive ways in which these different forms of
friendship, taken separately or together, contribute to the development of the moral and intellectual character.

Duties to God

Piety

The third branch of morality consists of the duties we owe to
God, and the virtue traditionally associated with the performance
of these obligations is piety. For different reasons, both classical and
Christian polities believed that the cultivation of piety was a legitimate concern of government. But the founders of modern liberalism, Thomas Hobbes and John Locke, argued that the purpose of
the state is to provide for bodily security and comfort, not to save
souls through the enforcement of true religion. As long as religious
belief does not endanger the civil peace, how individuals worship
and what religious dogmas they believe are of no concern to the
government. Modern liberalism has no business enforcing piety.
Indeed, as Jefferson himself would later argue, the presumption of
legislators and rulers, acting on their own fallible reason, to impose
their religious beliefs on others is the very definition of impiety.[107]

But is piety even a private virtue? Is it desirable for individuals on their own to continue to worship God according to the rituals and creeds of their revealed religions?[108] In letters to trusted
correspondents, and for their information alone, Jefferson makes
clear that the answer is no, since piety is in tension with both intellectual and moral virtue as he understands them. By making
knowledge of God dependent on faith and revelation, piety places
too great a premium on unquestioning obedience and authority

and so conflicts with wisdom and the pursuit of knowledge through reason. Moreover, by seeking to convert others, through fear and disapproval, to believe what cannot rationally be proved, piety clashes with the Christian virtue of charity. In place of piety, Jefferson believes that the duties we owe to God can best be fulfilled by honoring our obligations to others and practicing toleration in matters of faith. Toleration, not piety, is the liberal virtue connected with our duty to God.

In trying to comprehend the idea of God, Jefferson confesses bewilderment. Jesus teaches that God is good and perfect, but he does not define precisely what these terms mean. Lacking both the words and the ideas to understand God's nature, Jefferson concludes that we should not trouble ourselves with metaphysical speculations or quarrels about vestments, sacraments, and ceremonies, which are "totally unconnected with morality, . . . unimportant to the legitimate objects of society,"[109] and serve only the interests of the priests. If all men would simply accept that the subject is "undefinable," there would be no sectarian strife. "It is the speculations of the crazy theologists which have made a Babel" of religion,[110] causing oceans of human blood to be spilled and whole regions of the earth to be desolated by war and persecutions. It is time to recognize "how insoluble these questions are by minds like ours, how unimportant, and how mischievous; and to consign them to the sleep of death, never to be awakened from it."[111] Elsewhere, in response to a proselytizing clergyman urging him to embrace Christianity for the sake of eternal salvation, Jefferson is even more emphatic in dismissing our obligations to the Deity. Putting aside his conviction that we cannot ever truly understand God's nature and, hence, cannot know what he requires of us, Jefferson here sounds almost Epicurean in suggesting that God does not care about how we worship him. For "in the perfection of his state, he can feel [no] pain or pleasure from any thing we may do: he is far above our power."[112] All that matters is how we treat others, not how we treat him, or, to put it another way, salvation depends entirely on moral virtue, and not dogmatic belief.[113]

What knowledge Jefferson does have of God comes entirely from reason and free inquiry. For true belief can only be grounded on ideas the human mind can investigate and comprehend. When once man surrenders his reason, he has "no guard against absurdities the most monstrous, and like a ship without a rudder, is the sport of every wind. With such persons, gullibility which they call faith, takes the helm from the hand of reason, and the mind becomes a wreck."[114] Thus when it came time for Jefferson to advise his nephew and ward Peter Carr on religion, he urged him to bring every fact and every opinion before the bar of reason. No article of belief is exempt: "Question with boldness even the existence of a god; because, if there be one, he must more approve of the homage of reason, than that of blindfolded fear." Jefferson counsels him to read the Old Testament in the same way that he would read Tacitus or Livy, and not to believe any accounts that contradict the law of nature. Proceeding to the New Testament, Jefferson instructs his ward to pay special attention to the "personage called Jesus," and especially to the pretensions of the Evangelists who claim that "he was begotten by god, born of a virgin, suspended and reversed the laws of nature at will, & ascended bodily into heaven." Anticipating that no rational young man would assent to such unintelligible propositions, Jefferson cautions him not to be frightened of the inquiry or to fear its consequences. Even if his nephew concludes that there is no God, he will still find ample inducements to be good. Morality is not grounded in the love of God[115] but in the pleasure and approval of the moral sense, as well as the esteem and approbation of others. Maintaining an attitude of benign indifference to whether or not his nephew believes in God, Jefferson does not insist on his own opinion that the moral sense itself is the gift of a Benevolent Creator.

Jefferson practiced what he preached. He relied on his own reason to sift out the authentic teachings of Jesus from the "stupidity" and "roguery" of his disciples, and then to challenge some of Jesus' doctrines directly. Jefferson not only denied the divinity of Jesus but also scandalized even his fellow Unitarians with his insistence that Jesus never laid claim to a divine mission. As Dr. Priestley confessed, "It is an opinion that I do not remember ever to have been heard before." Priestley went on to point out that by this means Jefferson prevented Jesus from being called an imposter, since he could not be charged with the follies and falsehoods that his disciples and the early church fathers attributed to him. But clearing Jesus of the charge of imposter came at the price of impugning the "great integrity and piety" of his followers who did believe that Jesus was divinely inspired and that he gave sufficient evidence of this. Moreover, Priestley wondered, if Jesus did not have a divine mission, where did his wisdom come from, and why should the Jews have abandoned their religion to follow him?[116]

Yet precisely because Jesus was a man, Jefferson sees no need to attribute to him superhuman wisdom. Some things Jesus understood extraordinarily well. Jefferson particularly admires the way in which he reformed the Jewish conception of God, removing every suggestion of cruelty, jealousy, and injustice, and endowing him with every human perfection, "wisdom, justice, goodness," and infinite power, thereby rendering him "really worthy" of human adoration. And, of course, he regards his moral code as the most sublime and benevolent known to man. But not even Jesus got everything right. Jefferson is willing to grant, for example, that Jesus himself conscientiously believed he was divinely inspired, but, Jefferson insists, Jesus was mistaken.[117] Moreover, Jesus was a "spiritualist," while Jefferson maintains that everything in the universe, including God and the soul, is matter. Finally, Jesus "preaches the efficacy of repentance towards forgiveness of sin," but Jefferson "require[s] a counterpoise of good works to redeem it." Jefferson is right when he claims to read Jesus exactly as he reads all other ancient and modern moralists, "with a mixture of approbation and dissent."[118] Indeed, as Sanford Kessler has suggested, on these key issues Jefferson seems to have preferred John Locke's theological teaching to that of Jesus himself.[119]

With Locke, Jefferson aims to make religion "reasonable" by banishing from it all doctrines and observances that, under the pretense of piety, inflame the imagination and set individuals and nations against each other, instead of teaching them their moral duties to each other. Religion, as Jefferson understands it, boils down to three simple doctrines, all tending to the happiness of man:

1. that there is one God, and he is all-perfect.
2. that there is a future state of rewards and punishments.
3. that to love God with all thy heart, and thy neighbor as thyself is the sum of religion.[120]

Yet as this list suggests, although Jefferson went further than most other reformers in stripping Christianity of its mysticisms, not even he succeeded in making religion completely reasonable. While Jefferson does believe that the existence of God, the order and design of his creation, including our moral obligations, can be defended rationally, there is no way he can prove that a future state of rewards and punishments exists, and he knows it.[121] It is difficult to escape the conclusion that the idea of a future state of rewards and punishments is simply necessary to reinforce the moral duties humans owe to each other here and now.[122] This is one of the few instances where for Jefferson what is useful and what is true seem to part company.

Ironically, in positing the existence of a future state of rewards and punishments that he cannot prove, Jefferson finds himself in close agreement not only with Locke but also with the Plato he despised. For, no less than Plato, Jefferson, too, is forced to resort to a noble lie to get men to treat each other as brothers. As Jefferson himself admits in the *Notes on Virginia*,[123] a thoroughly reasonable religion is inadequate to secure either the liberties or the virtue of the people.

Toleration

In making toleration the first of the virtues connected with religious duty, Jefferson closely follows Locke's *Letter on Toleration*, whose main arguments he recorded in his "Notes on Locke and Shaftesbury" in 1776 in preparation for disestablishing the Church of England and instituting freedom of worship in Virginia. Echoing Locke, Jefferson's defense of toleration consists of five distinct arguments. The first is epistemological. Although Jefferson believes it is possible for humans to discover the one true religion by bringing every false one before the tribunal of reason as he has done,[124] he also insists that it is not given to men to know which, if any, of the sectarian dogmas dividing the different religions is right, since each is based not on reason but on revelation.[125] And where such uncertainty exists, neither rulers nor priests are justified in coercing others to submit to any particular articles of faith. Rival sects must be left free to pursue salvation as they see fit. Second is what William Galston, discussing Locke, calls the "conscience-based" argument.[126] Even if we could *know* what God requires of us, true belief must be uncoerced. "The life and essence of religion," Jefferson notes in his paraphrase of Locke, "consists in the internal persuasion or belief of the mind." Followers of religious sects are free to argue and to try to persuade others to adopt their views, but they may not compel them to believe. Nor would such coercion achieve its intended goal, for no one can be saved by professing a faith he disbelieves and abhors. "External forms [of wor]ship, when against our belief are hypocrisy [and im]piety."[127] In creating the human mind free, God himself prefers that we think for ourselves rather than submit blindly to his will; what matters is not the "rightness" of our beliefs but their "uprightness."[128] The third argument is moral and psychological. Although rulers and priests *claim* to be concerned with piety and the salvation of souls, they are really interested in their own power and privileges, earthly goods that in fact corrupt their character and make it more difficult for them to perform their sacred duties. By guaranteeing priests a steady income regardless of their personal conduct, the alliance between church and state removes the incentive for them to work hard for the moral instruction and improvement of their flock. At the same time, by bribing those who externally profess and support its doctrines "with a monopoly of worldly honors and emoluments," established churches encourage hypocrisy in their followers and undermine the principles of the very religion they seek to promote.[129] Jefferson's fourth argument for religious toleration is political. Individuals enter into civil society in order to protect their persons and their property; the legitimate powers of government extend only to the protection of these rights. Magistrates have no power to concern themselves with the salvation of souls because no man has the right to give up the care of his soul to another. Government is concerned only with the injuries men do to one another, not with the injuries they do to themselves. Since, in Jefferson's piquant phrase, religious differences neither pick his pocket nor break his leg, they remain outside the legitimate scope of government.[130] A liberal republic must recognize the natural right of conscience and practice, as well as promote, the corresponding moral virtue of toleration. Finally, Jefferson, once again quoting Locke, and without any sense of how strange this might sound to the pious believer, finds a religious dimension in the case for toleration.

In their unorthodox reading, toleration is not simply a secular virtue; it is the essence of Christian charity. "If any man err from the right way, it is his own misfortune, no injury to thee, nor therefore art thou to punish him in the things of this life because thou supposeth he will be miserable in that which is to come. On the contrary accdg to the spirit of the gospel, charity, bounty, liberality is due him." The "genius" of the Christian religion lies not in compelling men to profess what they do not believe but in the toleration of rival sects.[131]

In his notes on Locke's doctrine of religious toleration, Jefferson recorded Locke's answer to the question "How far does the duty of toleration extend?"[132] And, following Locke, Jefferson asserts that political societies may not legitimately deprive any persons of their civil rights because of their religious beliefs. For both Locke and Jefferson, this includes Jews, Muslims, and Hindus and not simply the different Christian denominations. Nevertheless, Jefferson finds Locke's doctrine too limiting. As he puts it, "It was a great thing to go so far, but where he stopped short, we may go on." In particular, Jefferson seems more ready to tolerate those religions whose doctrines endanger the peace and preservation of society, by asserting, for example, that faith need not be kept with those of different religions, that excommunicated sovereigns forfeit their political power, that political authority rests on divine grace, that obedience is due to a foreign ruler, that toleration need not be practiced, and that God does not exist. It is not that Jefferson is indifferent to the political and moral consequences of such doctrines (his Bill for Establishing Religious Freedom does acknowledge that the magistrate has the power to "interfere when principles break out into overt acts against peace and good order," even if these principles are religiously motivated), but on the whole he thinks there is a better and more liberal way to deal with them. For example, Jefferson believes that Locke should follow his own "excellent rule" and, rather than deny toleration to the offending sect, punish the assertion that a foreign prince has power within the commonwealth as a civil offense. In other words, Jefferson would not suppress any religion outright, but he would still punish certain religious opinions and actions that clearly endanger the public welfare. And for those ideas that pose no immediate threat, Jefferson is far more inclined than Locke to trust in the good sense of the people. In the case of atheists, Jefferson is again willing to go beyond Locke in extending toleration, though he is prepared to reject their testimony in a court of law.[133] The only issue on which he seems to agree with Locke is the question of toleration itself: "Perhaps the single thing which may be required to others before toleration to them would be an oath that they would allow toleration to others."

While in these important respects Jefferson is willing to go beyond Locke's idea of toleration, his understanding of the term is much more limited than what is commonly understood by toleration today.[134] For one thing, Jefferson, like Locke, confines toleration primarily to religious differences. And even here he is not prepared to acknowledge an absolute and unqualified right of conscience. Governments may not forbid any religious group from performing in its sacred rites what it permits other citizens to do in the ordinary course of events; for example, if killing calves or lambs is legal, then religions cannot be barred from such practices in their ceremonies and rituals. But, even more important, neither is the state required to permit as a matter of religious freedom what is ordinarily forbidden to other citizens.[135] Though not as emphatically as Locke, Jefferson nevertheless affirms the Lockean principle that considerations of the public good set some limits to the general principle of religious toleration.

Nor for all his opposition to established churches, and the special privileges they conveyed upon their members, is he willing to interfere with established religions in other states. The famous "wall of separation" that Jefferson believes the First Amendment erects between church and state is specifically intended to apply only to the federal government.[136] Moreover, in the Second Inaugural Jefferson acknowledges that the state governments have the power to issue Thanksgiving proclamations and to appoint days of fasting and prayer.[137] In the clash between religious liberty and federalism, Jefferson threw his weight behind the federal principle. If states wished to establish churches or otherwise to enforce piety and religious worship, Jefferson was prepared, however grudgingly, to countenance these actions for the sake of republican self-government, trusting that with proper instruction the people in the different states would eventually get it right without any interference from the national government.

Finally, Jefferson's understanding of religious toleration does not imply that we must *approve* of every sectarian belief. On the contrary, if a sect should arise whose tenets threaten to "subvert good morals" or endanger "peace and order," Jefferson counts upon the "good sense" of the people to reason and laugh it out of doors. Pernicious doctrines, like the ones Locke mentions, *should* be "despised."[138] Thus, instead of denying toleration to such sects, as Locke would do, Jefferson relies on the natural desire for the approval and approbation of others to serve as a spontaneous check on novel and irrational religious sects, "without suffering the state to be troubled."[139] Although Jefferson occasionally recognizes the danger that public opinion may be tempted to "substitute itself into that tyranny over religious faith which the laws have so justly abdicated,"[140] and never more so than where his own religious beliefs are concerned, on the whole, he trusts in the "unbounded tolerance" and common sense of the people not to abuse their power. The fear that a dull and plodding majority might stifle the moral or creative impulses of the individual, which figures so strongly in both Thoreau's and J. S. Mill's defenses of individual conscience and liberty, stands in stark contrast to Jefferson's solid faith in the decency and moral sense of ordinary men and women.

As Jefferson makes clear in the First Inaugural, he is also willing, at least in principle, to extend the idea of toleration to political opinions: "Having banished from our land that religious intolerance under which mankind so long bled and suffered, we have yet gained little if we countenance a political intolerance as despotic, as wicked, and as capable of as bitter and bloody persecutions." What Jefferson is referring to, of course, were the criminal prosecutions of Republicans for seditious libel by the federal government under the Alien and Sedition Acts. Under the new Republican dispensation, Jefferson assures his political opponents, Federalists and even monarchists will be permitted to "stand undisturbed as monuments of the safety with which error of opinion may be tolerated where reason is left free to combat it."[141]

But, in fact, the case for political toleration rests on somewhat different theoretical grounds and in practice was much more narrowly applied. Consider first the theoretical arguments. Where the argument for religious toleration rests on the inability of humans to know that part of God's will which is made manifest through revelation, the epistemological argument for political toleration starts from the premise that reason itself is fallible. Wherever men are free to think and speak, they will form a variety of opinions, owing to "difference[s] of perception and the imperfection of reason."[142] But Jefferson also believes that where these different opinions are allowed to "purify themselves by free discussion,"[143] the truth will ultimately prevail. Thus, toleration is desirable not because, as in religion, the truth cannot be known but precisely because rational argument exposes "error" and allows the truth to emerge.

Still, Jefferson's free marketplace of ideas is not Mill's. Where Mill invites opponents to slug it out in the ring, Jefferson believes that the free expression of political opinion can be perverted if pushed too far. A too vigorous confrontation of political views may actually threaten social harmony and, ironically, lessen toleration of opinion.[144] If toleration is to succeed, all parties must practice civility, moderation, and forbearance. It goes without saying that Jefferson has in mind political *opinions*; the whole tenor of his argument, with its emphasis on rational deliberation and exchange leading to the discovery of truth, suggests that he would have regarded the broadening of free speech protections to include nonverbal forms of expression as profoundly misguided and even dangerous.

While the "conscience-based" and religious arguments that figure in Jefferson's defense of religious toleration are not relevant here, it is significant that Jefferson ignores altogether the corrupting effect of political power on the character of those who exercise it. Nowhere does he argue, as he did against rulers and priests, that republican leaders who clamp down on dissenters may also be interested in their own power and glory. So convinced is he of the purity and disinterestedness of his, and his allies', motives that he remains blind to this danger.

But the biggest difference between Jefferson's toleration of religious differences and his toleration of dissenting opinions lies in the political argument. Although Jefferson pays lip service to the idea that government has no more business telling people what to *think* than it has telling them what to *believe*, his fear that the very existence of the republican experiment may be endangered by rival political principles leads him to conclude that the government does have an interest in what its citizens think about politics.

Thus, despite his ringing proclamation that "truth is great and will prevail if left to herself,"[145] in practice he is less willing to take chances and tries to stack the deck in favor of his particular brand of republicanism. Two examples will suffice. First, although Jefferson opposed the Alien and Sedition Acts on the ground that the national government has no power to regulate the rights of speech and press, he has no objections to the states abridging these very liberties. Indeed, he urges Governor Thomas McKean of Pennsylvania to use his powers to punish seditious libel. In language reminiscent of Machiavelli, Jefferson counsels the governor that a few carefully chosen prosecutions will have a "wholesome effect in restoring the integrity of the presses."[146] And second, although Jefferson believes, at least in principle, that the University of Virginia should "tolerate" erroneous political opinions, in practice he deliberately sought to keep "heretical" views out of the curriculum. Far from encouraging "the illimitable freedom of the human mind,"[147] Jefferson goes out of his way to ensure that Tory philosophers will not be read and Federalist professors will not be hired. In contrast to his views on religious toleration, which arose out of the conviction that differing religious beliefs caused no political harm, Jefferson was convinced that certain political principles might very well threaten the future of republican government in America. Accordingly, he sees no need for the state to remain scrupulously neutral as it does in religious disputes where, from Jefferson's perspective, nothing vital is at stake.[148]

But however much Jefferson's conception of political toleration differs from the contemporary civil libertarian position, the principal difference between his conception of toleration and our present understanding is that Jefferson emphatically does not extend toleration to moral issues, that is, to competing notions of good and bad, virtue and vice. For unlike religious truths, which cannot be rationally known, or political opinions, which rest on fallible reason, moral knowledge is accessible to all through the operation of the moral sense, with the help of a few commonsense rules of prudence. There is, therefore, no good reason to tolerate what we *know* to be wrong and detrimental to republican self-government. And Jefferson nowhere suggests that we should.

The author of the Declaration of Independence is no moral relativist. He never doubts that certain practical truths are self-evident, and that the moral sense, acting together with unassisted human reason, can discover what they are. Nor does he doubt that the moral sentiments are natural and universal; that all human beings, in every society, are motivated by feelings of sympathy, justice, gratitude, benevolence, and friendship. To be sure, most of the world has not yet wakened to the rights of man. And different societies have radically opposed ideas of right and wrong, so much so that "the same actions are deemed virtuous in one country and vicious in another."[149] But, as Jefferson's remarks about the Spanish-American colonies, Spain, England, and even France suggest, he is hardly neutral about this moral diversity. Those societies that acknowledge the equal rights of man, and seek through education to prepare the people for moral and political self-government, are vastly superior to those that, through "ignorance and bigotry," render them "incapable of self-government."[150] Moreover, even in republican America, Jefferson does not invite every man and woman to fashion for themselves their own distinctive and individual understanding of right and wrong. The "expressive" individualism so characteristic of Thoreau, Emerson, and Whitman in America and of J. S. Mill in England is completely foreign to Jefferson's moral vision.[151] Jefferson's moral principles are the shared principles of the political community. The moral sense affirms society's collective judgment about right and wrong; it actively seeks the approbation of the larger community, though it must be emphasized to those who fear the danger of majority tyranny that the majority does not create these principles. They are inscribed in human nature by a Benevolent Creator so that human beings everywhere can develop the moral and intellectual capacity for self-government. To deny these truths is to deny "the laws of nature and Nature's God." And that is why Jefferson is unwilling to make a virtue out of toleration on moral questions.[152]

Hope

Just as Jefferson transformed the Christian virtues of faith and charity into the secular virtue of toleration, so, too, did he reinterpret the Christian virtue of hope, directing it away from eternal salvation and toward the continuing success of the republican experiment. Jefferson did not, of course, initiate this process; the secularization of hope had been going on for more than a century.

But he was one of its most enthusiastic proponents. Wherever republicanism was under attack, his constant wish was to see the doomsayers proved wrong: "My theory has always been, that if we are to dream, the flatteries of hope are as cheap, and pleasanter than the gloom of despair."[153]

If Jefferson resisted the counsels of despair, so, too, did he refuse to succumb to nostalgia. Despite the heroic achievements of his generation, he remained confident that, if properly educated, the rising generation would be every bit as capable of preserving republican institutions as his own had been in establishing them.[154] However much he feared that the government was moving in the wrong direction, he never lost faith in the people or in their cause. To the end, he continued to insist, "My temperament is sanguine. I steer my bark with Hope in the head, leaving Fear astern." So contagious was his optimism that even the crotchety John Adams confessed: "I admire your Navigation and should like to sail with you, either in your Bark or in my own, along side of yours; Hope with her gay Ensigns displayed at the Prow; fear with her Hobgoblins behind the Stern."[155]

Part of Jefferson's enduring appeal is precisely this quality of hopefulness. As his namesake William Jefferson Clinton, the self-described man from Hope, so shrewdly understood, Americans have always preferred the bridge to the future to a golden age in the past. It is part of the American character to believe that the best days are still to come, and Jefferson, more than any other Founder, speaks to this longing. From him, we too have learned to prefer "the dreams of the future to the history of the past."[156]

At the same time, however, there is something undeniably simplistic about his optimism and, by extension, ours. Jefferson is unwilling to admit that the people, his people, can ever knowingly or deliberately do wrong. He is unprepared to set any limits to progress, or to consider that progress in science and technology may lead to a decline in morals and virtue. He fails to see that the activities that bring happiness and pleasure to an individual may not be so easily reconciled with service to one's fellow citizens. The opposite side of Jefferson's hopefulness is his failure to recognize the tensions between doing good for others and doing good for oneself, moral virtue and intellectual virtue, the duties we owe to God and the duties we owe to others, as well as to ourselves. For

Jefferson, all our obligations are meshed together into a seamless web of social utility. This was the Benevolent Creator's plan. No wonder Jefferson could be so hopeful, and we as a people are the heirs to his hope. There is no problem Americans cannot solve, no defect that cannot be overcome through effort, ingenuity, and goodwill. We may not go as far as Jefferson in denying original sin, but it does not much limit our expectations.

On only one issue did Jefferson's hopes utterly fail him. In the critical area of race relations, Jefferson could never envision emancipated blacks living side by side with white Americans. What makes his pessimism so striking is his belief that both Native Americans and immigrants, including those who lack knowledge and experience of republican self-government, can be assimilated into American society. By contrast, blacks, who already shared a common language and religion with their masters, and who for more than a century had observed firsthand the Anglo-American political tradition, would nevertheless be compelled to leave. Jefferson is prepared to tolerate every conceivable religion, from no gods to twenty gods, but he draws the line at racial differences. Where "these unfortunate people" are concerned, the only "hope" Jefferson permits himself is that somehow they can be emancipated and gotten rid of.[157]

As Jefferson predicted, the founding generation would not solve the problem of slavery and what to do with emancipated blacks. And on the whole, Jefferson has not been of much assistance to future generations on how to integrate black Americans into a republic he hoped they would leave. But one aspect of his thought has continued to resonate with black leaders for much of our history, and that is the whole question of character. As Frederick Douglass observed, slavery had degraded the character of the blacks, and it would have to be rebuilt before blacks could participate successfully in American society and politics. Since ultimately the success of the American republic would hinge on how well the country succeeded in extending its political principles, whites had a powerful stake in the outcome of this struggle. But, Douglass insisted, it was the blacks who bore the largest responsibility, since character was not something someone else could give them; they would have to get it for themselves. And in our own time, Martin Luther King's dream that African Americans would one day be judged by the content of their character finds powerful affirmation in the speeches and writings of a growing number of Americans of all races.[158]

If, for the most part, the extended, heterogeneous, multiracial Republic has proved more successful than even our most optimistic Founder could have imagined, it is largely because, for much of our history, Americans have continued to cultivate the virtues that Jefferson understood were necessary for self-government. To be sure, there were always a few artists and intellectuals who challenged this moral order as too confining and repressive. But it was not until the 1960s that the assault on traditional morality reached epidemic proportions, as growing numbers of Americans, instructed by elite opinion makers in government, the academy, the media, and the entertainment industry, systematically overthrew the core moral principles that had bound the country together since the Founding.[159] It is, however, a tribute to the overall soundness of Jefferson's moral vision that these virtues have refused to die and that, as we approach the two-hundredth anniversary of the "revolution of 1800," the concern with character, after a silence of several decades, is once again being heard. In increasing numbers, Americans have begun to recognize that the preservation of republican government depends, first and foremost, not on institutional contrivances (however important they might be) but on the character and virtue of the people. For only when we start by asking what kind of people we ought to be can it truly be said that America represents "the last best hope" of mankind.

Notes

Chapter 1. The Declaration and the American Character

1. TJ to Dr. James Mease, September 26, 1825, in *The Writings of Thomas Jefferson*, ed. Albert Ellery Bergh (Washington D.C.: Thomas Jefferson Memorial Association, 1907), XVI:122–123 (hereafter cited as *WTJ*).

2. Mary Ann Glendon, *Rights Talk* (New York: Free Press, 1991); Richard E. Morgan, *Disabling America: The "Rights Industry" in Our Time* (New York: Basic Books, 1984).

3. See, for example, the Federalist criticism of Jefferson's preoccupation with rights. According to one critic, Jefferson talked endlessly of rights "and loved them so much he even promoted the rights of weeds to flourish. And why not? Doesn't each plant have 'an equal right to live?' 'And why should wheat and barley thrive / Despotic tyrants of the field?'" (quoted in Gordon Wood, "The Trials and Tribulations of Thomas Jefferson," in *Jeffersonian Legacies*, ed. Peter Onuf [Charlottesville: University Press of Virginia, 1993], pp. 395–417, at p. 399). For a contemporary restatement of this argument, in which the Declaration is only a symptom of modern liberalism, see Robert Bork, *Slouching Toward Gomorrah: Modern Liberalism and American Decline* (New York: Regan Books/HarperCollins, 1996).

4. Carl Becker, *The Declaration of Independence: A Study in the History of Political Ideas* (New York: Vintage Books, 1942); Martin Diamond, "Ethics and Politics: The American Way," in *The Moral Foundations of the American Republic*, ed. Robert H. Horwitz (Charlottesville: University Press of Virginia, 1977), pp. 39–72. More recently, Thomas L. Pangle, *The Spirit of Modern Republicanism: The Moral Vision of the American Founders and the Philosophy of John Locke* (Chicago: University of Chicago Press, 1988), and *The Ennobling of Democracy: The Challenge of the Postmodern Age* (Baltimore, Md.: Johns Hopkins University Press, 1992); Michael Zuckert, "Thomas Jefferson on Nature and Natural Rights," in *The Framers and Fundamental Rights*, ed. Robert A. Licht (Washington, D.C.: American Enterprise Institute, 1991), pp. 137–169, esp. pp. 152–169.

5. Zuckert, "Thomas Jefferson on Nature and Natural Rights," p. 154.

6. Harry Jaffa, *Crisis of the House Divided* (Garden City, N.Y.: Doubleday, 1959), pp. 308–329.

7. John Locke, *Second Treatise of Government*, ed. Richard Cox (Arlington Heights, Ill.: Harlan Davidson, 1982), chap. 2, para. 6.

8. John Patrick Diggins, *The Lost Soul of American Politics: Virtue, Self-Interest, and the Foundations of Liberalism* (New York: Basic Books, 1984); cf. Harvey C. Mansfield, *America's Constitutional Soul* (Baltimore, Md.: Johns Hopkins University Press, 1991), esp. chap. 15.

9. J. G. A. Pocock, *The Machiavellian Moment: Florentine Political Thought and the Atlantic Republic* (Princeton, N.J.: Princeton University Press, 1975); Gordon Wood, *The Creation of the American Republic* (Chapel Hill: University of North Carolina Press, 1969); and Hannah Arendt, *On Revolution* (New York: Viking Press, 1963); but cf. Lance Banning, "The Republican Interpretation: Retrospect and Prospect," in *The Republican Synthesis Revisited*, ed. Milton M. Klein, Richard D. Brown, and John B. Hench (Worcester, Mass.: American Antiquarian Society, 1992), pp. 91–117. More recently, Michael J. Sandel seeks to revive the civic republican tradition against the claims of "procedural" republicans or liberals. Lost in his analysis, however, is any recognition that the civic republicanism of the Founders and their successors is committed to preserving the natural rights of individuals. In trying to rein in "procedural" liberals, Sandel errs too far in the direction of communitarianism. See Michael J. Sandel, *Democracy's Discontent* (Cambridge, Mass.: Belknap Press of Harvard University Press, 1996).

10. Garry Wills, *Inventing America* (Garden City, N.Y.: Doubleday, 1978); cf. the criticism of Wills by Ronald Hamowy, "Jefferson and the Scottish Enlightenment," *William and Mary Quarterly* 36 (1979): 503–523. For a far more persuasive discussion of the political significance of the Scottish school and its affinity to Lockean liberalism, see Frank D. Balog, "The Scottish Enlightenment and the Liberal Political Tradition," in *Confronting the Constitution*, ed. Allan Bloom (Washington, D.C.: AEI Press, 1990), pp. 191–208. For Adam Smith on these themes, see Joseph Cropsey, *Polity and Economy* (The Hague: M. Nijhoff, 1957).

11. For example, even in the state of nature, "no man has a natural right to commit aggression upon the equal rights of another" or "to be the judge between himself and another" (TJ to Francis W. Gilmer, June 7, 1816, *WTJ* XV: 23–27); cf. Locke, *Second Treatise*, chap. 2, para. 13.

12. Here again, Jefferson seems to follow the Scots rather than Locke. See the similar argument made on behalf of Alexander Hamilton by Gerald Stourzh, *Alexander Hamilton and the Idea of Republican Government* (Stanford, Calif.: Stanford University Press, 1970), esp. pp. 90–95; David F. Epstein, *The Political Theory of "The Federalist"* (Chicago: University of Chicago Press, 1984); and Mansfield, *America's Constitutional Soul*, esp. chaps. 6–7.

13. Locke, *Second Treatise*, chap. 2, paras. 5, 15. And see the discussion of how Locke has wrongly been assimiliated to Hooker and the Christian natural law tradition in Paul Rahe, *Republics: Ancient and Modern* (Chapel Hill: University of North Carolina Press, 1994), vol. 2, pp. 263–268. For a superb discussion of Locke's state of nature, one that distinguishes between the natural sociality of man as an anthropological fact and the selfishness and individualism of man as moral phenomena, see Ruth W. Grant, "Locke's Political Anthropology and Lockean Individualism," *Journal of Politics* 50 (February 1988): 42–63.

14. For an assessment of Kames's influence on Jefferson, see Adrienne

Koch, *The Philosophy of Thomas Jefferson* (Chicago: Quadrangle Books, 1964), p. 17 n. 6. Francis Hutcheson makes the same point in *A Short Introduction to Moral Philosophy* (1747), reprinted in facsimile edition as volume 4 in *Collected Works of Francis Hutcheson* (New York: George Olms Verlag, 1990), 4:139.

15. TJ, *The Commonplace Book of Thomas Jefferson: A Reportory of His Ideas on Government*, ed. Gilbert Chinard (Baltimore, Md.: Johns Hopkins University Press, 1926), p. 107.

16. TJ to P. S. DuPont de Nemours, April 24, 1816, *WTJ* XIV:487–493.

17. TJ to Francis W. Gilmer, June 7, 1816, *WTJ* XV:23–27.

18. TJ to James Madison, January 30, 1787, *WTJ* VI:256–262. And this, even though when an Indian seriously violates the rights of another, "he is tomahawked as a dangerous enemy." Also TJ to Francis W. Gilmer, June 7, 1816, *WTJ* XV:23–27; TJ to John Adams, January 21, 1812, in *The Adams-Jefferson Letters*, ed. Lester J. Cappon (New York: Simon and Schuster, 1971), p. 291 (hereafter cited as *Adams-Jefferson Letters*).

19. TJ, *Notes on the State of Virginia*, ed. William Peden (Chapel Hill: University of North Carolina Press, 1955), Query VI, p. 60 (hereafter cited as *Notes*).

20. Compare for example, Locke's discussion of the executive prerogative in chapter 14 of the *Second Treatise* with Jefferson's attack on an expansive reading of implied powers.

21. TJ to P. S. DuPont de Nemours, April 24, 1816, *WTJ* XIV:487–493.

22. TJ to Thomas Law, June 13, 1814, *WTJ* XIV: 138–144.

23. Second Inaugural Address, March 4, 1805, in *The Works of Thomas Jefferson*, ed. Paul Leicester Ford (New York: Putnam, 1904), X:127–136 (hereafter cited as *Works*); also TJ to James Monroe, May 4, 1806, *WTJ* XI:106–111; TJ to George Logan, November 12, 1816, *Works* XII:42–44.

24. For an excellent discussion of the Lockean liberal virtues, one that complements the political teaching of the *Second Treatise*, see Nathan Tarcov, *Locke's Education for Liberty* (Chicago: University of Chicago Press, 1984). And for more recent approaches to this question that range beyond Locke, see William A. Galston, *Liberal Purposes: Goods, Virtues and Diversity in the Liberal State* (Cambridge: Cambridge University Press, 1991); Stephen G. Salkever, *Finding the Mean: Theory and Practice in Aristotelian Political Philosophy* (Princeton, N.J.: Princeton University Press, 1990); Stephen Macedo, *Liberal Virtues: Citizenship, Virtue, and Community in Liberal Constitutionalism* (Oxford: Clarendon Press, 1991); Steven Kautz, *Liberalism and Community* (Ithaca, N.Y.: Cornell University Press, 1995), esp. chap. 3; and Donald McCloskey, "Bourgeois Virtue," *American Scholar* 63 (Spring 1994): 177–191.

25. See Jefferson's original draft of the Declaration of Independence, *Works* II:199–217.

26. For the argument that for Jefferson these two are basically the same, see Daniel Boorstin, *The Lost World of Thomas Jefferson* (Chicago: University of Chicago Press, [1943] 1981), pp. 29ff.; also Eva T. H. Brann, "Concerning the Declaration of Independence," *Saint John's Review* 28 (July 1976): 1–16, at p. 7; Zuckert, "Thomas Jefferson on Nature and Natural Rights," n. 17, pp. 182–183; Jean Yarbrough, "Race and the Moral Foundations of the American Republic: Another Look at the Declaration and the *Notes on Virginia*," *Journal of Politics* 53 (February 1991): 90–105.

27. A Bill for Proportioning Crimes and Punishments in Cases Heretofore

Capital, November 1778, in *The Papers of Thomas Jefferson*, ed. Julian P. Boyd (Princeton, N.J.: Princeton University Press, 1954), II:492–507 (hereafter cited as *Papers*).

28. TJ to James Ross, May 8, 1786, *WTJ* V:320–324.

29. Opinion on the French Treaties, April 28, 1793, *WTJ* III:226–243.

30. Ibid.

31. Herbert Storing, "Slavery and the Moral Foundations of the American Republic," in Horwitz, *Moral Foundation of the American Republic*, p. 226; Harry Jaffa, *Crisis of the House Divided* (Garden City, N.Y.: Doubleday, 1959), pp. 308–329.

32. TJ to John Holmes, April 22, 1820, *WTJ* XV:248–250

33. TJ, A Summary View of the Rights of British Americans, July 1774, *Works* II:87.

34. TJ to M. d'Ivernois, February 6, 1795, *WTJ* IX:299; also Argument in the Case of *Howell vs. Netherlands*, April 1770, *Works* I:470–481.

35. TJ to Isaac H. Tiffany, April 4, 1819, in *The Political Writings of Thomas Jefferson*, ed. Edward Dumbauld (New York: Bobbs-Merrill), p. 55.

36. TJ to P. S. DuPont de Nemours, April 24, 1816, *WTJ* XIV:487–493.

37. TJ to David Humphreys, March 18, 1789, *WTJ* VII:319–321.

38. TJ, Summary View of the Rights of British America, July 1774, *WTJ* II:87; TJ, Thoughts on Lotteries, *Works* XII:435–450; TJ to David Humphreys, March 18, 1789, *WTJ* VII:319–321; TJ to James Madison, October 28, 1785, in *The Republic of Letters: The Correspondence Between Thomas Jefferson and James Madison 1776–1826*, ed. James Morton Smith (New York: Norton, 1995), I:389–391 (hereafter cited as *Correspondence of Jefferson and Madison*).

39. Jaffa, *Crisis of the House Divided*, pp. 378–381.

40. See especially Vernon Louis Parrington, *Main Currents in American Thought: The Colonial Mind, 1620–1800* (New York: Harcourt, Brace, 1927); Charles M. Wiltse, *The Jeffersonian Tradition in American Democracy* (Chapel Hill: University of North Carolina Press, 1935); and Ursula von Eckhardt, *The Pursuit of Happiness in the Democratic Creed* (New York: Praeger, 1959). For a survey of the attempts to reconcile Jefferson's political philosophy with the New Deal, see Merrill D. Peterson, *The Jeffersonian Image in the American Mind* (New York: Oxford University Press, 1960), esp. pp. 355–376.

41. TJ to James Madison, October 28, 1785, *Correspondence of Jefferson and Madison*, I:389–391. Even here, Jefferson insists only that the unemployed should be allowed to cultivate the land, "paying a moderate rent." See also Zuckert, "Thomas Jefferson on Nature and Natural Rights," p. 161.

42. Note accompanying Jefferson's revision of Destutt de Tracy's *Treatise on Political Economy* included in the "Prospectus" sent by TJ to Joseph Milligan, April 6, 1816, *WTJ* XIV:456–466.

43. Eva Brann, *Paradoxes of Education in a Republic* (Chicago: University of Chicago Press, 1979), p. 10.

44. First Inaugural Address, March 4, 1801, *WTJ* III:317–323.

45. See especially Bill No. 64 of the Revisal of the Laws of Virginia in *Papers* II:497. For the full text of the Committee of Revisors, see *Papers* II:305–665; also TJ to Edmund Pendleton, August 26, 1776, Papers I:503–506; TJ to Samuel Kercheval, July 12, 1816, *WTJ* XV:29; also Ralph Lerner, "Jefferson's Pulse of Republican Reformation," in *The Thinking Revolutionary: Principle and Practice in the New Republic* (Ithaca, N.Y.: Cornell University Press, 1979), pp.

60–90; Rahe, *Republic,* 3:17–23. For a discussion of First Amendment rights, see Walter Berns, *Virtue, Freedom and the First Amendment* (Chicago: Henry Regnery, 1965), p. 28.

46. Consider Locke's defense of the prerogative in chapter. 14 of the *Second Treatise,* and compare with Jefferson's view of executive power, especially in the case of the Louisiana Purchase.

47. For a discussion of these themes in *The Federalist,* see David Epstein, *The Political Theory of "The Federalist"* (Chicago: University of Chicago Press, 1984), pp. 88–93, 162–192.

48. On the natural right of self-government, see Opinion on the Constitutionality of the Residence Bill, July 15, 1790, *WTJ* III:59–67; on self-government and republicanism, see TJ to Samuel Kercheval, July 12, 1816, *WTJ* XV:29, and September 5, 1816, *WTJ* XV:70–73; TJ to John Taylor, May 28, 1816, *WTJ* XV:17–23; TJ to Joseph Cabell, February 2, 1816, *WTJ* XIV:417–423; TJ to John Cartwright, June 5, 1824, *WTJ* XVI:42–52;

49. Mansfield, *America's Constitutional Soul,* p. 83; Harvey C. Mansfield, "Self-Interest Rightly Understood," *Political Theory* (February 1995): 48–66. On the twin passions of modern political philosophy, Joseph Cropsey, "The United States as a Regime and the Sources of the American Way of Life," in *Political Philosophy and the Issues of Politics* (Chicago: University of Chicago Press, 1977), pp. 1–15.

50. Louis Hartz, *The Liberal Tradition in America: An Interpretation of American Political Thought Since the Revolution* (New York: Harcourt, 1955); Becker, *The Declaration of Independence;* more recently, Martin Diamond, "Ethics and Politics: The American Way," in Horwitz, *Moral Foundations of the American Republic,* pp. 39–72; Walter Berns, "The New Pursuit of Happiness," *Public Interest,* no. 86 (1987): 65–76; Diggins, *Lost Soul of American Politics,* p. 37.

51. John Schaar, "And the Pursuit of Happiness," *Virginia Quarterly Review* 46 (Winter 1970): 1–27, esp. p. 19; Diggins, *Lost Soul of American Politics,* pp. 37–39.

52. Zuckert, "Thomas Jefferson on Nature and Natural Rights," pp. 161–163.

53. Adrienne Koch, "Jefferson and the Pursuit of Happiness," in *Power, Morals, and the Founding Fathers* (Ithaca, N.Y.: Great Seal Books, 1961), p. 31.

54. Pangle, *Spirit of Modern Republicanism,* pp. 207–209.

55. Richard Matthews, *The Radical Politics of Thomas Jefferson* (Lawrence: University Press of Kansas, 1984), p. 27; von Eckhardt, *Pursuit of Happiness,* p. 130.

56. Harry Jaffa, "Another Look at the Declaration," and "Inventing the Past: Garry Wills' *Inventing America* and the Pathology of Ideological Scholarship," both in *American Conservatism and the American Founding* (Durham, N.C.: Carolina Academic Press, 1984), pp. 18–25; Forrest McDonald, *Novus Ordo Seclorum* (Lawrence: University Press of Kansas, 1985), pp. ix–x; Brann, *Paradoxes of Education,* p. 12.

57. Wills, *Inventing America,* pp. 248–255.

58. TJ to Mrs. Trist, August 18, 1785, *WTJ* V:80–82, where Jefferson describes as "fallacious" the pursuits of happiness engaged in by the French.

59. TJ to J. Correa de Serra, April 19, 1814, *WTJ* XIX:209–211.

60. *Notes,* Query XIV, p. 147; TJ to Peter Carr, August 6, 1788, *Papers* XIII:470.

61. Koch, *Philosophy of Thomas Jefferson,* p. 1.

62. For a different view, which argues that at the time of the Declaration Jefferson was still a Lockean, who had not yet discovered the moral sense, see Garrett Ward Sheldon, *The Political Philosophy of Thomas Jefferson* (Baltimore, Md.: Johns Hopkins University Press, 1991), pp. 45–52, 155.

63. TJ to Henry Lee, May 8, 1825, *Works* XII:408–409.

64. Herbert Lawrence Ganter, "Jefferson's 'Pursuit of Happiness' and Some Forgotten Men," *William and Mary Quarterly* 16 (October 1936): 558–585, esp. p. 577.

65. Howard Mumford Jones, *The Pursuit of Happiness* (Cambridge, Mass.: Harvard University Press, 1953), pp. 63–64. Also note 50.

66. Harold Hellenbrand, *The Unfinished Revolution: Education and Politics in the Thought of Thomas Jefferson* (Newark: University of Delaware Press, 1990), esp. chap. 2, n. 55, p. 176. Moreover, the eighteenth-century understanding of the word "pursuit" would also seem to support this reading. According to the historian Arthur M. Schlesinger, Jr., the eighteenth century understood "pursuit" in two different senses. It could have meant "chase," as we commonly assume today or, what is now nearly obsolete, "practice," in the sense of a profession or a business. This latter usage fits well with Jefferson's suggestion in the *Notes* that the people be taught "how to work out their greatest happiness" by showing them that it "is always the *result* of good conscience, good health, occupation, and freedom in all just pursuits" (emphasis added). It is the practice of, and not merely the search after, these objects that produces true happiness. Also, Brann, *Paradoxes of Education,* p. 12.

67. TJ to Amos J. Cook, January 21, 1816, *WTJ* XIV:403–406.

68. TJ to John Page, July 15, 1763, *WTJ* IV:8–11. Also, Carl J. Richard, *The Founders and the Classics: Greece, Rome, and the American Enlightenment* (Cambridge, Mass.: Harvard University Press, 1994).

69. TJ, *The Literary Bible,* ed. Gilbert Chinard (New York: Greenwood Press, 1969), pp. 76–78; also the selection from Virgil, p. 120.

70. Ibid., p. 126.

71. Ibid., p. 180.

72. Ibid., p. 184.

73. See Douglas L. Wilson, ed., *Jefferson's Literary Commonplace Book: The Papers of Thomas Jefferson,* 2nd ser. (Princeton, N.J.: Princeton University Press, 1989), pp. 6–8. This is the same work that Chinard called *The Literary Bible.*

74. Ibid., p. 12.

75. TJ to Robert Skipwith, August 3, 1771, *Papers* I:76–81.

76. *Catalogue of the Library of Thomas Jefferson,* compiled with annotations by E. Millicent Sowerby (Washington, D.C.: Library of Congress, 1953), II:11–12. If it is true, as Jefferson wrote to Thomas Law in 1814, that he had read the book fifty years earlier, he would have read it in 1764. Even allowing for some exaggeration, there seems to be little doubt that he had read it before 1776. See also the discussion of the significance of this notation in Koch, *Philosophy of Thomas Jefferson,* pp. 17–18.

77. TJ to Maria Cosway, October 12, 1786, *WTJ* V:430–448.

78. Ibid.

79. TJ to Benjamin Rush, April 21, 1803, *WTJ* X:379–385.

80. Ibid.

81. TJ to Thomas Law, June 13, 1814, *WTJ* XIV:138–144.

82. But see Adam Smith's critique of Hutcheson on just this point (*Theory of Moral Sentiments* [Indianapolis: Liberty Classics, 1969], pp. 478–480).

83. TJ to Thomas Law, June 13, 1816, *WTJ* XIV:138–144.

84. TJ to Miles King, September 26, 1814, *WTJ* XIV:196–198.

85. Pangle, *Ennobling of Democracy*, pp. 91–92. See also James Q. Wilson, *The Moral Sense* (New York: Free Press, 1993).

86. In this connection see also James Wilson who, following the Scots, grounded rights on both the selfish and the social passions and spoke of the "rights and duties of benevolence" (*The Works of James Wilson*, 2 vols., ed. Robert Green McCloskey [Cambridge, Mass.: Belknap Press, 1967], I:242, II:592–594). See also Hutcheson's discussion of liberality and beneficence in connection with perfect and imperfect natural rights (*Introduction*, pp. 122–123).

87. Abraham Lincoln, "Speech on the Repeal of the Missouri Compromise," October 16, 1854.

88. TJ to Francis W. Gilmer, June 7, 1816, *WTJ* XV:23–27.

89. Wilson, *Lectures on Law*, "Natural Rights," in *Works of James Wilson*, II:594.

90. Francis Hutcheson, *A System of Moral Philosophy* (New York: Augustus M. Kelly, 1968), p. 51.

91. von Eckhardt, *Pursuit of Happiness*, esp. chap. 5, p. 130. More recently, Zuckert too stresses the comprehensiveness of happiness but lays undue emphasis on the variety of objects individuals desire, while saying nothing about the connection between happiness and virtue ("Thomas Jefferson on Nature and Natural Rights,"esp. pp. 162–163).

92. TJ to David Rittenhouse, July 19, 1778, *WTJ* IV:42–43.

93. TJ to Henry Lee, May 8, 1825.

94. See note 2.

95. For a criticism of nature as providing permanent standards as it relates to Jefferson, see Joyce Oldham Appleby, *Capitalism and a New Social Order: The Republican Vision of the 1790's* (New York: New York University Press, 1984), pp. 101–105, and, by the same author, "Introduction: Jefferson and His Complex Legacy," in Onuf, *Jeffersonian Legacies,* esp. pp. 10–11.

96. For a longer discussion, see Mansfield, *America's Constitutional Soul,* pp. 185 ff.

Chapter 2. The Moral Sense Virtues and Character Formation

1. TJ to Mary Jefferson Eppes, January 7, 1798, in *The Family Letters of Thomas Jefferson,* ed. Edwin Morris Betts and James Adam Bear, Jr. (Columbia: University of Missouri Press, 1996), p. 152 (hereafter cited as *Family Letters*).

2. For a contemporary examination of the moral sense, see Wilson, *The Moral Sense.*

3. TJ to Peter Carr, August 10, 1787, *WTJ* VI:256–262.

4. TJ to Thomas Law, June 13, 1814, *WTJ* XIV:138–144.

5. TJ to William Short, October 31, 1819, with "Syllabus of the doctrines of Epicurus," *WTJ* XV:219–224.

6. Cf. Aristotle, *Nichomachean Ethics,* ed. T. E. Page (Cambridge: Loeb Classical Library, [1926] 1962), book II, 1104b 10–15.

7. TJ to Maria Cosway, October 12, 1786, *WTJ* V:430–448.

8. See Henry Home Kames's criticism of Locke, *Essays on the Principles of Morality and Natural Religion 1751* (New York: Garland, 1976), pp. 2–15.

9. Here it may be useful to distinguish between the claim made by Aristotle that "man is by nature a political animal" (*Politics*, trans. Carnes Lord [Chicago: University of Chicago Press, 1985], book I, 1253al 3) and the Scottish assertion that he is by nature social. For Aristotle, man's political nature is linked to his capacity for speech, which in turn rests on his ability to reason and deliberate about the right way to live. Aristotle's emphasis upon reason as the distinctively human faculty points to what is most excellent in human nature. It does not mean that all human beings actually do reason about justice, only that the capacity to reason is what separates us from the animals. Indeed, since not all human beings possess the capacity for reasoned judgment, the claim that man is by nature political has decidedly aristocratic, or at least nondemocratic, implications.

Moreover, in the *Ethics*, Aristotle argues that the moral virtues are largely the result of habituation. He rejects outright the suggestion that there exists a distinct moral faculty, akin to the sense organs, for perceiving right and wrong. Similarly, he rejects the idea that virtue arises out of the social passions. All passions stand in need of correction so that they achieve a mean between excess and deficiency. No passion can by itself give rise to virtue. Ultimately, it is prudence or practical wisdom that establishes what is right in any given situation. In contrast to the moral sense philosophers, then, the argument that man is by nature political points to the supremacy of practical reason over sentiment, and of habit over impulse, in determining moral virtue.

10. Francis Hutcheson, *Illustrations on the Moral Sense*, ed. Bernard Peach (Cambridge, Mass.: Belknap Press of Harvard University Press, 1971), pp. 118–119.

11. Kames, *Principles of Morality*, pp. 61, 84.

12. Ibid., p. 85.

13. Ibid., p. 55.

14. Ibid., p. 81.

15. In fairness, Hutcheson had not argued in favor of such universal benevolence. But because Kames seeks to ground moral obligation in those sentiments that give rise to universal duty and can be enforced by the state, he rejects benevolence. Indeed, for Kames it is not clear if, strictly speaking, we have any "duty" to act for the positive good of others at all. Though such actions merit the highest approbation, the neglect of them is not enforceable (Kames, *Principles of Morality*, pp. 126–127).

16. Ibid., pp. 87–88.

17. Ibid., p. 103.

18. Ibid., pp. 112, 133.

19. Aristotle, *Ethics*, book II, 1103a 15–1103b 5.

20. David Hume, *A Treatise of Human Nature*, book III, pt. II, chap. 1; *An Enquiry Concerning the Principles of Morals*, sec. III, both in *Hume's Moral and Political Philosophy*, ed. Henry D. Aiken (New York: Hafner, 1972).

21. Smith, *Theory of Moral Sentiments*, pp. 47–53.

22. TJ to Peter Carr, August 10, 1787, *WTJ* VI:256–262; TJ to Thomas Law, June 13, 1814, *WTJ* XIV:138–144.

23. On this latter point, see Zuckert, "Appendix I: On Reading Jefferson," in "Thomas Jefferson on Nature and Natural Rights," pp. 167–168.

24. See in particular his observation that both Indians and Negro slaves possessed a moral sense in the *Notes,* Query XIV, pp. 140–149; TJ to Robert Skipwith, August 3, 1771, *WTJ* IV:237–240; TJ to Peter Carr, August 19, 1785, *WTJ* V:82–87.

25. TJ to Thomas Law, June 13, 1814, *WTJ* XIV:138–144; TJ to John Adams, October 14, 1816, *Adams-Jefferson Letters,* p. 492; TJ to Maria Cosway, October 12, 1786, *WTJ* V:430–448.

26. TJ to Peter Carr, August 10, 1787, *WTJ* VI:256–262.

27. David Daiches Raphael, *The Moral Sense* (London: Oxford University Press, 1947), pp. 1–14.

28. TJ to Martha Jefferson, December 11, 1783, *Family Letters,* pp. 20–21.

29. TJ to Maria Cosway, October 12, 1786, *WTJ* V:430–448.

30. TJ to James Fishback, September 27, 1809, *WTJ* XII:314–316; also to Dr. John Manners, June 12, 1817, *WTJ* XV:124–126. But cf. Morton White, *The Philosophy of the American Revolution* (New York: Oxford University Press, 1978), who argues that at the time of the Revolution Jefferson was more of a rationalist in moral matters and that only later did he "abandon" his early insistence that "the moral sense is subordinate to reason" (pp. 124–125).

31. TJ to Peter Carr, August 10, 1787, *WTJ* VI:256–262. Also TJ, Opinion on the French Treaties, where reason shares equally with the moral sense in its claim to moral knowledge: "Questions of natural right are triable by conformity with the moral sense and reason of man" (Opinion on the French Treaties, April 28, 1793, *WTJ* III:226–243).

32. TJ to Thomas Jefferson Randolph, November 24, 1808, *Family Letters,* pp. 362–365; also TJ to Mary Jefferson Eppes, January 7, 1798, *Family Letters,* p. 152.

33. TJ to Peter Carr, August 10, 1787, *WTJ* VI:256–262. The contrast with Kames on this point is striking. Where for the Scotsman abstract reason helps to refine the original moral impulses and to promote moral improvement, Jefferson, despite his agreement with Kames on the larger point, tends to stress the ways in which reason can lead the heart astray.

34. Ibid.; TJ to Francis Wayles Eppes, June 27, 1821, *Family Letters,* pp. 439–440.

35. TJ to Thomas Law, June 13, 1814, *WTJ* XIV:138–144; see also Kames's critique of the modern rationalists (*Principles of Morality,* pp. 95–100).

36. See especially Plato, *Republic,* trans. Allan Bloom (New York: Basic Books, 1968), 544a; Aristotle, *Politics,* book III, 1268bl 4–9; book IV, 1239bl 15–20; book VII, 1328bl 25–40; Marcus Tullius Cicero, *On the Commonwealth,* trans. George Holland Smith and Stanley Barney Smith (Indianapolis: Bobbs-Merrill Educational Publishing, 1984), book I, sections XXVII–XXXV.

37. TJ to Thomas Law, June 13, 1814, *WTJ* XIV:138–144.

38. Ibid.

39. In this regard, see especially White, *Philosophy of the American Revolution,* pp. 97–141.

40. Kames, *Principles of Morality,* p. 143.

41. Cited in Koch, *The Philosophy of Thomas Jefferson,* p. 18. And see the discussion in Kames, *Principles of Morality,* pp. 145–149.

42. This position would, moreover, accord with Jefferson's faith in the natural aristocracy to rule in the interests of the people, an argument we shall consider more fully in chapter 4.

43. TJ to Thomas Law, June 13, 1814, *WTJ* XIV:138–144.

44. Raphael, *Moral Sense,* p. 25 n. 2.

45. TJ to Thomas Law, June 13, 1814, *WTJ* XIV:138–144.

46. TJ to John Adams, October 14, 1816, *Adams-Jefferson Letters,* pp. 490–493.

47 TJ to John Bannister, Jr., October 15, 1785, *WTJ* V:185–188.

48. Smith, *Theory of Moral Sentiments,* pp. 194–199; also Kames, *Principles of Morality,* pp. 132–135.

49. TJ to Thomas Jefferson Randolph, November 24, 1808, *Family Letters,* pp. 362–365. To be sure, one must first possess the good judgment to identify those worthy of emulation, but that is not Jefferson's point here. And cf. TJ to Richard Price, February 7, 1788, *Memoir, Correspondence, and Miscellanies, from the Papers of Thomas Jefferson,* ed. Thomas Jefferson Randolph (Charlottesville, Va.: F. Carr, 1829), II:290, where Jefferson observes that reason becomes more important in moral judgment as it "grows stronger by time and experience."

50. TJ to Robert Skipwith, August 3, 1771, *WTJ* IV:237–240. For some reason, the Pangles do not discuss this important letter and so fault Jefferson for failing to appreciate the role that literature can play in stimulating the moral imagination. Lorraine Smith Pangle and Thomas L. Pangle, *The Learning of Liberty: The Educational Ideas of the American Founders* (Lawrence: University Press of Kansas, 1993), pp. 258–259.

51. TJ to Robert Skipwith, August 3, 1771, *WTJ* IV:237–240. Unless otherwise noted, all quotations in this section are from this letter. See also Jefferson's Shakespeare entries in his *Literary Commonplace Book.*

52. TJ to Peter Carr, August 10, 1787, *WTJ* XI:256–262.

53. But cf. TJ to Nathaniel Burwell, Esq., March 14, 1818, *WTJ* XV:165–168, where Jefferson criticizes popular and trashy novels, aimed at girls, for their tendency to produce, among other things, "a bloated imagination" and "sickly judgment." On the other hand, certain popular works, like "Modern Griselda," apparently can instruct by the "rule of contraries," that is, showing us how not to behave (TJ to Anne Randolph Bankhead, May 26, 1811, *Family Letters,* pp. 400–401).

54. TJ to Peter Carr, August 19, 1785, *WTJ* V:82–87.

55. TJ to Thomas Law, June 13, 1814, *WTJ* XIV:138–144. But cf. Jefferson's recollection with the discussion in Kames, *Principles of Morality,* p. 77. What Kames is arguing is that we have no moral obligations to which we are not prompted by some natural impulse. All our duties are grounded on our nature. Jefferson shifts Kames's emphasis on the naturalness of morality to an argument for moral majoritarianism.

56. As we shall see more clearly in chapter 4, this is a confusion that runs throughout Jefferson's political thought. As a statesman, he also tended to confuse the approbation of the wise few with that of his countrymen as a whole, until the distinction was made painfully clear to him.

57. Raphael, *Moral Sense,* pp. 44–46; Arthur O. Lovejoy, *Reflections on Human Nature* (Baltimore, Md.: Johns Hopkins University Press, 1961), Lecture VII, esp. pp. 228ff.

58. Consider, for example, his reference to the "wise and honest part of mankind" in the Opinion on the French Treaties, April 28, 1793, *WTJ* III:226–243.

59. TJ to Edward Coles, August 25, 1814, *Works* XI:416–420.

60. *Notes*, Query XVIII, p. 162; TJ to Edward Coles, August 25, 1814, *Works* XI:416–420. For the way in which slavery has corrupted the moral sense of the slaves, see *Notes*, Query XIV, p. 142.

61. *Notes*, Query XVIII, p. 163.

62. TJ to Dr. Benjamin Rush, April 21, 1803, *WTJ* X:379–385.

63. Only Thomas and Lorraine Smith Pangle have focused on this aspect of moral development in Jefferson (see *Learning of Liberty*, esp. chap. 13), though Hellenbrand takes note of it in passing (*Unfinished Revolution*, chap. 2). It is worth noting that Hutcheson and Kames both consider the importance of good habits in developing the moral sense.

64. See especially Martha Jefferson Randolph to TJ, November 18, 1808, *Family Letters*, pp. 359–361. It was this letter that provoked Jefferson's famous advice to his grandson Thomas Jefferson Randolph, written later that month.

65. TJ to Peter Carr, August 10, 1787, *WTJ* VI:256–262.

66. See especially Jan Lewis, "'The Blessings of Domestic Society': Thomas Jefferson's Family and the Transformation of Republican Politics," in Onuf, *Jeffersonian Legacies*, pp. 109–146, at p. 115.

67. TJ to Martha Jefferson, May 21, 1787, *Family Letters*, pp. 41–42; also, TJ to Martha Jefferson, March 6, 1786, *Family Letters*, p. 30; TJ to Martha Jefferson, April 7, 1787, *Family Letters*, pp. 36–37; TJ to Mary Jefferson, April 11, 1790, *Family Letters*, p. 52.

68. TJ to Anne Cary, Thomas Jefferson, and Ellen Wayles Randolph, March 2, 1802, *Family Letters*, p. 218.

69. TJ to Robert Skipwith, August 3, 1771, *WTJ* IV:237–240.

70. Despite the importance of the imagination, sympathy, as Hume and Smith understood it, that is, the capacity to enter imaginatively into the joys and sorrows of others and to have them enter imaginatively into ours, does not figure prominently in Jefferson's analysis.

71. Wills, *Inventing America*, esp. pp. 193–206.

72. TJ to Thomas Law, June 13, 1814, *WTJ* XIV:138–144.

73. TJ to Francis Gilmer, June 7, 1816, *WTJ* XV:23–27.

74. TJ to John Adams, October 14, 1816, in *Adams-Jefferson Letters*, pp. 490–493; also, TJ to William Johnson, June 12, 1823, *WTJ* XV:439–452.

75. TJ to Dr. Benjamin Rush, April 21, 1803, *WTJ* X:379–385; TJ to Maria Cosway, October 12, 1786, *WTJ* V:430–448; TJ to P. S. duPont de Nemours, April 24, 1816, *Works* XIV:487–493.

76. TJ to John Adams, October 14, 1816, *Adams-Jefferson Letters*, pp. 490–493; TJ to Francis Gilmer, June 7, 1816, *WTJ* XV:23–27.

77. TJ to Francis Gilmer, June 7, 1816, *WTJ* XV:23–27; also, TJ to John Adams, October 14, 1816, *Adams-Jefferson Letters*, pp. 490–493; and TJ to William Johnson, June 12, 1823, *WTJ* XV:439–452. Context is important here too, as Jefferson is again reacting to the argument that justice is conventional and is not developing an argument about the moral sense in general.

78. Opinion on the French Treaties, April 28, 1793, *WTJ* III:226–243.

79. Like Hutcheson, Jefferson speaks of benevolence both as a passion that the moral sense perceives and as the virtue that ensues (Raphael, *Moral Sense*, p. 22).

80. Prospectus on Political Economy, enclosed in a letter from TJ to Joseph Milligan, April 6, 1816, *WTJ* XIV:456–466.

81. See especially the discussion in Kames, *Principles of Morality*, pp. 126–127, 132–133; Smith, *Theory of Moral Sentiments*, pp. 155–160.

82. TJ to John Adams, July 5, 1814, *Adams-Jefferson Letters*, pp. 433–434.

83. Paul Conkin, "The Religious Pilgrimage of Thomas Jefferson," in Onuf, *Jeffersonian Legacies*, pp. 19–49.

84. Jefferson misses the irony of his rationalist attempt to persuade Americans that Jesus was only a man in order to prove the naturalness and superiority of sentiment over reason in matters of morality.

85. TJ to Dr. Benjamin Rush, April 21, 1803, *WTJ* X:379–385; also, TJ to Edward Dowse, April 19, 1803, *WTJ* X:376–378.

86. TJ to Dr. Benjamin Rush, April 19, 1803, *WTJ* X:379–385.

87. Ibid.

88. Ibid.

89. Jefferson actually compiled two digests. The first, which he entitled *The Philosophy of Jesus*, is now lost. The second, compiled much later, is the *Life and Morals of Jesus of Nazareth*, which sifts through the same materials, with a few changes, except that Jefferson later offers his selections in four languages. Ironically, the so-called Jefferson Bible was later reprinted and distributed to members of Congress for their personal instruction and edification.

90. TJ to John Adams, October 12, 1813, *Adams-Jefferson Letters*, pp. 383–386; TJ to Francis Adrian Van der Kemp, April 25, 1816, *WTJ* XV:1–3; TJ to William Short, October 31, 1819, *WTJ* XV:219–224. Although no edition of the extract still exists, an annotated copy of the table of contents in Jefferson's own hand has enabled the editors of the second series of Jefferson *Papers* to reconstruct the volume. See *Jefferson's Extracts from the Gospels: The Papers of Thomas Jefferson*, 2nd ser., ed. Dickenson W. Adams (Princeton, N.J.: Princeton University Press, 1983).

91. TJ to Ezra Stiles Ely, June 25, 1819, *WTJ* XV:202–204.

92. TJ to William Short, October 31, 1819, *WTJ* XV:219–224.

93. TJ to Ezra Stiles Ely, June 25, 1819, *WTJ* XV:202–204.

94. See the table of contents in Jefferson's *Extracts from the Gospels*, p. 59. It is this example that he offers in his discussion of the moral sense with Thomas Law (TJ to Thomas Law, June 13, 1814, *WTJ* XIV:138–144).

95. TJ to George Thacher, January 26, 1824, *Works* XII:332–339.

96. Jefferson to John Adams, October 12, 1813, *Adams-Jefferson Letters*, pp. 383–386.

97. On this point, see Arendt on the corruptions of the French Revolution in *On Revolution*, chap. 2, and Jean Bethke Elshtain, *Democracy on Trial* (New York: Basic Books, 1995), pp. 122–123.

98. TJ to Mary Jefferson Eppes, January 1, 1799, *Family Letters*, p. 170; TJ to Martha Jefferson Randolph, July 17, 1790, *Family Letters*, pp. 60–61.

99. TJ to Mary Jefferson, April 11, 1790, *Family Letters*, p. 52.

100. TJ to Martha Jefferson Randolph, July 17, 1970, *Family Letters*, p. 61; cf. TJ to Thomas Jefferson Randolph, November 24, 1808, *Family Letters*, pp. 362–365.

101. TJ to Thomas Jefferson Randolph, November 24, 1808, *Family Letters* pp. 362–365.

102. Pangle and Pangle, *Learning of Liberty*, pp. 262–264.

103. Gordon Wood, *The Radicalism of the American Revolution* (New York: Knopf, 1992), pp. 224–225.

Chapter 3. Work, Property, and Character:
Agrarian Virtue and Commercial Virtue

1. *Notes* Query XIX, pp. 164–165. For a twentieth-century reaffirmation of the agrarian tradition, see Twelve Southerners, *I'll Take My Stand: The South and the Agrarian Tradition* (New York: Harper and Brothers, 1930). Jefferson differs from these latter-day agrarians in his faith in science and progress and in his refusal to link the cultivation of the earth with religion and the maintenance of traditional society.

2. Peterson, *The Jeffersonian Image in the American Mind,* esp. chap. 7.

3. Alexander Hamilton, June 21, 1788, New York Ratifying Convention, in *The Debates in the Several State Conventions on the Adoption of the Federal Constitution,* ed. Jonathan Elliot (Philadephia: Lippincott, 1901), II:256.

4. Indeed, Jefferson would later oppose the Missouri Compromise because it foreclosed his and Madison's misguided strategy of "diffusing" slavery throughout the territories, a policy they hoped would encourage Southern states to emancipate the much smaller number of slaves remaining within their jurisdictions. See TJ to John Holmes, April 22, 1820, *WTJ* XV: 248–250; see also James Madison to Robert J. Evans, June 15, 1819; JM to Robert Walsh, November 27, 1819, in Marvin Meyers, ed., *The Mind of the Founder: Sources of the Political Thought of James Madison* (Hanover, N.H.: University Press of New England, 1981), pp. 314–327.

5. For a discussion, see especially Harry V. Jaffa, "Agrarian Virtue and Republican Freedom," in *Equality and Liberty: Theory and Practice in American Politics* (New York: Oxford University Press, 1965); Rahe, *Republics,* 3:203. See also McDonald, *Novus Ordo Seclorum,* pp. 74–75; Drew McCoy, *The Elusive Republic: Political Economy in Jeffersonian America* (Chapel Hill: University of North Carolina Press, 1980), esp. pp. 250–252. And, for a different perspective, Richard K. Matthews argues that Jefferson's desire to restrict manufacturing in the United States contributed to European wage slavery (*Radical Politics of Thomas Jefferson,* p. 40).

6. See, for example, the suggestive essay by Lance Banning, "Political Economy and the Creation of the Federal Republic," in *Devising Liberty: Preserving and Creating Freedom in the New American Republic,* ed. David Thomas Konig (Stanford, Calif.: Stanford University Press, 1995), pp. 11–49.

7. Aristotle, *Politics,* book I, chap. 8, 1256al 35, and chap. 9, 1257al 5–40; *Jefferson's Literary Commonplace Book,* pp. 63, 78–80, 81–82, 143, 149.

8. Elizabeth Fox-Genovese, *The Origins of Physiocracy: Economic Revolution and Social Order in Eighteenth-Century France* (Ithaca, N.Y.: Cornell University Press, 1976). On Adam Smith, see Cropsey, *Polity and Economy.*

9. TJ to General Washington, August 14, 1787, *WTJ* VI:274–278; TJ to James Madison, December 20, 1787, in *Correspondence of Jefferson and Madison* I:511–515; also, TJ to John Blair, August 13, 1787, *WTJ* VI:272–273; TJ to Abbe Salimankis, March 14, 1810, *WTJ* XII:379–380.

10. TJ to Thomas Mann Randolph, May 30, 1790, *WTJ* VIII:29–33.

11. Smith, *Wealth of Nations,* pp. 734–735.

12. Ibid. Whether the state can, however, succeed in overcoming the "contemptible," "mutilated," and "deformed" character of the inferior ranks remains highly problematic for Smith, despite the obvious interest of a free society in doing so.

13. Ibid., pp. 249–250, 395, 460.

14. Ibid., p. 358.

15. Ibid., p. 359.

16. TJ to General Thaddeus Kosciusko, February 26, 1810, in *The Garden and Farm Books of Thomas Jefferson*, ed. Robert C. Baron (Golden, Colo.: Fulcrum, 1987), p. 197. As the selections in this volume make clear, Jefferson's correspondence is filled with information about the newest plants, the latest inventions, and the most promising methods of cultivation.

17. TJ to David Williams, November 14, 1803, *WTJ* X:428–431.

18. TJ to Samuel Kercheval, July 12, 1816, *WTJ* XV:32–44; TJ to William Crawford, June 20, 1816, *WTJ* XV:27–31.

19. TJ to St. John de Crevecoeur, January 15, 1787, *WTJ* VI:53–55. And see the discussion in Matthews, *Radical Politics of Thomas Jefferson*, pp. 47–48.

20. See the discussion of "inferior" and "superior prudence" in Smith, *Theory of Moral Sentiments*, pp. 353–354. Note also that in describing superior prudence as the "utmost perfection of all the intellectual and of all the moral virtues" (p. 354), Smith leaves no place for the pursuit of theoretical wisdom for its own sake.

21. TJ to G. K. Van Hogendorp, October 13, 1785, *WTJ* V:180–184; also *Notes*, Query XXII, p. 175.

22. TJ to G. K. Van Hogendorp, October 13, 1785, *WTJ* V:180–184; also, TJ to General Washington, March 15, 1784, *Papers* VII:25–27.

23. *Notes*, Query XXII, p. 175; TJ to John Jay, August 23, 1785, *WTJ* V:93–96.

24. *Notes*, Query XXII, p. 175. Jefferson may have underestimated the danger of a "landboard" attack, but he was quick to recognize the dangers from the sea.

25. *Notes*, Query XXII, pp. 175–176; also, Report on the Privileges and Restrictions on the Commerce of the United States in Foreign Countries, December 16, 1793, *Works* VIII:98–119; TJ to Elbridge Gerry, January 26, 1799, *WTJ* X:74–86; First Annual Message, December 8, 1801, *Works* IX:321–342. For a discussion of Jefferson's naval policy, see Merrill Peterson, *Thomas Jefferson and the New Nation* (New York: Oxford University Press, 1970), pp. 834–837.

26. TJ to John Jay, August 23, 1785, *WTJ* V:93–96; also *Notes*, Query XXII, p. 175. For a reiteration of this argument, see TJ to Benjamin Austin, January 9, 1816, *WTJ* XIV:387–393.

27. Plato, *The Laws of Plato*, trans. Thomas L. Pangle (New York: Basic Books, 1980), book II 704b; Aristotle, *Politics*, book VII, chap. 6, 1327a11–1327b17; Cicero, *On the Commonwealth*, book II, sections III–V. See also the discussion of sailing and its relationship to republican virtue in Montesquieu, *The Spirit of the Laws*, trans. Anne Cohler, Basia Miller, and Harold Stone (Cambridge: Cambridge University Press, 1989), book XXI, chap. 13; David Hume, "Of Commerce," in *Essays: Moral, Political, and Literary*, ed. Eugene F. Miller (Indianapolis: Liberty Classics, 1985), p. 259.

28. James Madison, *Papers of James Madison*, ed. Robert A. Rutland et al. (Charlottesville: University Press of Virginia, 1984), XIV:244–246. Madison had considered this question a few years earlier in a letter to Jefferson and had arrived at a somewhat more paradoxical position. Then, taking notice of the simplicity of manners fostered by a society composed largely of farmers, Madison wondered if there would be a market for the manufactured superfluities that might otherwise have provided employment for the surplus population,

and he saw little hope that mariners would absorb the excess population, especially when a "juster government" would reduce the need for soldiers to control the citizens (Madison to TJ, June 19, 1786, in *Correspondence of Jefferson and Madison* I:423–428).

29. TJ to John Jay, August 23, 1785, *WTJ* V:93–96.

30. Report on the Privileges and Restrictions on the Commerce of the United States in Foreign Countries, December 16, 1793, *Works* VIII:98–119.

31. First Annual Message, December 8, 1801, *Works* IX:321–342; TJ to President Madison, May 21, 1813, in *Correspondence of Jefferson and Madison* II: 1719–1721; also TJ to John Adams, May 27, 1813, in *Adams-Jefferson Letters,* pp. 323–325; TJ to James Monroe, January 1, 1815, *WTJ* XIV:226–230; TJ to Benjamin Austin, January 9, 1816, *WTJ* XIV:387–393.

32. "Answers to Demeusnier's First Queries," January 24, 1786, *Papers* X:11–20. For a general statement of Jefferson's views, see TJ to Elbridge Gerry, January 26, 1799, *WTJ* X:74–86; First Inaugural Address, March 4, 1801, *Works* IX:193–200.

33. TJ to Dr. Thomas Cooper, September 10, 1814, *WTJ* XIV:179–190. In his Eighth Annual Message, Jefferson sought to give greater power to Congress to produce a "uniform state of preparation" among the state militias, but his proposal failed; Eighth Annual Message, November 8, 1808, *Works* XI:56–72.

34. TJ to John Wayles Eppes, September 9, 1814, *Works* XI:422–426.

35. First Annual Message, December 8, 1801, *Works* IX:321–342; TJ to James Madison, June 29, 1812, in *Correspondence of Jefferson and Madison* II:1698–1699.

36. Alexis de Tocqueville, *Democracy in America,* ed. J. P. Mayer (Garden City, N.Y.: Doubleday, 1969), vol. I, pt. ii, chap. 6.

37. For a thoughtful reflection on the way in which the agrarian life shapes character, see Charles Fish, *In Good Hands: The Keeping of a Family Farm* (New York: Farrar, Straus and Giroux, 1995), esp. pp. 142–148.

38. See the useful literature review of recent economic history by Gordon Wood, "Inventing American Capitalism," *New York Review of Books,* June 9, 1994, pp. 44–49.

39. See especially TJ to Mary Jefferson, June 13, 1790, *Family Letters,* pp. 58–59; to Anne Cary Randolph, November 24, 1807, *Family Letters,* p. 316; and to Ellen Wayles Randolph, June 29, 1807, *Family Letters,* pp. 309–310.

40. *Notes,* Query XIX, p. 165; also TJ to William Short, November 28, 1814, *WTJ* XIV:211–218, but cf. TJ to Col. Charles Yancey, January 6, 1816, *WTJ* XIV:379–384. For the persistence of this view, see the 1853 essay by Henry Lester, "Man Made for Agriculture," in Fish, *In Good Hands,* pp. 186–194. For a discussion, see Matthews, *Radical Politics of Thomas Jefferson,* pp. 42–52; also, Leo Marx, *The Machine in the Garden: Technology and the Pastoral Ideal in America* (New York: Oxford University Press, 1964), chap. 3.

41. TJ to General George Washington, August 14, 1787, *WTJ* VI:274–278.

42. For a more extended discussion of this theme, see James Madison, "Fashion," *National Gazette,* March 20, 1792, in *Papers of James Madison* XIV:257–259. See also Daniel Vickers, "Competency and Competition: Economic Culture in Early America," *William and Mary Quarterly* 47 (January 1990): 3–29.

43. For this suggestion, I am indebted to Fish, *In Good Hands,* pp. 145–146.

44. Harry Jaffa, "The Virtue of a Nation of Cities: On the Jeffersonian Paradoxes," in *The Condition of Freedom* (Baltimore, Md.: Johns Hopkins University Press, 1975), p. 100.

45. *Notes,* Query XIX, p. 165; see also Madison, "Fashion."

46. TJ to John Jay, August 23, 1785, *WTJ* V:93–96.

47. TJ to Thomas Law, June 13, 1814, *WTJ* XIV:138–144.

48. TJ to Dr. Thomas Cooper, September 10, 1814, *WTJ* XIV:179–190.

49. Although Rahe is ultimately critical of the claims made by Jefferson on behalf of agrarian virtue, he nonetheless observes that in our own century, "those intent on establishing totalitarian tyranny" clearly understood that the spirit and independence of the farmer must be broken before complete political control can be established (*Republics,* 3:196).

50. TJ to James Madison, October 28, 1785, *Correspondence of Jefferson and Madison* I:389–391.

51. *Notes,* Query XIV, p. 133.

52. Ibid., pp. 133–134.

53. For further elaboration of this point and its applicability to farmers both north and south, see Fish, *In Good Hands,* esp. chap. 7, and Jane C. Nylander, *Our Own Snug Fireside: Images of the New England Home 1760–1860* (New York: Knopf, 1994), esp. chaps. 7 and 9.

54. *Papers* II:419–423; see also Lerner, "Jefferson's Pulse of Republican Reformation," esp. pp. 63–69.

55. See note 5.

56. *Notes,* Query XVIII, p. 163. It is telling that Jefferson used the word "commerce" to describe the relations between master and slave. On the vices of the South, see also TJ to Chastellux, September 2, 1785, *Papers* VIII:467–470, where Jefferson, writing to his French correspondent, echoes the argument of Montesquieu and attributes these vices solely to the effect of a warm climate. In this letter he remains silent about the institution of slavery. On the contradictory treatment of farmers in the *Notes,* see Peter Onuf, "The Scholars' Jefferson," *William and Mary Quarterly* 50 (October 1993): 682.

57. Aristotle, *Politics,* book VI, 1318bl 10–25, and cf. book VII, 1329al 20–25. For a superb discussion of this issue, see Darrell Dobbs, "Natural Right and the Problem of Aristotle's Defense of Slavery," *Journal of Politics* 56 (February 1994): 69–94.

58. On the power of the imagination to triumph over "hugely altered conditions, and also of a huge mass of negative fact," see the suggestive essay by Larry McMurtry, "How the West Was Won or Lost," *New Republic,* October 22, 1990, pp. 32–38. And consider especially McMurtry's assertion that historians "so rarely do justice to the quality of the imagination that constitutes part of the truth" (p. 37).

59. Jaffa, "Agrarian Virtue and Republican Freedom," p. 63.

60. For the moral economic argument, see James A. Henretta, "Families and Farms: *Mentalité* in Pre-Industrial America," *William and Mary Quarterly* 35 (January 1978): 3–32; and cf. Joyce Appleby, "The 'Agrarian Myth' in the Early Republic," reprinted in *Liberalism and Republicanism in the Historical Imagination* (Cambridge, Mass.: Harvard University Press, 1992), pp. 253–276. For a discussion of these two interpretations, see Wood, "Inventing American Capitalism."

61. McCoy, *Elusive Republic;* Albert O. Hirschman, *The Passions and the Interests* (Princeton, N.J.: Princeton University Press, 1977); Ralph Lerner, "Commerce and Character," in *The Thinking Revolutionary,* pp. 195–221; Jean Yarbrough, "The Constitution and Character: The Missing Critical Principle?"

in *To Form a More Perfect Union: The Critical Ideas of the Constitution*, ed. Herman Belz, Ronald Hoffman, and Peter J. Albert (Charlottesville: University Press of Virginia, 1992), pp. 217–249; James Q. Wilson, "Capitalism and Morality," *The Public Interest*, no. 121 (Fall 1995): 42–60; McClosky, "Bourgeois Virtue"; Sandel, *Democracy's Discontent*, esp. part 2, chap. 5.

62. Montesquieu, *Spirit of the Laws*, book XX, chap. 2, pp. 338–339; book V, chap. 6, p. 48. See also Anne Cohler, *Montesquieu's Comparative Politics and the Spirit of American Constitutionalism* (Lawrence: University Press of Kansas, 1988); and Thomas L. Pangle, *Montesquieu's Philosophy of Liberalism* (Chicago: University of Chicago Press, 1974).

63. David Hume, "Of Commerce," in *Essays*, p. 261.

64. Ibid., p. 259.

65. Ibid., p. 261.

66. David Hume, "Of Refinement in the Arts," in *Essays*, pp. 268–280. Still, even Hume recognized that the principle of commercial exchange could be carried too far, as evidenced by his distinction between "innocent" and "vicious luxury."

67. Antoine-Louis-Claude Destutt de Tracy, *A Commentary and Review of Montesquieu's Spirit of the Laws*, trans. Thomas Jefferson (New York: Burt Franklin, 1969), pp. 232–233. For a different analysis of the relation between Tracy and Jefferson, which argues that Jefferson was persuaded by Tracy to take a more positive view of commerce, see Joyce Appleby, "What Is Still American in Jefferson's Political Philosophy?" in *Liberalism and Republicanism*, pp. 291–319. I am more inclined to agree with Gordon Wood's suggestion that Jefferson did not fully comprehend the import of Tracy's argument, in Wood, *Radicalism of the American Revolution*, p. 338.

68. Tracy criticizes Smith for not sufficiently developing the connection between these two or between *The Wealth of Nations* and *The Theory of Moral Sentiments*.

69. For two contrasting views of Jefferson's pastoralism, see Douglas L. Wilson, "The American *Agricola:* Jefferson's Agrarianism and the Classical Tradition," *South Atlantic Quarterly* 80 (1981): 339–354; cf. Marx, *Machine in the Garden*, chap. 3.

70. TJ to the U.S. Minister to France (Robert R. Livingston), April 18, 1802, *WTJ* X:311–316.

71. TJ to William Johnson, October 27, 1822, *Works* XII:246–252. On Jefferson's own attempts at commercial farming, see TJ to John Taylor, December 29, 1794, *WTJ* XVIII:192–200: "I am for throwing the whole force of my husbandry on the wheat-field, because it is the only one which is to go to market to produce money."

72. TJ to Jean-Baptiste Say, February 1, 1804, *WTJ* XI:1–3.

73. Appleby, "'Agrarian Myth' in the Early Republic," p. 258. But as Lance Banning persuasively argues, Appleby uses the term so loosely that it covers those like Jefferson who favored nothing more than free exchange and those who favored more elaborate forms of capitalism based on "entrepreneurial activities and investment." See Lance Banning, "Jeffersonian Ideology Revisited: Liberal and Classical Ideas in the New American Republic," *William and Mary Quarterly*, 3rd ser., 48 (January 1986): 3–19, at p. 10 n. 24. For a different, but less persuasive, criticism of Appleby, which argues that Jefferson's political economy was noncapitalist, see Matthews, *Radical Politics of Thomas Jefferson*,

pp. 138–139. And, for a general discussion, see James T. Kloppenberg, "The Virtues of Liberalism: Christianity, Republicanism, and Ethics in Early American Political Discourse," *Journal of American History* 74 (1987): 9–33.

74. TJ to M. De Meusnier, April 29, 1795, *Works* VIII:173–176; TJ to John Adams, February 28, 1796, *Adams-Jefferson Letters*, pp. 259–260, and also October 28, 1813, *Adams-Jefferson Letters*, pp. 387–392. See also Tocqueville, *Democracy in America,* vol II, pt. 2, chap. 18.

75. *Notes,* Query XIX, p. 165.

76. Vickers, "Competency and Competition," esp. pp. 9–11. I am grateful to Richard Vernier, an independent scholar living in Chicago, for first having suggested this essay to me. My argument in this section draws heavily on Vickers's article.

77. For an extended discussion, see McCoy, *Elusive Republic.*

78. *Notes,* Query XXII, p. 174, and cf. Query XVII, p. 161. Although free trade and the pursuit of comparative advantage were Jefferson's first priorities, he signaled his willingness to retaliate against foreign restrictions and to have the state governments encourage those manufactures that were appropriate in his "Report on the Privileges and Restrictions on the Commerce of the United States in Foreign Countries," December 16, 1793, *Works* VIII:98–119.

79. TJ to Mr. Lithgow, January 4, 1805, *WTJ* XI:55–56.

80. TJ to John Adams, January 21, 1812, *Adams-Jefferson Letters,* pp. 290–292.

81. TJ to John Melish, January 13, 1813, *WTJ* XI:55–56; TJ to Eli Whitney, November 16, 1793, *Works* VIII:70–71; TJ to M. De Meusnier, April 29, 1795, *Works* VIII:173–176; also, Peterson, *TJ and the New Nation,* pp. 536–537, 938–941.

82. TJ to Mr. Lithgow, January 4, 1805, *WTJ* XI:55–56. Note also the shift in Jefferson's understanding of dependency. Although the artificer may still take orders from another and, if outside the family, remain "dependent" on customers, he is never reduced to subservience because there is a ready market for his goods. Moreover, if working for others should become too demeaning, the laborer can always leave and take up farming for himself. The availability of vacant lands serves as a safety valve to ensure that no worker need remain too dependent or exploited for long.

83. TJ to John Adams, January 21, 1812, *Adams-Jefferson Letters,* pp. 290–292; TJ to John Melish, January 13, 1813, *WTJ* XIII:206–213.

84. TJ to Charles Wilson Peale, cited in Peterson, *TJ and the New Nation,* pp. 940–941.

85. James Madison, Seventh Annual Message, December 5, 1815, in *The Writings of James Madison,* ed. Gaillard Hunt (New York: Putnam, 1908), VIII:335–344. See McCoy, *Elusive Republic,* chap. 10.

86. TJ to Charles Wilson Peale, cited in Peterson, *TJ and the New Nation,* pp. 940–941.

87. TJ to William Short, November 28, 1814, *WTJ* XIV:211–218.

88. TJ to Benjamin Austin, January 9, 1816, *WTJ* XIV:387–393; TJ to John Melish, January 13, 1813, *WTJ* XIII:206–213; Peterson, *TJ and the New Nation,* pp. 940–941.

89. TJ to William Crawford, June 20, 1816, *WTJ* XV:27–31; First Annual Message, December 8, 1801, *Works* IX:321–342.

90. TJ to Governor James Jay, April 7, 1809, *WTJ* XII:270–371.

91. TJ to William Crawford, June 20, 1816, *WTJ* XV:27–31; TJ to Governor James Jay, April 7, 1809, *WTJ* XII:270–371.

92. *Notes*, Query XIX, p. 165.

93. See especially Daniel Green, *To Colonize Eden: Land and Jeffersonian Democracy* (London: Gordon and Cremonesi, 1977), p. 4. Green is speaking of landed property in general, but the point also applies to farming: value "cannot entirely be measured in terms of money values, since the ownership of farmland or of a house adds more to a man's security, independence and freedom of action than anything else can."

94. See note 74. Although in his letter to M. De Meusnier, Jefferson declared that in America "every honest employment is deemed honorable," he is here comparing the social situation in America with that of France. In other contexts, he continued to insist that certain occupations must be discouraged because they were harmful to morals and character. See especially TJ to William Crawford, June 20, 1816, *WTJ* XV:27–31.

95. At first sight, this distinction may seem quaintly moralistic, but even in our own more advanced commercial society, makers of X-rated movies, "rap" singers, owners of legitimate gambling establishments, topless dancers, and "ambulance-chasing" lawyers, to name but a few "honest" jobs, are still not universally considered "honorable," despite the best efforts of their supporters to make them so.

96. Tocqueville, *Democracy in America*, vol. II, pt. ii, chap. 19; but cf. TJ to David Williams, November 14, 1803, *WTJ* X:428–431, where he does take note of the "general desire of men to live by their heads rather than their hands." It is, moreover, important to keep in mind that Tocqueville is speaking comparatively. By the standards of aristocratic France, there is considerably more mobility and speculation in America, but many farmers stayed in one place for generations and, though aware of their farms as an investment that *could* be sold, nevertheless declined to treat their land as a commodity. On this last point, see Fish, *In Good Hands*, pp. 124–132.

97. TJ to Dr. Benjamin Rush, September 23, 1800, *WTJ* X:173–176.

98. Daniel Bell, *The Cultural Contradictions of Capitalism* (New York: Basic Books, 1979); Irving Kristol, "When Virtue Loses All Her Loveliness," reprinted in *Two Cheers for Capitalism* (New York: Basic Books, 1978), pp. 239–253.

99. John Adams to TJ, December 21, 1819, in *Adams-Jefferson Letters,* pp. 550–551.

100. James Q. Wilson, "Capitalism and Morality," pp. 43–44. For criticisms across the political spectrum, see the writings of Christopher Lasch, Eugene Genovese, Jean Bethke Elshtain, Daniel Bell, and Irving Kristol.

101. Hamilton's actual words were "A national debt, if it is not excessive, will be to us a national blessing" (AH to Robert Morris, April 30, 1781, in *Papers of Alexander Hamilton*, ed. Harold C. Syrett [New York: Columbia University Press, 1961], II:604–635).

102. TJ to James Madison, September 6, 1789, in *Correspondence of Jefferson and Madison* I:631–636; TJ to John Wayles Eppes, June 24, 1813, *WTJ* XIII:269–279; TJ to Samuel Kercheval, July 12, 1816, *WTJ* XV:32–44. Consider Madison's original response to TJ, February 4, 1790, in *Correspondence of Jefferson and Madison* I:650–653, and cf. "Perpetual Peace," *National Gazette*, January 31, 1792, in *Papers of James Madison* XIV:206–209.

103. Second Annual Message, December 15, 1802, *Works* IX:406–415; TJ to

John Wayles Eppes, November 6, 1813, *WTJ* XIII:404–432. For illuminating discussions of these themes, see Herbert J. Sloan, "The Earth Belongs in Usufruct to the Living," in Onuf, *Jeffersonian Legacies,* pp. 281–315; Lance Banning, "'The Earth Belongs to the Living': Property and Public Debt in a Republic," in *Jefferson and Madison: Three Conversations* (Madison, Wis.: Madison House, 1995), pp. 27–55.

104. TJ to Samuel Kercheval, July 12, 1816, *WTJ* XV:32–44 (emphasis in original).

105. James Q. Wilson, "The Rediscovery of Character: Private Virtue and Public Policy," in *On Character* (Washington, D.C.: American Enterprise Institute, 1991), pp. 11–23, esp. 17–19.

106. For a different approach, see Lance Banning, who regards the return to more progressive rates of taxation beginning in 1990 as a sign of "our increasing consciousness of our responsibilities" (Banning, "'The Earth Belongs to the Living,'" pp. 47, 55).

107. TJ to John Taylor, May 28, 1816, *WTJ* XV:17–23; TJ to Col. Charles Yancey, January 6, 1816, *WTJ* XIV:379–384; TJ to Dr. Thomas Cooper, September 10, 1814, *WTJ* XIV:179–190; TJ to Dr. Thomas Cooper, January 16, 1814, *WTJ* XIV:54–63. For an extended and more dispassionate assessment of the banking situation, see TJ to John Wayles Eppes, November 6, 1813, *WTJ* XIII:404–432. The latter communication makes clear that, despite his opposition to banks, Jefferson preferred the National Bank to the even more irresponsible state banks and also favored a policy of hard currency, positions that set him apart from later populist critics. On the question of bankruptcy, see Notes on the Bankrupt Bill, December 1792, *Works* VII:193–194; TJ to Thomas Mann Randolph, December 21, 1792, *Papers* XXIV:774–775; TJ to John Francis Mercer, December 19, 1792, *WTJ* VIII:445–446. The Savings and Loan scandals of the 1980s, now estimated to have cost taxpayers more than $132 billion, testify to the continuing relevance of Jefferson's concerns regarding the strict regulation of banks. See James Sterngold, "For Some, It's Still a Wonderful Life," in News of the Week in Review, *New York Times,* December 8, 1996, p. 3.

108. TJ to Edward Rutledge, August 25, 1791, *WTJ* VIII:232–234; TJ to Colonel Charles Yancey, January 6, 1816, *WTJ* XIV:379–384. On the diversion of capital from useful investments, see TJ to Edmund Pendleton, July 24, 1791, *Works* VI:286–287; TJ to Abbe Salimankis, March 14, 1810, *WTJ* XII:379–380.

109. William A. Galston and David Wasserman "Gambling Away Our Moral Capital," *Public Interest,* no. 126 (Spring 1996): 58–71.

110. Marx, *Machine in the Garden,* pp. 146–150.

111. See the suggestive essay by Thomas C. Kohler, "Civic Virtue at Work: Unions as Seedbeds of the Civic Virtues," in *Seedbeds of Virtue: Sources of Competence, Character, and Citizenship in American Society,* ed. Mary Ann Glendon and David Blankenhorn (Lanham, Md.: Madison Books, 1995), pp.131–162. Also, Arendt's discussion of the workers' councils, in *On Revolution,* chap. 6.

112. TJ to Dr. Benjamin Rush, September 23, 1800, *WTJ* X:173–176.

113. Jaffa, "Agrarian Virtue and Republican Freedom" and "The Virtue of a Nation of Cities"; for a modest reassessment, see George F. Will, "Mr. Jefferson Comes to Town," *Public Interest,* no. 112 (Summer 1993): 50–59; Andrew Peyton Thomas, "The Death of Jeffersonian America?" *Weekly Standard,* August 26, 1996, pp. 26–29. Although it might be argued that much of what is wrong with our cities is the result of a characteristically Jeffersonian anti-urban

policy bias (e.g., highways and home mortgage subsidies), these have been *federal* policies. And in considering white flight, one has to consider as well the effect of *federal* court decisions mandating integration and busing.

114. Robert Kaplan, "Cities of Despair," *New York Times*, June 6, 1996, p. A29.

115. TJ to James Madison, December 20, 1787, in *Correspondence of Jefferson and Madison* I:511–515.

116. James Q. Wilson, "The Enduring Problem of Business Ethics," in *On Character*, pp. 139–148, at p. 148; also from the same volume, "The Rediscovery of Character," pp. 11–23; Irving Kristol, "Of Decadence and Tennis Flannels," in *Two Cheers for Capitalism*, pp. 234–238. For a more sustained treatment, see Myron Magnet, *The Dream and the Nightmare: The Sixties' Legacy to the Underclass* (New York: Morrow, 1993).

117. As Jefferson warned in the *Notes*, deep-rooted prejudice among whites, resentment and anger among blacks, and "natural" differences in intellect would keep the races eternally divided into warring parties. Not even this foremost representative of the Enlightenment could envision a biracial society. See Yarbrough, "Race and the Moral Foundations of the American Republic," 90–105. And as Douglas L. Wilson points out in a stinging critique of Conor Cruise O'Brien, Jefferson was hardly alone in seeing "no future for a multiracial society, something which had no precedent in history, particularly in a society made up of former masters and slaves" (Conor Cruise O'Brien, "Thomas Jefferson: Radical and Racist," *Atlantic Monthly*, October 1996, pp. 53–74; and Douglas L. Wilson, "Counter Points: Jefferson Scholar Douglas L. Wilson Responds to Conor Cruise O'Brien," *Atlantic Monthly On-Line*, http://www.TheAtlantic.com/atlantic/issues/96oct/obrien/response.htm).

118. *Notes*, Query XIV, pp. 142–143; Query XVIII, p. 163. TJ to Jared Sparks, February 4, 1824, *WTJ* XVI: 8–14.

119. Charles Murray, "The Coming White Underclass," *Wall Street Journal*, October 29, 1993, p. A14. See also Gertrude Himmelfarb, *The De-Moralization of Society* (New York: Knopf, 1995), esp. pp. 221–257.

120. James Q. Wilson, "Capitalism and Morality," pp. 52–55; David Brooks, "'Civil Society' and Its Discontents," *Weekly Standard*, February 5, 1996, pp. 18–21. Of course, many of the virtues Brooks admires can also be found in Jefferson, even if they are missing from the softer, more caring, "civil society" supporters.

121. Bell, *Cultural Contradictions of Capitalism*; Kristol, "When Virtue Loses All Her Loveliness"; Will, "Mr. Jefferson Comes to Town."

122. Even if there is a new kind of puritanism taking hold among the intellectual elite clustered principally in university towns and beautiful rural surroundings, this chic brand of self-denial is unlikely to reverse "the cultural contradictions of capitalism." See David Brooks, "The Rise of the Latte Town," *Weekly Standard*, September 15, 1997, pp. 17–22.

123. On the general right of individuals to choose their own occupations, see Thoughts on Lotteries, 1826, but cf. TJ to David Williams, November 14, *WTJ* X:428–431, on the responsibility of the government to try to influence such decisions.

124. For suggestive comments, see Eugene Genovese, *The Southern Tradition: The Achievement and Limitations of an American Conservative* (Cambridge, Mass.: Harvard University Press, 1994); Allan C. Carlson, *From Cottage to Work*

Station: The Family's Search for Harmony in an Industrial Age (San Francisco: Ignatius Press, 1993), esp. chap. 1; Christopher Lasch, *Women and the Common Life: Love, Marriage, and Feminism,* ed. Elisabeth Lasch–Quinn (New York: Norton, 1997).

125. Charles Murray, "Limiting Government and the Pursuit of Happiness," *Cornell Journal of Law and Public Policy* 4 (1995): 449–455. Still, it is difficult to predict how the technological revolution will affect the American character, and not all the changes may be for the better. As Andrew Peyton Thomas sensibly notes, it is too soon to tell whether rural life will change the character of these new transplants, or whether they will alter the character of rural life by bringing with them their libertarian and individualistic habits (see note 113).

126. TJ to Isaac McPherson, August 13, 1813, *WTJ* XIII:326–338. Unless otherwise noted, all quotations in the next two paragraphs are from this letter.

127. TJ to James Madison, September 6, 1789, in *Correspondence of Jefferson and Madison* I:631–636.

128. I do not, however, wish to suggest that Kames's understanding of property differs in any fundamental respect from Locke's, merely that their approach to these questions is different.

129. TJ, *Commonplace Book,* pp. 107–108; see also TJ to James Madison, September 6, 1789, in *Correspondence of Jefferson and Madison* I:631–636.

130. TJ to Du Pont de Nemours, April 24, 1816, *WTJ* XIV:487–493. Also, David N. Mayer, *The Constitutional Thought of Thomas Jefferson* (Charlottesville: University Press of Virginia, 1994), pp. 77–88.

131. See the discussion of Madison in Jennifer Nedelsky, *Private Property and the Limits of American Constitutionalism: The Madisonian Framework and Its Legacy* (Chicago: University of Chicago Press, 1990).

132. TJ to James Madison, October 28, 1785, in *Correspondence of Jefferson and Madison* I:389–391.

133. Aristotle, *Politics,* book I, chap. 9, 1257al–1258al.

134. For a full discussion of this point, see Hirschman, *Passions and the Interests.*

135. Locke, *Second Treatise,* chap. 5, para. 42; cf. Aristotle, *Politics,* book I, chap. 8, 1256al 1–1256bl 23; book II, chap. 5, 1263bl 1–14; *Ethics,* book II, 1107b5–15.

136. Smith, *Wealth of Nations,* pp. 358ff.

137. TJ, *Commonplace Book,* pp. 107–108.

138. TJ to James Madison, October 28, 1785, in *Correspondence of Jefferson and Madison* I:389–391. See also The Batture at New Orleans, July 31, 1810, where Jefferson observes, "He who plants fields keeps possession till he has gathered the produce, after which one has as good a right as another to occupy it. Government must be established, and laws provided, before lands can be separately appropriated, and their owner protected in his possession" (*WTJ* XVIII:1–132).

139. TJ to Maria Cosway, October 12, 1286, *WTJ* V:430–448.

140. Ibid.

141. *Notes,* Query XIV, p. 133.

142. TJ to Samuel Kercheval, January 15, 1810, *WTJ* XII:341–343.

143. TJ to Drs. Rogers and Slaughter, March 2, 1806, *WTJ* XI:92–93.

144. TJ to Michael Megear, May 29, 1823, *WTJ* XV:433–434.

145. TJ to Drs. Rogers and Slaughter, March 2, 1806, *WTJ* XI:92–93; also, TJ

to Charles Christian, March 21, 1812, *WTJ* XIII:134–135; see also *Notes*, Query XIV, p. 133, where Jefferson observes that it is only foreigners, "who have never obtained a settlement in any parish," who have been reduced to begging.

146. TJ to Drs. Rogers and Slaughter, March 2, 1806, *WTJ* XI:92–93.

147. Cf. Wills, who argues in *Inventing America* that Jefferson's view of property was far more "communitarian" and so presumably linked more with benevolence than with justice.

148. TJ to Bishop Henri Gregoire, February 25, 1809, *WTJ* XII:254–255.

149. TJ, *Autobiography*, in *Thomas Jefferson: Writings*, ed. Merrill Peterson (New York: Library of America, 1984), p. 39.

150. TJ, Bill to Enable Tenants in Fee Tail to Convey Their Land in Fee Simple, October 14, 1776, *Papers* I:560. Also, Locke, *Second Treatise*, chap. VI, para. 72–73.

151. TJ to James Madison, September 6, 1789, in *Correspondence of Jefferson and Madison* I:631–636; TJ to James Madison, October 28, 1785, in *Correspondence of Jefferson and Madison* I:389–391.

152. Matthews, *Radical Politics of Thomas Jefferson*; Wills, *Inventing America*.

153. TJ to James Madison, September 6, 1798, in *Correspondence of Jefferson and Madison* I:631–636.

154. *Papers* II:553–554. And see the useful discussion by Lerner in "Jefferson's Pulse of Republican Reformation," pp. 76–77.

155. James Madison to TJ, February 4, 1790, in *Correspondence of Jefferson and Madison* I:650–653.

156. Sloan, "The Earth Belongs in Usufruct to the Living," pp. 301–302.

157. Banning, " 'The Earth Belongs to the Living,' " n. 11, p. 50; Banning's emphasis.

158. TJ to James Madison, October 28, 1785, in *Correspondence of Jefferson and Madison* I:389–391.

159. TJ to William Carmichael, August 18, 1785, *WTJ* V:78–80. Jefferson's earlier proposal in his draft Constitution of 1776 to grant to every Virginia citizen who did not already possess it fifty acres of public land had already failed, and he was writing from Paris to encourage other means of broadly distributing property.

160. Prospectus on Political Economy, enclosed in TJ to Joseph Milligan, April 6, 1816, *WTJ* XIV:456–466.

161. Second Inaugural Address, March 4, 1805, *Works* X:127–136; Reply to Vermont Address, December 10, 1807, *WTJ* XVI:293–294.

162. TJ to Joseph Milligan, April 6, 1816, *WTJ* XIV:456–466; emphasis in original.

163. TJ to Monsieur Du Pont de Nemours, April 15, 1811, *WTJ* XIII:37–40.

164. TJ to Samuel Smith, 1823, *Works* XII:283–286. For Jefferson's opposition to an earlier proposed tax on pleasure horses, see TJ to Dr. George Gilmer, December 15, 1792, *WTJ* VIII:444–445.

165. TJ to Joseph Milligan, April 6, 1816, *WTJ* XIV:456–466.

166. Ibid.

167. TJ to Du Pont de Nemours, April 15, 1811, *WTJ* XIII:37–40; *Autobiography*, in Peterson, *Writings*, p. 44.

168. On this point, see TJ to Cornelius Camden Blatchly, October 21, 1822, *WTJ* XV:399–400.

169. TJ to Thomas Cooper, September 10, 1814, *WTJ* XIV:179–190.

170. TJ to Du Pont de Nemours, December 31, 1815, *WTJ* XIV:369–373.

171. TJ to Thomas Cooper, September 10, 1814, *WTJ* XIV:179–190.

172. TJ to John Adams, February 28, 1796, in *Adams-Jefferson Letters*, pp. 259–260.

173. See especially the treatment of Jefferson's ideas during the Progressive Era and the New Deal, where Jefferson's faith in the rights of the people was used by the philosopher John Dewey to justify "political action to bring about the equalization of economic conditions in order that the equal rights of all to free choice and free action be maintained," in Peterson, *Jeffersonian Image*, pp. 255–376, at p. 359.

174. TJ to John Wayles Eppes, November 6, 1813, *WTJ* XIII:404–432; TJ to William H. Crawford, June 20, 1816, *WTJ* XV:27–31.

175. For an interesting contemporary discussion, see Irving Kristol's comment on Bertrand de Jouvenal's *The Ethics of Redistribution* in Kristol, "Taxes, Poverty, and Equality," in *Two Cheers for Capitalism*, pp. 208–209.

Chapter 4. Civic Virtue, Statesmanship, and
Republican Self-Government

1. Aristotle, *Politics*, book I, chap. 2, 1253al 1–20; Cicero, *On the Commonwealth*, book I; also Hannah Arendt, *The Human Condition* (Chicago: University of Chicago Press, 1958), pp. 12–17; Paul Rahe, "The Primacy of Politics in Classical Greece," *American Historical Review* 89 (April 1984): 265–293.

2. Opinion on the Constitutionality of the Residence Bill, July 15, 1790, *WTJ* III:59–67.

3. TJ to John Adams, October 28, 1813, in *Adams-Jefferson Letters*, pp. 387–392; TJ to Major John Cartwright, June 5, 1824, *WTJ* XVI:42–52.

4. See especially Arendt in *On Revolution* and Pocock in *The Machiavellian Moment*; but cf. Diggins, who argues that because Jefferson was a liberal republican, his notion of virtue is "devoid of civic content" (*Lost Soul of American Politics*, p. 41).

5. For a more comprehensive discussion of the meaning and requirements of classical republicanism, see especially Pangle, *Spirit of Modern Republicanism*, and Rahe, *Republics*.

6. TJ to John Adams, December 10, 1819, *Adams-Jefferson Letters*, pp. 548–550. On the rejection of the Roman model, see TJ to Thomas Leiper, June 12, 1815, *WTJ* XIV:306–311; and *Notes*, Query XIII, pp. 128–129; for the inappropriateness of Sparta, see TJ to A. Coray, October 31, 1823, *WTJ* XV:480–490; on the primacy of citizenship, see Second Inaugural Address, March 4, 1805, *Works* X:127–136.

7. Eighth Annual Message, November 8, 1808, *Works* XI:56–72.

8. TJ to Edward Everett, 1824, *WTJ* XVI:20–22; Rockfish Gap Report, August 4, 1818, in Peterson, *Writings*, pp. 457–473. Both statements, however, are ambiguous: does Jefferson mean that these virtues do not develop spontaneously but require nurturing, or does he mean that they are conventional?

9. TJ to Samuel Kercheval, July 12, 1816, *WTJ* XV: 32–44; *Notes*, Query XIX, p. 165.

10. Klein, Brown, and Hench, *Republican Synthesis Revisited*.

11. On the way in which interest and pride combine, see Mansfield, *America's Constitutional Soul*, pp. 73–83.

12. See especially Felix Raab, *The English Face of Machiavelli: A Changing Interpretation, 1500–1700* (London: Routledge and K. Paul, 1964); Stourzh, *Alexander Hamilton*, pp. 30–37; Mayer, *Constitutional Thought of Thomas Jefferson*, pp. 297–302; Jean Yarbrough, "Republicanism Reconsidered: Some Thoughts on the Foundation and Preservation of Republican Government," *Review of Politics* 41 (January 1979): 61–95; but cf. Paul Rahe, who argues that Jefferson was influenced directly by the writings of the Florentine: "Thomas Jefferson's Machiavellian Political Science," *Review of Politics* 57 (Summer 1995): 449–481, and see also his discussion in *Republics*, 3:155–159.

13. TJ to Dr. Joseph Priestley, March 21, 1801, *Works* IX:216–219; TJ to William Green Munford, June 18, 1799, in Peterson, *Writings*, pp. 1063–1066; TJ to John Adams, June 15, 1813, in *Adams-Jefferson Letters*, pp. 331–333; Rockfish Gap Report, August 4, 1818, in Peterson, *Writings*, pp. 457–473.

14. *Notes*, Query XIV, p. 148.

15. Cf. Aristotle, *Politics*, book IV, chap. 1, 1289al 1–5, with TJ to Isaac Tiffany, August 26, 1816, *WTJ* XV:66.

16. TJ to John Adams, October 28, 1813, *Adams-Jefferson Letters*, pp. 387–392.

17. TJ to Monsieur D'Ivernois, February 6, 1795, *WTJ* IX:299.

18. *Notes*, Query XIV, p. 148.

19. *Notes*, Query XVII, p. 161, and *Autobiography*, in Peterson, *Writings*, p. 71.

20. TJ to Archibald Stuart, January 25, 1786, *Papers* IX:217–219; TJ to John Page, May 4, 1786, *Papers* IX:444–445.

21. Tocqueville, *Democracy in America*, vol. II, pt. 2, chaps. 2, 10. Also Mansfield, *America's Constitutional Soul*, chap. 13.

22. TJ to Colonel William Stephens Smith, November 13, 1787, *WTJ* VI:371–373; TJ to Thomas Pinckney, May 29, 1797, *Works* VIII:291–294. For Jefferson's earliest concerns about lethargy, see *Autobiography*, in Peterson, *Writings*, pp. 8–9.

23. TJ to F. A. VanderKemp, March 22, 1812, *WTJ* XIII:136.

24. TJ to Colonel Edward Carrington, January 16, 1787, *WTJ* VI:58.

25. Consider, in this context, Jefferson's prediction about future American corruption in *Notes*, Query XIII, p. 121. And see the discussion in Rahe, *Republics*, vol. 3, chap. 4.

26. *Anas*, in Peterson, *Writings*, p. 670.

27. Ibid., p. 671.

28. Ibid., p. 682; TJ to the President of the United States, May 23, 1792, *WTJ* VIII:341–349; TJ to the President of the United States, September 9, 1792, *Papers* XXIV:351–360.

29. TJ to Gideon Granger, August 13, 1800, *WTJ* X:167–168; TJ to William T. Barry, July 2, 1822, *WTJ* XV:388–390; TJ to the President of the United States, May 23, 1792, *WTJ* VIII:341–349.

30. TJ to Thomas McKean, February 19, 1803, *Works* IX:449–452; TJ to Moses Robinson, March 23, 1801, *WTJ* X:236–237; TJ to Elbridge Gerry, January 26, 1799, *WTJ* X:74–86.

31. First Annual Message, December 8, 1801, *Works* IX:321–342; Second Inaugural Address, March 4, 1805, *Works* X:127–136.

32. For a spirited defense of Hamilton that nevertheless confirms the extent of private speculation and stock manipulation, along with a withering

critique of Jefferson, see Forrest McDonald, *Alexander Hamilton: A Biography* (New York: Norton, [1979] 1982), esp. chaps. 10–11.

33. TJ to Samuel Kercheval, July 12, 1816, *WTJ* XV:39.

34. *Notes*, Query XIX, p. 165. Cf. Tocqueville, *Democracy in America*, vol. I, pt. II, chap. 9.

35. Niccolò Machiavelli, *The Prince and the Discourses* (New York: Modern Library, 1950), III, i; also Harvey C. Mansfield, *Machiavelli's New Modes and Orders* (Ithaca, N.Y.: Cornell University Press, 1979), and *Machiavelli's Virtue* (Chicago: University of Chicago Press, 1996).

36. Sowerby, *Catalogue of the Library of Thomas Jefferson*, III:22.

37. TJ to John Cartwright, June 5, 1824, *WTJ* XVI:42–52.

38. In this connection Jefferson recommended regular exercise with firearms to his nephew Peter Carr because, unlike other forms of recreation, it would stamp the mind with "boldness, enterprize, and independence," qualities essential to the character of free men. Armed citizens could then be organized into militia units, where they would stand as a warning to all potential tyrants and usurpers. See TJ to Peter Carr, August 19, 1785, *WTJ* V:82–87; TJ to Destutt de Tracy, January 26, 1811, *Works* XI:181–189. Also Joyce Lee Malcolm, *To Keep and Bear Arms: The Origin of an Anglo-American Right* (Cambridge, Mass.: Harvard University Press, 1994); Robert E. Shalhope, "The Ideological Origins of the Second Amendment," *Journal of American History* 69 (December 1982): 599–614; Don B. Kates, Jr., "Handgun Prohibition and the Original Meaning of the Second Amendment," *Michigan Law Review* 82 (November 1983): 204–273.

39. A Summary View of the Rights of British America, *Works* II:87.

40. TJ to James Madison, January 30, 1787, *Correspondence of Jefferson and Madison* I:460–464. For a more cautious assessment, see Lance Banning, "Public Spirit," in *Three Conversations*, pp. 57–99.

41. See the initial reaction of John Adams to TJ, November 30, 1786, *Adams-Jefferson Letters*, p. 156. Without approving the rebellion, Adams was not at first alarmed by it; TJ to John Adams, December 20, 1786, *Adams-Jefferson Letters*, pp. 157–158. And as Peter Onuf has recently noted in his review of Conor Cruise O'Brien's *The Long Affair: Thomas Jefferson and the French Revolution 1785–1800*, Jefferson was more inclined to support rebellion from a distance. He penned his comments on Shays's Rebellion from Paris and endorsed the French Revolution after he had returned to America (Peter Onuf, "Reconsidering an American Icon," *Washington Post Book World*, November 24, 1996).

42. TJ to Colonel Edward Carrington, January 16, 1787, *WTJ* VI:58.

43. Ibid.; TJ to Abigail Adams, February 22, 1787, in *Adams-Jefferson Letters*, pp. 172–173.

44. TJ to Abigail Adams, February 22, 1787, *Adams-Jefferson Letters*, pp. 172–173; TJ to James Madison, December 20, 1787, in *Correspondence of Jefferson and Madison* I:511–515; TJ to Col. William Stephens Smith, November 13, 1787, *WTJ* VI:371–373. For other letters approving the rebellion, see TJ to Ezra Stiles, December 24, 1786, *WTJ* VI:25–26; TJ to William Carmichael, December 26, 1786, *WTJ* VI:29–32. And see Rahe, "Thomas Jefferson's Machiavellian Political Science."

45. TJ to James Madison, January 30, 1787, in *Correspondence of Jefferson and Madison* I:460–464.

46. TJ to Colonel William Stephens Smith, November 13, 1787, *WTJ* VI:371–373.

47. TJ to James Madison, January 30, 1787, in *Correspondence of Jefferson and Madison* I:460–464.

48. Ibid.; TJ to Samuel Kercheval, July 12, 1816, *WTJ* XV:32–44.

49. TJ to James Madison, December 20, 1787, in *Correspondence of Jefferson and Madison* I:511–515.

50. TJ to Colonel William Stephens Smith, November 13, 1787, *WTJ* VI:371–373.

51. TJ to Robert R. Livingston, February 23, 1799, *WTJ* X:117–119.

52. Rahe, "Thomas Jefferson's Machiavellian Political Science"; Banning, "Public Spirit"; and for a one-sided caricature, O'Brien, "Thomas Jefferson: Radical and Racist," pp. 53–74.

53. See TJ to James Madison, December 28, 1794, in *Correspondence of Jefferson and Madison* II:866–868.

54. Kentucky Resolutions, November 16, 1798, in *Documents of American History*, ed. Henry Steele Commager (New York: Appleton, Century, Crofts, 1949), p. 181.

55. Wilson, "Counter Points."

56. Jefferson did not reveal himself to be the author of the published version of the Kentucky Resolutions until 1821. And it was not until 1834, eight years after his death, that his own more extreme version was made public. This suggests that Jefferson did not want his name associated with these more radical ideas. In this connection, see TJ to John C. Breckinridge, December 11, 1821, *Works* VIII:459–460; but cf. the discussion in Rahe, *Republics*, 3:150–152. Moreover, Jefferson could also counsel moderation in political disputes. See, for example, TJ to John Taylor, June 1, 1798, *WTJ* X:44–47.

57. TJ to Judge Spencer Roane, September 6, 1819, *Works* XII:135–140; TJ to Thomas Lomax, March 12, 1799, *Works* IX:62–64.

58. TJ to Joseph Priestley, March 2, 1801, *WTJ* X:227–230; TJ to Benjamin Waring, March 23, 1801, *WTJ* X:235–236; First Annual Message, December 8, 1801, *Works* IX:321–342; Eighth Annual Message, November 8, 1808, *Works* XI:56–72.

59. First Inaugural Address, March 4, 1801, *Works* IX:196.

60. TJ to the Republican Mechanics of Leesburg, March 29, 1809, *WTJ* XVI:352–353; also TJ to Governor Daniel D. Tompkins, February 24, 1809, *WTJ* XVI:341–342.

61. That Jefferson appreciated these qualities from the beginning, see his respectful account of the civic virtue of Virginians during the colonial and revolutionary eras in *Notes*, Query XIII. For a perceptive discussion, see Jack P. Greene, "The Intellectual Reconstruction of Virginia in the Age of Jefferson," in Onuf, *Jeffersonian Legacies*, p. 232. That he continued to hold them until the end, TJ to Judge William Johnson, June 12, 1823, *WTJ* XV:439–452.

62. Reply to Public Address, General Assembly of Virginia, February 16, 1809, *WTJ* XVI:333–334; Eighth Annual Message, *Works* XI:56–72, and see notes 58 and 59.

63. TJ to William Branch Giles, December 26, 1825, *WTJ* XVI:146–151; TJ to Judge William Johnson, June 12, 1823, *WTJ* XV:439–452; The Solemn Declaration and Protest of the Commonwealth of Virginia, on the Principles of the Constitution of the United States of America, and on the Violations of them, December 1825 (unpublished), *WTJ* XVII:442–448, and cf. the discussion in Rahe, *Republics*, 3:150–152.

64. See especially his enthusiastic support for the French Revolution even in its most violent phases (TJ to Abigail Adams, February 22, 1787, *Adams-Jefferson Letters,* pp. 172–173; TJ to Diodati, August 3, 1789, *Papers* XV:325–327; and TJ to William Short, January 3, 1793, *WTJ* IX:9–13). Merrill Peterson suggests that Jefferson was convinced that the fate of the American experiment was somehow tied to the success of the French Revolution. See Merrill Peterson, *Adams and Jefferson: A Revolutionary Dialogue* (Athens: University of Georgia Press, 1976), pp. 46–54; and also TJ to George Mason, February 4, 1791, *Papers* IX:241–243.

65. Cf. the discussion of civic virtue in Pangle and Pangle, *Learning of Liberty,* chap. 6, which rightly emphasizes jealousy and armed resistance but errs in suggesting that this was the sum total of Jefferson's understanding of civic virtue. They fault him for failing to teach citizens obedience to the law or sober expectations about what politics can achieve.

66. *Notes,* Query XIII, p. 129.

67. *Notes,* Appendix 2, p. 221.

68. TJ to James Madison, December 20, 1787; July 31, 1788, *Correspondence of Jefferson and Madison* I:511–515, I:543–546; TJ to Edward Carrington, May 27, 1788, *WTJ* VII:36–39; TJ to T. Lee Shippen, June 19, 1788, *WTJ* VII:52–54; TJ to Colonel William Stephens Smith, February 2, 1788, *Papers* XII:557–559.

69. TJ to Comte de Moustier, May 17, 1788, *Papers* XIII:173–176; TJ to John Brown, May 26, 1788, *WTJ* VII:23–26.

70. TJ to James Madison, September 6, 1789, *Correspondence of Jefferson and Madison* I:631–636. See also Sloan, "The Earth Belongs in Usufruct to the Living," pp. 281–315; Banning, " 'The Earth Belongs to the Living,' " pp. 27–55. Nevertheless, the closing paragraph of Jefferson's Bill for Establishing Religious Freedom suggests that from a moral, as opposed to a legal, perspective, succeeding generations are bound to respect the permanent and unchanging rights of man (*Papers* II:545–553, at pp. 546–547).

71. TJ to Samuel Kercheval, July 12, 1816, *WTJ* XV:32–44; TJ to Major John Cartwright, June 5, 1824, *WTJ* XVI:42–52; TJ to Thomas Earle, September 24, 1823, *WTJ* XV:470–471.

72. For critical appraisals, see Rahe, *Republics,* 3:130–131; Mansfield, *America's Constitutional Soul,* pp. 180–181; *Correspondence of Jefferson and Madison* I:640–642. For more sympathetic readings see Sloan, "The Earth Belongs in Usufruct to the Living," pp. 281–315; Banning, " 'The Earth Belongs to the Living,' " pp. 27–55. But note that Sloan and Banning focus on the problem of burdening future generations with debt, not remaking the Constitution every generation.

73. Alexander Hamilton, James Madison, and John Jay, *The Federalist Papers,* ed. Jacob E. Cooke (Middletown, Conn.: Wesleyan University Press, 1961), no. 49; for the second of these objections, see also no. 37.

74. James Madison to TJ, February 4, 1790, in *Correspondence of Jefferson and Madison* I:650–653.

75. TJ to Samuel Kercheval, July 12, 1816, *WTJ* XV:32–44; Rockfish Gap Report, August 4, 1818, in Peterson, *Writings,* pp. 457–473.

76. TJ to Samuel Kercheval, July 12, 1816, *WTJ* XV:32–44. On Jefferson's own moderation in revising the laws of Virginia after Independence, see *Autobiography,* in Peterson, *Writings,* pp. 38–39.

77. James Madison to TJ, February 4, 1790, in *Correspondence of Jefferson and*

Madison I:650–653. But cf. TJ to Thomas Earle, September 24, 1823, *WTJ* XV:470–471, where Jefferson finally acknowledges the idea of implied assent.

78. Sixth Annual Message to Congress, December 2, 1806, *Works* X:302–320; TJ to William T. Barry, July 2, 1822, *WTJ* XV:388–390; TJ to Robert J. Garnett, February 14, 1824, *WTJ* XVI:14–16; but cf. TJ to Jared Sparks, February 4, 1824, *Works* XII:334–339, where Jefferson recommends both a "liberal construction" of the Constitution and a constitutional amendment to pay for the emancipation and expatriation of slaves.

79. TJ to Wilson C. Nicholas, September 7, 1803, *WTJ* X:417–420; TJ to William Charles Jarvis, September 28, 1820, *WTJ* XV:276–279; TJ to Judge William Johnson, June 12, 1823, *WTJ* XV:439–452. Although Jefferson's insistence that the people must be "as independent of the one preceding, as that was of all which had gone before" bears a superficial resemblance to the "living constitution" argument expounded by Justice Brennan, the two are radically different. According to Jefferson, only the people, acting in their sovereign capacity, can alter the Constitution. Moreover, Jefferson does not believe that the Constitution must keep pace with a historically evolving conception of rights. For Jefferson, the rights of man are immutable and unchangeable; they are rooted in a permanent understanding of human nature. Under changing political conditions, powers may have to be expanded to secure these rights, but the rights themselves are fixed. Finally, Jefferson's own list of amendments suggests that in most cases it is not the expansion of powers but their redistribution that will be the object of constitutional reform. See also Mayer, *Constitutional Thought of Thomas Jefferson*, pp. 313 ff.; Sloan, "The Earth Belongs in Usufruct to the Living," pp. 281–315. For a history of the amendment process, see David E. Kyvig, *Explicit and Authentic Acts: Amending the U.S. Constitution 1776–1995* (Lawrence: University Press of Kansas, 1996).

80. See especially the recent debate over how best to respond to judicial usurpation and restore self-government organized by Richard John Neuhaus in *First Things*, no. 67 (November 1996): 18–42, and further comments in January 1997 issue.

81. TJ to Spencer Roane, September 6, 1819, *WTJ* XV:212–216.

82. TJ to Nathaniel Macon, November 21, 1821, *WTJ* XV:341.

83. Mansfield, *Machiavelli's Virtue*, p. 85. Still, as Gordon Wood points out, Jefferson's defense of party division is a far cry from the two-party system that gradually began to emerge during the Jacksonian era. For Jefferson, the Federalists were never a legitimate political party, but the enemy of republican government. See Gordon Wood, "Politics Without Party," *New York Review of Books*, October 11, 1984, pp. 18–21.

84. For this last point, see Marc Landy and Sidney Milkis, *Presidential Greatness* (New York: Free Press, forthcoming), chap. 3.

85. TJ to William T. Barry, July 2, 1822, *WTJ* XV:388–390 (emphasis added); also TJ to William Branch Giles, December 31, 1795, *Works* VIII:201–204; TJ to John Taylor, June 1, 1798, *WTJ* X:44–47.

86. TJ to Edward Livingston, March 25, 1825, *WTJ* XVI:112–117; TJ to Spencer Roane, March 19, 1821, *Works* XII:201–202.

87. TJ to P. S. Du Pont de Nemours, April 24, 1816, *WTJ* XIV:487–493; TJ to Samuel Kercheval, July 12, 1816, *WTJ* XV:32–44.

88. TJ to Samuel Kercheval, July 12, 1816, *WTJ* XV:32–44.

89. TJ to John Taylor, May 28, 1816, *WTJ* XV:17–23.

90. TJ to Edmund Pendleton, August 26, 1776, *Papers* II:507–508; but cf. TJ to Samuel Kercheval, July 12, 1816, *WTJ* XV:32–44.

91. Draft Constitution for Virginia, 1776, *Papers* II:337–364.

92. TJ to John Taylor, May 28, 1816, *WTJ* XV:17–23.

93. TJ to Samuel Kercheval, July 12, 1816, *WTJ* XV:32–44.

94. TJ to Robert J. Garnett, February 14, 1824, *WTJ* XVI:14–16. In this letter Jefferson mysteriously omits all reference to the judiciary and recommends instead amending the Constitution to give Congress power over internal improvement.

95. TJ to William Barry, July 2, 1822, *WTJ* XV:388–390; TJ to Judge William Johnson, March 4, 1823, *WTJ* XV:419–423; and cf. TJ to Samuel Kercheval, July 12, 1816, *WTJ* XV:32–44, where TJ flirts with the idea of making judges elective.

96. TJ to John Taylor, November 26, 1798, *Works* VIII:479–483.

97. TJ to Robert J. Garnett, February 14, 1824, *WTJ* XVI:14–16.

98. For the best discussion of the way in which populism is at war with constitutional government, see Mansfield, *America's Constitutional Soul*, chaps. 2, 13, 14.

99. TJ to Major John Cartwright, June 5, 1824, *WTJ* XVI:42–52. In this letter, Jefferson suggested two methods by which bicameralism in the state legislatures might be reformed so as to accord with natural right: "Either by requiring a greater age in one of the bodies, or by electing a proper number of representatives of persons, dividing them by lots into two chambers, and renewing the divisions at frequent intervals."

100. TJ to Joseph C. Cabell, February 2, 1816, *WTJ* XIV:417–423; *Autobiography*, in Peterson, *Writings*, pp. 74–75.

101. TJ to Judge William Johnson, June 12, 1823, *WTJ* XV:439–452.

102. TJ to Joseph C. Cabell, February 2, 1816, *WTJ* XIV:417–423; for a criticism of centralization in France and a defense of federalism, see also TJ to Destutt de Tracy, January 26, 1811, *WTJ* XIII:13–21. See also Arendt, *On Revolution*, pp. 252–259.

103. Tocqueville, *Democracy in America,* vol. II, bk. iv, chap. 7; and see the discussion in Mansfield, *America's Constitutional Soul*, pp. 189–192.

104. For a discussion of this point, see Arendt, *On Revolution*, pp. 122–123, 236–239.

105. Bill for the More General Diffusion of Knowledge, 1779, *Works* II:414–426. Even as he defended Shays's Rebellion, Jefferson held that the way to prevent such "irregular interpositions" was to inform the people (TJ to Edward Carrington, January 16, 1787, *WTJ* VI:58).

106. TJ to John Norvell, June 14, 1807, *Works* X:415–419.

107. *Notes*, Query 14, p. 148.

108. TJ to Robert Skipwith, August 3, 1771, *WTJ* IV:237–240.

109. *Notes*, Query XIV, p. 147. In 1785, Jefferson had not yet discovered the sublime morality of true Christian (i.e., Unitarian) principles.

110. *Notes*, Query XIV, p. 147.

111. Rockfish Gap Report, August 4, 1818, in Peterson, *Writings*, pp. 457–473.

112. For Jefferson's changing view of the role of newspapers in enlightening and then deceiving the people, see TJ to Edward Carrington, January 16, 1787, *WTJ* VI:55–59; TJ to Thomas Seymour, February 11, 1807, *Works*

X:366–369; but cf. TJ to John Norvell, June 14, 1807. *Works* X:415–419. And see the discussion in Banning, "Public Spirit," pp. 69–70.

113. TJ to Robert Skipwith, August 3, 1771, *WTJ* IV:237–240; TJ to Peter Carr, August 19, 1785, *WTJ* V:82–87; TJ to Thomas Mann Randolph, Jr., August 27, 1786, *Works* V:174–179; TJ to John Norvell, June 14, 1807, *Works* X:415–419; TJ to Nathaniel Burwell, Esq., March 14, 1818, *WTJ* XV:165–168.

114. An Act for Establishing Elementary Schools, September 9, 1817, in *The Complete Jefferson*, ed. Saul K. Padover (New York: Duell, Sloan & Pearce, 1943), pp. 1072–1076; TJ to Chevalier de Onis, April 28, 1814, *WTJ* XIV:129–131; TJ to Du Pont de Nemours, April 24, 1816, *WTJ* XIV:487–493.

115. Rockfish Gap Report, August 4, 1818, in Peterson, *Writings*, pp. 457–473; Arendt, *On Revolution*, p. 62.

116. TJ to Nathaniel Burwell, Esq., March 14, 1818, *WTJ* XV:165–168.

117. See especially Frederick Rudolph, ed., *Essays on Education in the Early Republic* (Cambridge, Mass.: Harvard University Press, 1965); for a useful discussion, see Pangle and Pangle, *Learning of Liberty*, pp. 101–105.

118. Christopher Lasch, "Bourgeois Domesticity, the Revolt Against Patriarchy, and the Attack on Fashion," in Lasch-Quinn, *Women and the Common Life*, pp. 67–89.

119. TJ to Robert Skipwith, August 3, 1771, *WTJ* IV:237–240.

120. TJ to Nathaniel Burwell, Esq., March 14, 1818, *WTJ* XV:165–168.

121. Ibid.

122. Jefferson exhorted both his daughter Martha and his granddaughter Anne Cary Randolph to study history (TJ to Martha Jefferson, March 28, 1787; TJ to Anne Cary Randolph, January 9, 1804, in *Family Letters*, pp. 34–36, 251).

123. Hume, *Essays*, pp. 563–564.

124. TJ to Samuel Kercheval, July 12, 1816, *WTJ* XV:32–44.

125. TJ to Albert Gallatin, January 13, 1807, *Works* X:339–340.

126. TJ to Nathaniel Burwell, Esq., March, 14, 1818, *WTJ* XVI:165–168.

127. Susan R. Stein, *The Worlds of Thomas Jefferson at Monticello* (New York: Harry N. Abrams Publishers, in association with the Thomas Jefferson Memorial Foundation, 1993), pp. 94–100, esp. p. 98. And see also TJ to Anne Cary Randolph, January 9, 1804, in *Family Letters*, p. 251.

128. For a discussion of "republican mothers," see Linda Kerber, *Women of the Republic: Intellect and Ideology in Revolutionary America* (New York: Norton, 1986); for "republican wives," see Jan Lewis, "The Blessings of Domestic Society," in Onuf, *Jeffersonian Legacies*, esp. pp. 134–136; also Rhys Isaac, "The First Monticello," in Onuf, *Jeffersonian Legacies*, pp. 77–108.

129. Lasch, "Bourgeois Domesticity."

130. In his discussion of the treatment of women among the Indians, Jefferson observes that every barbarous society mistreats its weaker members. The crucial difference between barbarism and civilization is that the latter compels those who are physically stronger to subdue their selfish passions and respect the rights of those who are weaker. Only a civilized society reinforces the moral impulse to protect the weak and so secures the equal rights of women (*Notes*, Query VI, p. 60; TJ to John H. Pleasants, April 19, 1824, *WTJ* XVI:26–30).

131. TJ to Mrs. William Bingham, May 11, 1788, *WTJ* V:390–391.

132. Tocqueville, *Democracy in America*, vol. II, pt. iii, chap. 8–12. For important discussions of Tocqueville on women, see Delba Winthrop, "Tocqueville's American Woman and the True Conception of Democratic Progess," *Political*

Theory 14 (May 1986): 239–261; F. L. Morton, "Sexual Equality and the Family in Tocqueville's *Democracy in America*," *Canadian Journal of Political Science* 17 (June 1984): 309–324; William Mathie, "God, Woman, and Morality: The Democratic Family in the New Political Science of Alexis de Tocqueville," *Review of Politics* 57 (Winter 1995): 7–30.

133. TJ to Charles Bellini, September 30, 1785, *WTJ* V:151–154; TJ to John Bannister, Jr., October 15, 1785, *WTJ* V:185–188; TJ to George Washington, December 4, 1788, *WTJ* VII:223–231.

134. TJ to Joseph C. Cabell, February 2, 1816, *WTJ* XIV:417–423.

135. *Notes*, Query XIV, p. 148.

136. TJ to Joseph C. Cabell, January 17, 1814, *WTJ* XIV:67–70.

137. TJ to Joseph C. Cabell, February 2, 1816, *WTJ* XIV:417–423; TJ to John Tyler, May 26, 1810, *WTJ* XII:391–394.

138. Response to the Citizens of Albemarle, February 12, 1790, *Papers* XVI:178–179; TJ to Richard Price, February 1, 1785, *Papers* VII:630–631. For TJ's most critical comment on the New England townships in delivering the 1796 election to Adams, see TJ to James Madison, January 1, 1797, in *Correspondence of Jefferson and Madison* II:952–955.

139. TJ to John Taylor, May 28, 1816, *WTJ* XV:17–23.

140. Tocqueville, *Democracy in America*, vol. II, part ii, chap. 4.

141. TJ to Major John Cartwright, June 5, 1824, *WTJ* XVI:42–52.

142. TJ to John Adams, October 28, 1813, *Adams-Jefferson Letters*, pp. 387–392; TJ to Joseph Cabell, February 2, 1816, *WTJ* XIV:417–423; TJ to Samuel Kercheval, July 12, 1816, *WTJ* XV:32–44; TJ to John Cartwright, June 5, 1824, *WTJ* XVI:42–52.

143. TJ to Joseph C. Cabell, February 2, 1816, *WTJ* XIV:417–423.

144. TJ to Joseph C. Cabell, November 28, 1820, *WTJ* XV:289–294.

145. TJ to Judge William Johnson, June 12, 1823, *WTJ* XV:439–452.

146. TJ to Samuel Kercheval, July 12, 1816, *WTJ* XV:32–44.

147. Note the parallel between Jefferson's solution and that proposed by Tocqueville, who agrees that the cure for the defects of democracy is more liberty, not less (Tocqueville, *Democracy in America*, vol. II, pt. ii, chap. 4).

148. TJ to Joseph C. Cabell, February 2, 1816, *WTJ* XIV:417–423.

149. Though, here again, Tocqueville's analysis of the relation between constitutional forms and local self-government is more complex than Jefferson's.

150. TJ to Samuel Kercheval, July 12, 1816, *WTJ* XV:32–44; TJ to John Cartwright, June 5, 1824, *WTJ* XVI:42–52.

151. I put aside the larger question, later posed by Stephen Douglas, of whether the natural right to self-government includes the right of establishing a government that enslaves others. For Jefferson, it clearly does not. All our natural rights, including the right of self-government, flow from our fundamental human equality. And this equality requires that all governments be established by the consent of the governed. Jefferson's opposition to the Missouri Compromise is not a defense of the absolute right of self-government but, on the contrary, a misguided attempt to encourage the self-governing states of the South to bring their constitutions into accord with the principles of the Declaration by making it in their interest voluntarily to abolish slavery.

152. *Notes*, Query XIV, p. 138; see also Yarbrough, "Race and the Moral Foundations of the American Republic."

153. TJ to Dr. Benjamin Rush, April 21, 1803, *WTJ* X:379–385; TJ to John Taylor, June 4, 1798, *WTJ* X:44–47.

154. TJ to John Taylor, June 4, 1798, *WTJ* X:44–47.

155. For a discussion of the tyranny of the majority in this broader sense, see Tocqueville, *Democracy in America*, vol. I, pt. ii, chap. 7.

156. Consider in this regard, the question posed by Eugene Genovese: "Who on the left is willing to show the slightest respect for the collective will of communities that choose to restrict abortion, resist affirmative action, oppose gay and lesbian rights, and provide religious instruction in their schools?" See Eugene Genovese, "Eugene Rivers's Challenge: A Response," *Boston Review* 18, no. 5 (October/November 1993): 34–36.

157. On the importance of community, see especially Glendon and Blankenhorn, *Seedbeds of Virtue*; Elshtain, *Democracy on Trial*; and Genovese, *The Southern Tradition*; Sandel, *Democracy's Discontent*.

158. Perhaps nowhere are the two sides of this dilemma clearer than in Tocqueville's discussion of majority tyranny in vol. I of *Democracy in America*, and his changed emphasis in vol. II, pt. iv, chap. 6.

159. *Notes*, Query XIV, p. 146.

160. See Tocqueville, *Democracy in America*, vol. I, pt. i, chap. 3.

161. Although Jefferson does in passing acknowledge that "in every government on earth is some trace of weakness, some germ of corruption and degeneracy, which cunning will discover, and wickedness insensibly open, cultivate, and improve," his proposals for education assume that the virtues of the best will be directed toward serving the people (*Notes*, Query XIV, p. 148).

162. TJ to John Adams, October 28, 1813, in *Adams-Jefferson Letters*, pp. 387–392.

163. TJ to Samuel Kercheval, September 5, 1816, *WTJ* XV:70–73; TJ to Samuel Kercheval, July 12, 1816, *WTJ* XV:32–44.

164. Arendt, *On Revolution*, pp. 115, 234–242; and, to a lesser extent, Matthews, *Radical Politics of Thomas Jefferson*, p. 83

165. TJ to Samuel Kercheval, July 12, 1816, *WTJ* XV:32–44.

166. Tocqueville, *Democracy in America*, vol. II, pt. ii, chap. 4.

167. See especially O'Brien, "Thomas Jefferson: Radical and Racist."

168. Rahe, *Republics*, 3:201. Rahe emphasizes the interested aspect of modern virtue, while minimizing Mansfield's argument about the way in which pride ennobles interest. See also the fine discussion in Lance Banning, "Some Second Thoughts on 'Virtue' and the Course of Revolutionary Thinking," in *Conceptual Change and the Constitution*, ed. Terrence Ball and J. G. A. Pocock (Lawrence: University Press of Kansas, 1988), pp. 194–212.

169. Tocqueville, *Democracy in America*, vol. II, pt. ii, chap. 8; see also Banning, "Public Spirit," pp. 73–75.

170. Rockfish Gap Report, August 4, 1818, in Peterson, *Writings*, pp. 457–473.

171. TJ to John Adams, October 28, 1813, in *Adams-Jefferson Letters*, pp. 387–392.

172. "Conversations with Aaron Burr," *Anas*, in Peterson, *Writings*, pp. 690–696.

173. *Anas*, in Peterson, *Writings*, p. 671.

174. TJ to Marquis de Lafayette, November 4, 1823, *Works* XII:321–325; TJ

to James Sullivan, February 9, 1797, WTJ IX:376–379. See also "Introduction," in Harvey C. Mansfield, Jr., ed., *Thomas Jefferson: Selected Writings* (Arlington Heights, Ill.: AHM, 1979).

175. TJ to Dr. Walter Jones, January 2, 1814, *WTJ* XIV:46–52.

176. Rockfish Gap Report, August 4, 1818, in Peterson, *Writings,* pp. 457–473.

177. Ibid. For a fuller discussion of Jefferson's educational philosophy, see Pangle and Pangle, *Learning of Liberty,* and Brann, *Paradoxes of Education.*

178. Minutes of the Board of Visitors of the University of Virginia, March 4, 1825, *WTJ* XIX:459–462.

179. TJ to James Madison, February 17, 1826, in *Correspondence of Jefferson and Madison* III:1964–1967; TJ to Joseph C. Cabell, February 3, 1825, *Works* XII:455–459; Minutes of the Board of Visitors of the University of Virginia, March 4, 1825, *WTJ* XIX:459–462.

180. David P. Peeler, "Thomas Jefferson's Nursery of Republican Patriots: The University of Virginia," *Journal of Church and State* 28 (Winter 1986): 79–93; Lorraine Smith Pangle, "Liberal Education and Politics: Lessons from the American Founding," *Academic Questions* 8 (Winter 1994–95): 33–44. And from the perspective of the civil libertarian, see Leonard Levy, *Jefferson and Civil Liberties: The Darker Side* (Cambridge, Mass.: Belknap Press of Harvard University Press, 1963), pp. 94–96, 100–101.

181. On Hume and Montesquieu, see TJ to William Duane, August 12, 1810, *WTJ* XII:404–409; on Blackstone, TJ to John Tyler, May 26, 1810, *Works* XI:141–143. While students could still read these works privately, Jefferson preferred "corrected" versions of Hume and Montesquieu.

182. Jaffa, *Crisis of the House Divided,* chap. IX.

183. TJ to William Roscoe, December 27, 1820, *WTJ* XV:302–304; also Second Inaugural Address, March 4, 1805, *Works* X:127–136.

184. TJ to the President of the United States, September 9, 1792, *Papers* XXIV:351–360. This is what Ralph Ketcham refers to as Jefferson's "muted partisanship." It is, however, only the president who claims to be disinterested. Legislators, even republican legislators, are expected to have interests, though they are not to pursue these interests at the expense of the people. But Ketcham goes too far when he asserts that Jefferson's attacks on Hamilton reveal his nonpartisan conception of executive leadership (Ralph Ketcham, *Presidents Above Party: The First American Presidency, 1789–1829* [Chapel Hill: University of North Carolina Press, 1984], pp. 102–103, 111).

185. TJ to J. Garland Jefferson, January 25, 1810, *WTJ* XII:353–355. For a more extended analysis, see Mansfield, "Introduction," pp. xxvii–xlii. For a discussion of the partisan nature of gossip in circulating accounts of virtue and vice in Federalist and Republican political circles, see Joanne B. Freeman, "Slander, Poison, Whispers and Fame: Jefferson's 'Anas' and Political Gossip in the Early Republic," *Journal of the Early Republic* 15 (Spring 19951): 25–57.

186. See especially the revealing letter to Chastellux, September 2, 1785, *Papers* VIII:467–470, where Jefferson is surprised to find that Chastellux believes the Southerners "attached to their interest," when Jefferson had always regarded them as "disinterested," in the sense of being "so careless of their interests, so thoughtless in their expences [*sic*], and in all their transactions of business." Jefferson mistakenly identifies interests with the commercial North and so fails to see the sense in which the South, too, has interests.

See also Michael Leinesch, "Thomas Jefferson and the American Democratic Experience: The Origins of the Partisan Press, Popular Political Parties, and Public Opinion," in Onuf, *Jeffersonian Legacies*, pp. 316–339.

187. TJ to John B. Colvin, September 20, 1810, *Works* XI:146–150.

188. Though, as Levy points out, in the Embargo Crisis this is precisely what Jefferson failed to do. He never adequately explained the policy to those who would be most affected by it, and he showed no sympathy for the sacrifices he demanded of them (Levy, *Jefferson and Civil Liberties*, chap. 5).

189. *Notes*, Query XVIII, p. 162; TJ to Edward Coles, August 25, 1814, *Works* XI:416–420; John Chester Miller, *The Wolf by the Ears: Thomas Jefferson and Slavery* (New York: Free Press, 1977).

190. As a result, Madison, "with more consistency and more success," practiced a more genuine "public spirit," in Banning, "Public Spirit," pp. 75–88.

191. TJ to the President of the United States (George Washington), May 23, 1792, *WTJ* VIII:341–349; TJ to P. S. Du Pont de Nemours, January 18, 1802, in Peterson, *Writings*, pp. 1099–1101.

192. TJ to Chastellux, September 2, 1785, *Papers* VIII:467–470; cf. Aristotle, *Politics*, book VII, chap. 7, 1328al 5–9; Thomas Hobbes, *Leviathan*, ed. Michael Oakeshott (New York: Collier Books, 1962), chap. 17, p. 129; Lincoln, "The Perpetuation of Our Political Institutions: Address Before the Young Men's Lyceum of Springfield, Illinois," January 27, 1838, pp. 76–85.

193. He is willing to grant that the "strongest feature" of Washington's character was prudence, which he equates with circumspection or "never acting until every circumstance, every consideration, was maturely weighed" (TJ to Dr. Walter Jones, January 2, 1814, *WTJ* XIV:46–52).

194. *Anas*, in Peterson, *Writings*, p. 673.

195. By contrast, Robert Bork argues that the principles of the Declaration are inherently defective. The belief that all human beings are endowed with equal rights necessarily gives rise to extravagant expectations that make genuine self-government impossible. I differ from Bork in holding that it is the misunderstanding of these principles, due in part to the failure of statesmen like Jefferson to educate the people about the true meaning and limitations of these altogether admirable ideas. See especially Bork, *Slouching Toward Gomorrah*.

196. TJ to James Monroe, May 20, 1782, *WTJ* IV:193–198, and again a decade later, TJ to James Madison, June 9, 1793; April 27, 1795, in *Correspondence of Jefferson and Madison* II:780–782, II:877–878.

197. TJ to John Adams, December 28, 1796, in *Adams-Jefferson Letters*, pp. 262–263. For Adams's reaction, see the discussion in Peterson, *Adams and Jefferson*, pp. 65–67. See also TJ to James Madison, April 27, 1795, in *Correspondence of Jefferson and Madison* II:877–878.

198. Mansfield, "Introduction," pp. xxxii–xlii.

199. TJ to Francis Hopkinson, March 13, 1789, *Papers* XIV:649–651.

200. But see the revealing letter to his daughter, in which Jefferson describes the "antisocial and misanthropic" effects of his withdrawal from the world during his retirement years (TJ to Mary Jefferson Eppes, March 3, 1802, in *Family Letters*, pp. 218–220).

201. TJ to John T. Mason, August 14, 1814, *Works* XI:410–415; cf. Plato, *Republic*, 361b–c.

202. TJ to the President of the United States, May 23, 1792, *WTJ* VIII:341–349.

203. TJ to Elbridge Gerry, June 21, 1797, *WTJ* IX:405–407.

204. *Autobiography*, in Peterson, *Writings*, pp. 98–99; contemplating retirement as secretary of state, Jefferson repeats the argument (TJ to James Madison, June 9, 1793, in *Correspondence of Jefferson and Madison* II:780–782).

205. TJ to the President of the United States, May 23, 1792, *WTJ* VIII:341–349; cf. Plato, *Republic*, 347a.

206. It is easier for Jefferson to recognize these motives in others; see TJ to the President of the United States, May 23, 1792, *WTJ*:341–349; TJ to Dr. Walter Jones, January 2, 1814, *WTJ* XIV:46–52.

207. TJ to James Monroe, May 20, 1782, *Papers* VI:184–187.

208. TJ to Martha Jefferson Randolph, February 11, 1800, in *Family Letters*, p. 184. In the same volume, see also TJ to MJR, January 15, 1792, p. 93; March 22, 1792, p. 97; June 8, 1797, p. 146; November 7, 1803, pp. 248–249; November 6, 1804, p. 263.

209. TJ to Thomas Mann Randolph, Jr., July 6, 1787. It is noteworthy that even as he encouraged his nephew to pursue a political career, Jefferson once again abstracted from all considerations of self-interest and offered no clue to the personal satisfactions that might motivate the best to devote their lives to public service.

210. TJ, Message Accepting Election as Governor, June 2, 1779, *Papers* II:277–278.

211. TJ to Harry Innes, June 25, 1799, *Works* IX:71–73.

212. TJ to Colonel Larkin Smith, April 25, 1809, *WTJ* XII:271–273.

213. TJ to Samuel Smith, August 22, 1798, *WTJ* X:55–59.

214. First Inaugural Address, March 4, 1801, *Works* IX:196.

215. See especially Douglass Adair, "Fame and the Founding Fathers," in *Fame and the Founding Fathers*, ed. Trevor Colbourn (New York: Norton, 1974), pp. 3–26.

216. TJ to James Monroe, January 13, 1803, *Works* IX:418–421.

217. TJ to David Rittenhouse, July 19, 1778, *WTJ* IV:42–43; TJ to Dr. Edward Jenner, May 14, 1806, *WTJ* XIX:152.

218. TJ to John Trumbull, February 15, 1789, *Papers* XIV:561; Adair, "Fame and the Founding Fathers."

219. See especially Thomas, "Death of Jeffersonian America?" pp. 25–29.

220. For a superb account, see Heather MacDonald, "The Billions of Dollars That Made Things Worse," *City Journal*, Autumn 1996, pp. 26–42.

Chapter 5. The Liberal Ideal: Duties to Self,
Friendship, and Duties to God

1. TJ to James Monroe, May 20, 1782, *Works* VII:373–377.

2. TJ to Dr. Benjamin Rush, January 3, 1808, *WTJ* XI:412–413; TJ to P. S. Du Pont de Nemours, March 2, 1809, *WTJ* XII:258–260.

3. TJ to Dr. Benjamin Rush, April 21, 1803, *WTJ* X:379–385; TJ to Dr. Joseph Priestley, April 9, 1803, *WTJ* X:374–376; TJ to Edward Dowse, April 19, 1803, *WTJ* X:379–385; TJ to William Short, October 31, 1819, *WTJ* XV:219–224.

4. In *Literary Commonplace Book*, ed. Wilson, pp. 56–61, esp. p. 58, sect. 68. (Note that Chinard first published this notebook as the *Literary Bible*.)

5. TJ to John Adams, April 8, 1816, in *Adams-Jefferson Letters,* pp. 466–469. And see the discussion in Karl Lehmann, *Thomas Jefferson: American Humanist* (New York: Macmillan, 1947), chap. 8.

6. TJ to Charles Thompson, January 9, 1816, *WTJ* XIV: 385–387.

7. TJ to William Short, October 31, 1819, *WTJ* XV:219–224.

8. Ibid.; also, TJ to Charles Thomson, January 9, 1816, *WTJ* XIV:385–387.

9. "Syllabus of the doctrines of Epicurus," included in TJ to William Short, October 31, 1819, *WTJ* XV:219–224.

10. Epicurus, "Letter to Menoeceus," in *The Stoic and Epicurean Philosophers: The Complete Extant Writings of Epicurus, Epictetus, Lucretius, Marcus Aurelius,* ed. Whitney J. Oates (New York: Random House, 1940), pp. 30–33; and see also the discussion of classical Epicureanism in James H. Nichols, Jr., *Epicurean Political Philosophy: The De Rerum Natura of Lucretius* (Ithaca, N.Y.: Cornell University Press, 1976).

11. Epicurus, "Letter to Menoeceus," p. 32; "Principal Doctrines," V, p. 35; TJ to Thomas Jefferson Randolph, November 24, 1808, *Family Letters,* pp. 362–365.

12. "Syllabus of the doctrines of Epicurus," included in TJ to William Short, October 31, 1819, *WTJ* XV:219–224.

13. TJ to Charles Bellini, September 30, 1785, *WTJ* V:151–154.

14. On the differences between classical and modern hedonism, see Nichols, *Epicurean Political Philosophy,* esp. chap. 5.

15. Cf. the discussion of courage in Aristotle, *Ethics,* book III, 1117a10–25; and consider Tarcov's treatment of courage in Locke, in *Locke's Education for Liberty,* pp. 153–163.

16. TJ to John Adams, December 10, 1819, in *Adams-Jefferson Letters,* pp. 548–550; TJ to Monsieur Coray, October 31, 1823, *WTJ* XV:480–490.

17. TJ to Thomas Jefferson Randolph, November 24, 1808, *Family Letters,* pp. 362–265. For an extended discussion, see Clifford Orwin, "Civility," *American Scholar* 60 (Autumn 1991): 553–564.

18. On this same point, see also Tarcov, *Locke's Education for Liberty,* pp. 137–141.

19. TJ to William Short, October 31, 1819, *WTJ* XV:219–224.

20. TJ to Martha Jefferson, March 28, 1787, in *Family Letters,* pp. 34–36; TJ to Dr. Joseph Priestley, January 27, 1800, *WTJ* X:146–149.

21. TJ to William Short, October 31, 1819, "Syllabus of the doctrines of Epicurus," *WTJ* XV:219–224.

22. TJ to P. S. Du Pont de Nemours, April 24, 1816, *Works* XI:519–525.

23. TJ to Thomas Jefferson Smith, February 21, 1825, *WTJ* XVI:110–111.

24. TJ to P. S. Du Pont de Nemours, March 2, 1809, *WTJ* XII:258–260.

25. TJ to Peter Carr, April 19, 1785, *WTJ* V:82–87.

26. Cf. Plato, *Republic,* book VI 491b–c; Aristotle, *Ethics,* book X, 1178a10–1178b10.

27. TJ to Henry Dearborn, June 22, 1807, *Works* X:430–431.

28. TJ to John Adams, July 5, 1814, in *Adams-Jefferson Letters,* pp. 430–434.

29. TJ to William Short, October 31, 1819, "Syllabus of the doctrines of Epicurus," *WTJ* XV:219–224.

30. By 1786, Jefferson already owned a copy of *De Rerum Natura,* and the following year, he included Lucretius under the heading "Morality" in the list of readings he drew up for his nephew Peter Carr (TJ to Peter Carr, August

10, 1787, *WTJ* VI:256–262). See Richard, *The Founders and the Classics*, esp. chap. 6.

31. Epicurus, "Letter to Menoeceus," pp. 30–33; Lucretius, *The Way Things Are*, trans. Rolphe Humphries (Bloomington: Indiana University Press, 1969).

32. Epicurus, Fragment LVIII, p. 43; Lucretius, *The Way Things Are*, book V, 1128–1135.

33. Nichols, *Epicurean Political Philosophy*, chap. 5.

34. Lehmann (*Thomas Jefferson: American Humanist*) alludes to the difficulty, but nowhere tries to account for it; Richard (*The Founders and the Classics*) makes no mention of it.

35. This last paragraph draws heavily on L. T. Sarasohn, "The Ethical and Political Philosophy of Pierre Gassendi," in *Essays on Early Modern Philosophers from Descartes and Hobbes to Newton and Leibniz*, vol. 2, *Grotius to Gassendi*, ed. Vere Chappell (New York: Garland, 1992) pp. 261–282. For a general discussion of Lucretius and the tranformation of Epicureanism by modern political philosophy, see Nichols, *Epicurean Political Philosophy*, chap. 5.

36. TJ to Richard Rush, May 31, 1813, *Works* XI:291–293; TJ to John Adams, June 27, 1813, in *Adams-Jefferson Letters*, pp. 335–338; TJ to William Short, November 28, 1814 *WTJ* XIV:211–218; TJ to William Short, October 31, 1819, *WTJ* XV:219–224.

37. TJ to William Short, October 31, 1819, *WTJ* XV:219–224; TJ to Charles Thomson, January 9, 1816, *WTJ* XIV:385–387.

38. TJ to John Adams, August 15, 1820, in *Adams-Jefferson Letters*, pp. 565–569.

39. Ibid.

40. TJ to John Adams, March 14, 1820, in *Adams-Jefferson Letters*, pp. 561–563.

41. Lucretius, *The Way Things Are*, book V, 195–236.

42. TJ to John Adams, April 11, 1823, in *Adams-Jefferson Letters*, pp. 591–594.

43. TJ to John Adams, April 8, 1816, in *Adams-Jefferson Letters*, pp. 466–469.

44. TJ to John Adams, October 14, 1816, in *Adams-Jefferson Letters*, pp. 490–493.

45 TJ to William Green Munford, June 18, 1799 in Peterson, *Writings*, pp. 1063–1066; TJ to Elbridge Gerry, January 26, 1799, *WTJ* X:74–86.

46. TJ to William Short, October 31, 1819, *WTJ* XV:219–224.

47. Indeed, Jefferson appeals to the nearly "unanimous sentiment" of mankind in favor of the preexistence of a Creator, as an additional argument in its favor (TJ to John Adams, April 11, 1823, in *Adams-Jefferson Letters*, pp. 591–594).

48. Consider, for example, Jefferson's comments on Platonic republicanism (TJ to John Adams, July 5, 1814, in *Adams-Jefferson Letters*, pp. 430–434).

49. Tocqueville, *Democracy in America*, vol. II, pt. 1, chap. 1.

50. Cicero, *On Friendship*, Epicurus, and Lucretius. Aristotle's *Nichomachean Ethics* devotes two whole books to the subject, compared with one book on justice.

51. Even the best American historians tend to confuse friendship and justice as the foundation of political community. See the literature review in Peter S. Onuf, "The Scholars' Jefferson," p. 694. The best discussion of this issue in American political thought is still Wilson Carey McWilliams, *The Idea*

of Fraternity in America (Berkeley: University of California Press, 1973), esp. chap. 9 on the Jeffersonians.

52. See especially William Galston and Steven Kautz, as well as Allan Bloom, *Love and Friendship* (New York: Simon and Schuster, 1993). Two exceptions are Montaigne's and Bacon's essays on friendship and see the discussion in Bloom, *Love and Friendship*, pp. 410–428.

53. Salkever, *Finding the Mean*, esp. chap. 6.

54. Kautz, *Liberalism and Community*.

55. TJ to Maria Cosway, October 12, 1786, *WTJ* V:430–448.

56. James Morton Smith, "Introduction: An Intimate Friendship," in *Correspondence of Jefferson and Madison*, I:1–36, at p. 6.

57. TJ to Dr. Benjamin Rush, August 17, 1811, *Works* XI:211–213.

58. Andrew Burstein, *The Inner Jefferson: Portrait of a Grieving Optimist* (Charlottesville: University Press of Virginia, 1995), esp. chaps. 4–5. And see also James Morton Smith, "Introduction: An Intimate Friendship," *Correspondence of Jefferson and Madison* I:1–36.

59. Of course, Jefferson never makes such clear-cut distinctions among the different kinds of friendship and, as the friendship with Adams indicates, he was able to cultivate more than one form of friendship with the same person. Nevertheless, since this typology helps to clarify the nature of friendship in a liberal republic and to distinguish it from the classical account of friendship so much admired by Aristotle and Epicurus, I have found it useful.

60. TJ to Maria Cosway, October 12, 1786, *WTJ* V:430–448; consider also Jefferson's comments to James Monroe regarding the nature of the friendship he hoped to strike up with Monroe's bride: "I must not philosophize too much with her lest I give her too serious apprehensions of a friendship I shall impose upon her" (cited in Burstein, *The Inner Jefferson*, p. 155). For a general discussion of Jefferson's epistolary friendships with women, see Burstein, pp. 75–111.

61. For a comprehensive analysis of this correspondence, see Burstein, *The Inner Jefferson*, chap. 3.

62. TJ to James Madison, February 17, 1826, in *Correspondence of Jefferson and Madison* III:1964–1967.

63. TJ to John Adams, August 15, 1820, in *Adams-Jefferson Letters*, pp. 565–569.

64. Onuf, "Scholars' Jefferson," p. 694; Burstein, *The Inner Jefferson*, chap. 6. On the relation between political friendship and spiritedness, see Salkever, *Finding the Mean*, pp. 197–199.

65. TJ to James Madison, February 20, 1784, in *Correspondence of Jefferson and Madison* I:292–299; TJ to James Madison, December 8, 1784, in *Correspondence of Jefferson and Madison* I:292–297, 353–355.

66. TJ to James Madison, February 17, 1826, in *Correspondence of Jefferson and Madison* III:1964–1967.

67. On this point, cf. the standard treatment by Adrienne Koch, *Jefferson and Madison: The Great Collaboration* (New York: Knopf, 1950), with the suggestive remarks of Harvey C. Mansfield, "Friends and Founders," *New Criterion* 13, no. 9 (May 1995): 69–72.

68. In this connection, see Michael Zuckert, "Appendix I: On Reading Jefferson," in "Thomas Jefferson on Nature and Natural Rights," pp. 167–169.

69. TJ to James Madison, December 20, 1787, in *Correspondence of Jefferson and Madison* I:511–515.

70. TJ to James Madison, February 17, 1826, in *Correspondence of Jefferson and Madison* III:1964–1967 (emphasis added).

71. TJ to John Adams, October 28, 1813, in *Adams-Jefferson Letters*, pp. 387–392.

72. Abigail Adams to TJ, June 6, 1785, in *Adams-Jefferson Letters*, pp. 28–31.

73. TJ to John Adams, August 22, 1813, in *Adams-Jefferson Letters*, pp. 367–370.

74. TJ to Dr. Benjamin Rush, January 16, 1811, *Works* XI:165–173.

75. The story is told by Cappon in *Adams-Jefferson Letters*, pp. 283–289.

76. TJ to Dr. Benjamin Rush, December 5, 1811, *WTJ* XIII:114–117; emphasis added.

77. TJ to John Adams, July 17, 1791, in *Adams-Jefferson Letters*, pp. 245–247.

78. Ibid. On this same point, see also TJ to William Hamilton of Woodlands, April 22, 1800, *Works* IX:129–131; TJ to John F. Mercer, Esq., October 9, 1804, *WTJ* XI:53–54; TJ to Judge David Campbell, January 28, 1810, *WTJ* XII:355–357; TJ to James Monroe, March 27, 1824, *Works* XII:346–347.

79. John Adams to TJ, July 29, 1791, in *Adams-Jefferson Letters*, pp. 247–250.

80. TJ to John Adams, June 27, 1813, in *Adams-Jefferson Letters*, pp. 335–338.

81. John Adams to TJ, July 15, 1813, in *Adams-Jefferson Letters*, pp. 357–358.

82. TJ to John Adams, October 31, 1813, in *Adams-Jefferson Letters*, pp. 387–392. One important exception was the Missouri Compromise (TJ to John Adams, December 10, 1819; January 22, 1821, in *Adams-Jefferson Letters*, pp. 548–550, 569–570).

83. TJ to John Adams, January 21, 1812, in *Adams-Jefferson Letters*, pp. 290–292.

84. TJ to John Adams, August 22, 1813, in *Adams-Jefferson Letters*, pp. 367–370.

85. John Adams to TJ, September 14, 1813; December 25, 1813, in *Adams-Jefferson Letters*, pp. 372–375, 409–413.

86. John Adams to TJ, March 2, 1816; September 14, 1813, in *Adams-Jefferson Letters*, pp. 372–375, 464–466.

87. TJ to John Adams, May 5, 1817, in *Adams-Jefferson Letters*, pp. 512–514.

88. TJ to James Smith, December 8, 1822; TJ to James Fishback, September 27, 1809, both in *Jefferson's Extracts from the Gospels*, pp. 343–345, 408–410.

89. TJ to John Adams, October 12, 1813, in *Adams-Jefferson Letters*, pp. 383–386; TJ to Dr. Benjamin Rush, April 21, 1803, with enclosed Syllabus, *WTJ* X:379–385.

90. John Adams to TJ, September 22, 1813, in *Adams-Jefferson Letters*, pp. 378–380 (emphasis in original). For Adams's more favorable estimate of the Jewish religion, see John Adams to TJ, October 4, 1813, in *Adams-Jefferson Letters*, pp. 380–383.

91. TJ to John Adams, October 12, 1813, in *Adams-Jefferson Letters*, pp. 383–386.

92. John Adams to TJ, September 24, 1813, in *Adams-Jefferson Letters*, pp. 372–375.

93. Though, once again, he insisted that the "atrocious" attributes of Calvin's God seemed "chiefly copied from that of the Jews" (TJ to John Adams, April 11, 1823, in *Adams-Jefferson Letters*, pp. 591–594).

94. John Adams to TJ, April 19, 1817, in *Adams-Jefferson Letters*, pp. 508–510.

95. Ibid.

96. John Adams to TJ, April 19, 1817; December 25, 1813; May 3, 1816, in *Adams-Jefferson Letters,* pp. 409–413, 469–471, 508–510.

97. John Adams to TJ, May 18, 1817, in *Adams-Jefferson Letters,* pp. 515–516.

98. John Adams to TJ, March 2, 1816, in *Adams-Jefferson Letters,* pp. 464–466.

99. John Adams to TJ, May 3, 1816; December 1, 1825, in *Adams-Jefferson Letters,* pp. 469–471, 611.

100. John Adams to TJ, May 3, 1816; December 8, 1818, in *Adams-Jefferson Letters,* pp. 469–471, 530.

101. I am indebted to my colleague William Watterson for pointing out that Jefferson's extracts from the Gospel end with the burial of Jesus and the great stone rolled before the door of the sepulchre. Jefferson omits all mention of the resurrection and ascension. See *The Life and Morals of Jesus of Nazareth,* prepared by Dr. Cyrus Adler, librarian of the Smithsonian Institution, for the use of Congress (Chicago: Mainz Engraving Company), p. 82.

102. TJ to John Adams, August 1, 1816; June 1, 1822, in *Adams-Jefferson Letters,* pp. 483–485, 577–579.

103. Citations for the preceding two paragraphs are TJ to John Adams, April 8, 1816; John Adams to TJ, May 6, 1816; John Adams to TJ, September 3, 1816; TJ to John Adams, October 14, 1816, in *Adams-Jefferson Letters,* pp. 466–469, 472–474, 487–488, 490–493.

104. Wood, "The Trials and Tribulations of Thomas Jefferson," in *Jeffersonian Legacies,* pp. 395–417, esp. p. 413.

105. John Adams to TJ, May 26, 1817, in *Adams-Jefferson Letters,* pp. 516–518.

106. TJ to David Rittenhouse, July 19, 1778, *WTJ* IV:42–43.

107. A Bill for Establishing Religious Freedom, *Papers* II:545–553.

108. Bear in mind that not all, and perhaps not even a majority, of Americans shared Jefferson's views. For a survey of the provisions in the revolutionary state constitutions on the usefulness of piety in maintaining republican institutions, see Yarbrough, "The Constitution and Character," pp. 217–249.

109. TJ to James Fishback, September 27, 1809, in *Jefferson's Extracts from the Gospels,* pp. 343–345. The citation is from a draft of the letter Jefferson did not send, which the editor has included in a footnote.

110. TJ to Ezra Stiles Ely, June 25, 1819, in *Jefferson's Extracts from the Gospels,* pp. 386–387; TJ to John Adams, August 15, 1820, in *Adams-Jefferson Letters,* pp. 565–569.

111. TJ to James Fishback, September 27, 1809, in *Jefferson's Extracts from the Gospels,* pp. 343–345. The citation is from a draft of the letter Jefferson did not send, which the editor has included in a footnote.

112. TJ to Miles King, December 20, 1814, in *Jefferson's Extracts from the Gospels,* pp. 360–361. Elsewhere, to a sympathetic Unitarian, Jefferson would qualify this statement. We must love God with our whole hearts, but we show this love by loving our brethren (TJ to Benjamin Waterhouse, June 26, 1822, in the same volume, pp. 405–406).

113. TJ to William Canby, September 18, 1813, in *Jefferson's Extracts from the Gospels,* pp. 349–351. Canby was a Quaker who had been trying for a decade to convert Jefferson to Christianity.

114. TJ to James Smith, December 8, 1822, in *Jefferson's Extracts from the Gospels,* pp. 408–410.

115. TJ to Thomas Law, June 13, 1814, *WTJ* XIV:138–144. Yet while Jefferson denies that morality is rooted in the love of God, he relies on the fear of God as an auxiliary precaution.

116. Joseph Priestley to TJ, May 7, 1803, in *Jefferson's Extracts from the Gospels*, pp. 338–340.

117. TJ to William Short, August 4, 1820, in *Jefferson's Extracts from the Gospels*, pp. 394–399.

118. TJ to William Short, April 13, 1820, in *Jefferson's Extracts from the Gospels*, pp. 391–394.

119. Sanford Kessler, "Locke's Influence on Jefferson's 'Bill for Establishing Religious Freedom,'" *Journal of Church and State* 25 (1983): 231–252, at p. 247. And see especially TJ to Thomas Cooper, August 14, 1820, *WTJ* XV:264–269.

120. TJ to Benjamin Waterhouse, June 26, 1822, in *Jefferson's Extracts from the Gospels*, pp. 405–406.

121. TJ to Rev. Isaac Story, December 5, 1801, in *Jefferson's Extracts from the Gospels*, pp. 325–326.

122. Accordingly, Jefferson sometimes asserts that we must not only love God but also fear him. Still, we fear him not (as the Jews believed) because we have failed in our duties toward him but because we have failed in our duties to our fellow men.

123. *Notes*, Query XVIII, p. 163.

124. *Notes*, Query XVII, p. 159. And for a fuller discussion of Locke's arguments, see Galston, *Liberal Purposes*, chap. 12.

125. TJ to Miles King, September 26, 1814, in *Jefferson's Extracts from the Gospels*, pp. 360–361.

126. Galston, *Liberal Purposes*, chap. 12.

127. TJ, "Notes on Locke and Shaftesbury," *Papers* I:544–548.

128. TJ to Peter Carr, August 10, 1787, *WTJ* XI:256–262; A Bill for Establishing Religious Freedom, in *Papers* II:545–553. And on this point, see Mansfield, "Introduction," pp. xiii–xv.

129. A Bill for Establishing Religious Freedom, *Papers* II:545–553.

130. *Notes*, Query XVII, p. 159.

131. In the fall of 1776, Jefferson took extensive notes on Locke's *A Letter on Toleration* and *The Reasonableness of Christianity*, which are entitled Notes on Locke and Shaftesbury, *Papers* I:544–548. On this point, see also Kessler, "Locke's Influence," and Orwin, "Civility."

132. Unless otherwise noted, all citations in this paragraph are from TJ's Notes on Locke and Shaftesbury, *Papers* I:544–548.

133. *Notes*, Query XVII, p. 159.

134. For a fuller discussion, see Kessler's fine article "Locke's Influence on Jefferson's 'Bill for Establishing Religious Freedom,'" and Adam Wolfson's two superb essays, "Toleration and Relativism: The Locke-Proast Exchange," *Review of Politics* 59 (Spring 1997): 213–231; "Two Theories of Toleration: Locke Versus Mill," *Perspectives in Political Science* 25, no. 4 (Fall 1996): 192–197. My only quarrel with Wolfson is that on the most casual of comments, he too readily places Jefferson in the camp of Mill and against Locke.

135. Jefferson offers the example of child sacrifice, but drug use and polygamy would also fall outside the protections of the free exercise of religion (Notes on Locke and Shaftesbury, *Papers* I:544–548). This is precisely what is at

stake in the Religious Freedom Restoration Act, which the Supreme Court recently struck down in *City of Boerne v. Flores*, 117 Sup. Ct. 2157 (1997).

136. TJ to Messrs. Nehemiah Dodge and Others, a Committee of the Danbury Baptist Association, in the State of Connecticut, January 1, 1802, in Peterson, *Writings*, p. 510. Consider also Daniel L. Dreisbach, "A New Perspective on Jefferson's Views on Church-State Relations: The Virginia Statute for Establishing Religious Freedom in its Legislative Context," *American Journal of Legal History* 35 (1991): 172–204.

137. Second Inaugural Address, March 4, 1805, *Works* X:127–136; TJ to Rev. Samuel Miller, January 23, 1808, *Works* XI:7–9.

138. Notes on Locke and Shaftesbury, in *Papers* I:544–548, n. 2, p. 551. Indeed, Jefferson himself carried the idea farther by ridiculing religious doctrines, such as Calvin's five points, which in no way endangered the public welfare or morals, but which he considered contrary to the spirit of true Christianity, though he did so only privately.

139. *Notes*, Query XVII, p. 161. Jefferson's answer to the contemporary self-esteem movement, which insists that the majority approve of minority opinions because it is vital to their self-esteem, is that the minority should act in ways that will win the approval of the majority. For a different argument against broadening toleration to approval, one which insists that the liberal republic envisioned by the Framers sees men and women as strong and self-sufficient and, therefore, not in need of the approval of others, see Kautz, *Liberalism and Community*, chap. 3.

140. TJ to Edward Dowse, April 19, 1803, in *Jefferson's Extracts from the Gospels*, pp. 329–330.

141. First Inaugural Address, March 4, 1801, *Works* IX:193–200.

142. TJ to Benjamin Waring, March 23, 1801, *WTJ* X:235–236. And so, it must have given him particular satisfaction to write to Abigail Adams, in the wake of the disastrous Alien and Sedition Acts: "I tolerate with the utmost latitude the right of others to differ from me in opinion without imputing to them criminality. I know too well the weakness and uncertainty of human reason to wonder at it's [*sic*] different results" (TJ to Abigail Adams, September 11, 1804, in *Adams-Jefferson Letters*, pp. 278–280). Such sentiments, however, were hardly designed to effect a reconciliation.

143. TJ to Benjamin Waring, March 23, 1801, *WTJ* X:235–236.

144. Reply to Address by Citizens of Washington, March 4, 1809, in *The Writings of Thomas Jefferson*, ed. H. A. Washington (Washington, D.C.:Taylor and Maury, 1854), VIII:157–158.

145. A Bill for Establishing Religious Freedom, *Papers* II:545–553.

146. TJ to Thomas McKean, February 19, 1803, *Works* IX:449–452. And consider also the Second Inaugural Address, March 4, 1805, *Works* X:127–136, where Jefferson publicly encourages the states to enforce their laws against "false and defamatory publications," in order to preserve "public morals and public tranquility."

147. TJ to William Roscoe, December 27, 1820, *WTJ* XV:302–304.

148. For a discussion of the psychological underpinnings of this view in Locke and a comparsion with Mill, see Wolfson, "Two Theories of Toleration," esp. pp. 194–195.

149. TJ to Thomas Law, June 13, 1814, *WTJ* XIV:138–144.

150. TJ to Marquis Layfayette, May 14, 1817, *WTJ* XV:114–118.

151. The term is from Robert Bellah, quoted in Galston, *Liberal Purposes*, p. 269. For a discussion of Mill and the extension of toleration to moral questions, see Wolfson, "Two Theories of Toleration."

152. Nevertheless, once skepticism is introduced in religious questions, it has a tendency to spread to other areas as well, especially when so many moral questions are at least partly reinforced by the teachings of revealed religion. On this point, see especially Wolfson, "Toleration and Relativism."

153. TJ to François de Marbois, June 14, 1817, *WTJ* XV:129–131.

154. Two exceptions were the crisis engendered by the Missouri Compromise and the use of national powers for internal improvements. Commenting on the first, Jefferson feared that the present generation might throw away "the fruits of their fathers' sacrifices of life and fortune, and render . . . desperate the experiment which was to decide ultimately whether man is capable of self-government." To do so would be "treason against human hope" (TJ to William Short, April 13, 1820, in *Jefferson's Extracts from the Gospels*, pp. 391–394).

155. TJ to John Adams, April 8, 1816; John Adams to TJ, May 3, 1816, in *Adams-Jefferson Letters*, pp. 466–471.

156. TJ to John Adams, August 1, 1816, in *Adams-Jefferson Letters*, pp. 483–485.

157. TJ to Jared Sparks, February 4, 1824, *WTJ* XVI:8–14. Here I would like to express my appreciation to my student Melvin Lee Rogers, whose senior seminar paper explored this topic with penetration and insight. I have also benefited from reading an early draft of Peter Onuf's forthcoming manuscript, "'To Declare Them a Free and Independent People': Race, Slavery, and National Identity in Jefferson's Thought."

158. Frederick Douglass, "What Are the Colored People Doing for Themselves," and Booker T. Washington, "Our New Citizen," both in *What Country Have I?* ed. Herbert J. Storing (New York: St. Martin's Press, 1970); James Q. Wilson, *On Character*; Glenn Loury, "Achieving the 'Dream': A Challenge to Liberals and Conservatives in the Spirit of Martin Luther King," in *American Political Thought*, ed. Kenneth M. Dolbeare (Chatham, N.J.: Chatham House, 1996), pp. 591–601; Shelby Steele, *The Content of Our Character: A New Vision of Race in America* (New York: Harper Perennial, 1991); and Galston, *Liberal Purposes*.

159. To be sure, the sixties generation claimed not to be rejecting morality but to be acting on a higher social morality. Instead of concerning itself with the virtues and vices of individuals, it focused on the virtues and vices of society as a whole. Thus, vice came to be associated with racism, sexism, assaults upon the environment, bourgeois materialism, and so forth, and virtue with their opposites. Still, the individual virtues were not entirely overlooked, but the virtues that generation celebrated had to do with personal liberation and self-fulfillment rather than the more old-fashioned virtues that seemed to be stifling individual development. From their perspective, the sixties generation was more moral than preceding generations, not less. Theirs was a generation marked by a certain kind of moral earnestness, at odds with past conceptions of morality, but also with the postmodern irony and doubt so pervasive today.

Works Cited

Primary American Sources

Cappon, Lester J., ed. *The Adams-Jefferson Letters*. New York: Simon and Schuster, 1971.

Commager, Henry Steele, ed. *Documents of American History*. New York: Appleton, Century, Crofts, 1949.

Elliot, Jonathan, ed. *The Debates in the Several State Conventions on the Adoption of the Federal Constitution*. 5 vols. Philadephia: Lippincott, 1901.

Hamilton, Alexander. *Papers of Alexander Hamilton*. 27 vols. Ed. Harold C. Syrett. New York: Columbia University Press, 1961.

Hamilton, Alexander, et al. *The Federalist Papers*. Ed. Jacob E. Cooke. Middletown, Conn.: Wesleyan University Press, 1961.

Jefferson, Thomas. *Autobiography*, in *Thomas Jefferson: Writings*. Ed. Merrill Peterson. New York: Library of America, 1984.

———. *The Commonplace Book of Thomas Jefferson: A Repertory of His Ideas on Government*. Ed. Gilbert Chinard. Baltimore, Md.: Johns Hopkins University Press, 1926.

———. *The Complete Jefferson*. Ed. Saul K. Padover. New York: Duell, Sloan and Pearce, 1943.

———. *The Family Letters of Thomas Jefferson*. Ed. Edwin Morris Betts and James Adam Bear, Jr. Columbia: University of Missouri Press, 1996.

———. *The Garden and Farm Books of Thomas Jefferson*. Ed. Robert C. Baron. Golden, Colo.: Fulcrum, 1987.

———. *Jefferson's Extracts from the Gospels: The Papers of Thomas Jefferson*. 2nd ser. Ed. Dickenson W. Adams. Princeton, N.J.: Princeton University Press, 1983.

———. *Jefferson's Literary Commonplace Book: The Papers of Thomas Jefferson*. 2nd ser. Ed. Douglas L. Wilson. Princeton, N.J.: Princeton University Press, 1989.

———. *The Life and Morals of Jesus of Nazareth*. Prepared by Dr. Cyrus Adler, Librarian of the Smithsonian Institution, for the use of Congress. Chicago: Mainz Engraving Company.

———. *The Literary Bible*. Ed. Gilbert Chinard. New York: Greenwood Press, 1969.

———. *Memoir, Correspondence, and Miscellanies, from the Papers of Thomas Jefferson*. Ed. Thomas Jefferson Randolph. Charlottesville, Va.: F. Carr, 1829.

―――. *Notes on the State of Virginia.* Ed. William Peden. Chapel Hill: University of North Carolina Press, 1955.

―――. *The Papers of Thomas Jefferson.* 27 vols. Ed. Julian P. Boyd. Princeton, N.J.: Princeton University Press, 1954.

―――. *The Political Writings of Thomas Jefferson.* Ed. Edward Dumbauld. New York: Bobbs-Merrill, 1955.

―――. *The Republic of Letters: The Correspondence Between Thomas Jefferson and James Madison 1776-1826.* 3 vols. Ed. James Morton Smith. New York: Norton, 1995.

―――. *The Works of Thomas Jefferson.* 12 vols. Ed. Paul Leicester Ford. New York: Putnam, 1904.

―――. *The Writings of Thomas Jefferson.* 20 vols. Ed. Albert Ellery Bergh and Andrew A. Lipscomb. Washington, D.C.: Thomas Jefferson Memorial Association, 1907.

―――. *The Writings of Thomas Jefferson.* 9 vols. Ed. H. A. Washington. Washington, D.C.: Taylor and Maury, 1854.

Lincoln, Abraham. *Abraham Lincoln: His Speeches and Writings.* Ed. Roy P. Basler. New York: Grosset and Dunlap, 1962.

Madison, James. *Papers of James Madison.* 17 vols. Ed. Robert A. Rutland et al. Charlottesville: University Press of Virginia, 1984.

―――. *The Writings of James Madison.* 9 vols. Ed. Gaillard Hunt. New York: Putnam, 1908.

Meyers, Marvin, ed. *The Mind of the Founder: Sources of the Political Thought of James Madison.* Hanover, N.H.: University Press of New England, 1981.

Sowerby, E. Millicent. *Catalogue of the Library of Thomas Jefferson.* 5 vols. Washington, D.C.: Library of Congress, 1953.

Wilson, James. *The Works of James Wilson.* 2 vols. Ed. Robert Green McCloskey. Cambridge, Mass.: Belknap Press, 1967.

Books

Appleby, Joyce Oldham. *Capitalism and a New Social Order: The Republican Vision of the 1790's.* New York: New York University Press, 1984.

―――. *Liberalism and Republicanism in the Historical Imagination.* Cambridge, Mass.: Harvard University Press, 1992.

Arendt, Hannah. *The Human Condition.* Chicago: University of Chicago Press, 1958.

―――. *On Revolution.* New York: Viking Press, 1963.

Aristotle. *Nichomachean Ethics.* Ed. T. E. Page. Cambridge, Mass.: Loeb Classical Library, [1926] 1962.

―――. *Politics.* Trans. Carnes Lord. Chicago: University of Chicago Press, 1985.

Ball, Terrence, and J. G. A. Pocock, eds. *Conceptual Change and the Constitution.* Lawrence: University Press of Kansas, 1988.

Banning, Lance. *Jefferson and Madison: Three Conversations.* Madison, Wis.: Madison House, 1995.

―――. *The Jeffersonian Persuasion: Evolution of a Party Ideology.* Ithaca, N.Y.: Cornell University Press, 1978.

Becker, Carl. *The Declaration of Independence: A Study in the History of Political Ideas*. New York: Vintage Books, 1942.

Bell, Daniel. *The Cultural Contradictions of Capitalism*. New York: Basic Books, 1979.

Belz, Herman, Ronald Hoffman, and Peter J. Albert, eds. *To Form a More Perfect Union: The Critical Ideas of the Constitution*. Charlottesville: University Press of Virginia, 1992.

Berns, Walter. *Virtue, Freedom, and the First Amendment*. Chicago: Henry Regnery, 1965.

Bloom, Allan. *Love and Friendship*. New York: Simon and Schuster, 1993.

———, ed. *Confronting the Constitution*. Washington, D.C.: AEI Press, 1990.

Boorstin, Daniel. *The Lost World of Thomas Jefferson*. Chicago: University of Chicago Press, [1943] 1981.

Bork, Robert. *Slouching Toward Gomorrah: Modern Liberalism and American Decline*. New York: Regan Books/HarperCollins, 1996.

Brann, Eva. *Paradoxes of Education in a Republic*. Chicago: University of Chicago Press, 1979.

Burstein, Andrew. *The Inner Jefferson: Portrait of a Grieving Optimist*. Charlottesville: University Press of Virginia, 1995.

Carlson, Allan C. *From Cottage to Work Station: The Family's Search for Harmony in an Industrial Age*. San Francisco: Ignatius Press, 1993.

Chappell, Vere, ed. *Essays on Early Modern Philosophers from Descartes and Hobbes to Newton and Leibniz*. Vol. 2, *Grotius to Gassendi*. New York: Garland, 1992.

Cicero, Marcus Tullius. *On the Commonwealth*. Trans. George Holland Smith and Stanley Barney Smith. Indianapolis: Bobbs-Merrill Educational Publishing, 1984.

Cohler, Anne. *Montesquieu's Comparative Politics and the Spirit of American Constitutionalism*. Lawrence: University Press of Kansas, 1988.

Colbourn, Trevor, ed. *Fame and the Founding Fathers*. New York: Norton, 1974.

Cropsey, Joseph. *Political Philosophy and the Issues of Politics*. Chicago: University of Chicago Press, 1977.

———. *Polity and Economy*. The Hague: M. Nijhoff, 1957.

Destutt de Tracy, Antoine-Louis-Claude. *A Commentary and Review of Montesquieu's Spirit of the Laws*. Trans. Thomas Jefferson. New York: Burt Franklin, 1969.

Diggins, John Patrick. *The Lost Soul of American Politics: Virtue, Self-Interest, and the Foundations of Liberalism*. New York: Basic Books, 1984.

Dolbeare, Kenneth M., ed. *American Political Thought*. Chatham, N.J.: Chatham House, 1996.

Elshtain, Jean Bethke. *Democracy on Trial*. New York: Basic Books, 1995.

Epstein, David F. *The Political Theory of "The Federalist."* Chicago: University of Chicago Press, 1984.

Fish, Charles. *In Good Hands: The Keeping of a Family Farm*. New York: Farrar, Straus and Giroux, 1995.

Fox-Genovese, Elizabeth. *The Origins of Physiocracy: Economic Revolution and Social Order in Eighteenth-Century France*. Ithaca, N.Y.: Cornell University Press, 1976.

Galston, William A. *Liberal Purposes: Goods, Virtues and Diversity in the Liberal State*. Cambridge: Cambridge University Press, 1991.

Genovese, Eugene. *The Southern Tradition: The Achievement and Limitations of an American Conservative.* Cambridge, Mass.: Harvard University Press, 1994.

Glendon, Mary Ann. *Rights Talk.* New York: Free Press, 1991.

Glendon, Mary Ann, and David Blankenhorn, eds. *Seedbeds of Virtue: Sources of Competence, Character, and Citizenship in American Society.* Lanham, Md: Madison Books, 1995.

Green, Daniel. *To Colonize Eden: Land and Jeffersonian Democracy.* London: Gordon and Cremonesi, 1977.

Hartz, Louis. *The Liberal Tradition in America: An Interpretation of American Political Thought Since the Revolution.* New York: Harcourt, 1955.

Hellenbrand, Harold. *The Unfinished Revolution: Education and Politics in the Thought of Thomas Jefferson.* Newark: University of Delaware Press, 1990.

Himmelfarb, Gertrude. *The De-Moralization of Society.* New York: Knopf, 1995.

Hirschman, Albert O. *The Passions and the Interests.* Princeton, N.J.: Princeton University Press, 1977.

Hobbes, Thomas. *Leviathan.* Ed. Michael Oakeshott. New York: Collier Books, 1962.

Horwitz, Robert H., ed. *The Moral Foundations of the American Republic.* Charlottesville: University Press of Virginia, 1977.

Hume, David. *David Hume: The Philosophical Works.* Ed. Thomas Hill Green and Thomas Hodge Grose. Aalen: Scientia Verlag, 1964.

———. *Essays: Moral, Political, and Literary.* Ed. Eugene F. Miller. Indianapolis: Liberty Classics, 1985.

———. *Hume's Moral and Political Philosophy.* Ed. Henry D. Aiken. New York: Hafner, 1972.

Hutcheson, Francis. *Collected Works of Francis Hutcheson.* New York: George Olms Verlag, 1990.

———. *Illustrations on the Moral Sense.* Ed. Bernard Peach. Cambridge, Mass.: Belknap Press of Harvard University Press, 1971.

———. *A System of Moral Philosophy.* New York: Augustus M. Kelly, 1968.

Jaffa, Harry V. *American Conservatism and the American Founding.* Durham, N.C.: Carolina Academic Press, 1984.

———. *The Conditions of Freedom.* Baltimore, Md.: Johns Hopkins University Press, 1975.

———. *Crisis of the House Divided.* Garden City, N.Y.: Doubleday, 1959.

———. *Equality and Liberty: Theory and Practice in American Politics.* New York: Oxford University Press, 1965.

Jones, Howard Mumford. *The Pursuit of Happiness.* Cambridge, Mass.: Harvard University Press, 1953.

Kames, Henry Home. *Essays on the Principles of Morality and Natural Religion 1751.* New York: Garland, 1976.

Kammen, Michael G. *A Machine That Would Go of Itself: The Constitution and American Culture.* New York: Alfred A. Knopf, 1986.

Kautz, Steven. *Liberalism and Community.* Ithaca, N.Y.: Cornell University Press, 1995.

Kerber, Linda. *Women of the Republic: Intellect and Ideology in Revolutionary America.* New York: Norton, 1986.

Ketcham, Ralph. *Presidents Above Party: The First American Presidency, 1789–1829.* Chapel Hill: University of North Carolina Press, 1984.

Klein, Milton M., Richard D. Brown, and John B. Hench, eds. *The Republican Synthesis Revisited*. Worcester, Mass.: American Antiquarian Society, 1992.

Koch, Adrienne. *Jefferson and Madison: The Great Collaboration*. New York: Knopf, 1950.

————. *The Philosophy of Thomas Jefferson*. Chicago: Quadrangle Books, 1964.

————. *Power, Morals, and the Founding Fathers*. Ithaca, N.Y.: Great Seal Books, 1961.

Konig, David Thomas, ed. *Devising Liberty: Preserving and Creating Freedom in the New American Republic*. Stanford, Calif.: Stanford University Press, 1995.

Kristol, Irving. *Two Cheers for Capitalism*. New York: Basic Books, 1978.

Kyvig, David E. *Explicit and Authentic Acts: Amending the U.S. Constitution*. Lawrence: University Press of Kansas, 1996.

Landy, Marc, and Sidney Milkis. *Presidential Greatness*. New York: Free Press, forthcoming.

Lasch, Christopher. *Women and the Common Life: Love, Marriage, and Feminism*. Ed. Elisabeth Lasch-Quinn. New York: Norton, 1997.

Lehmann, Karl. *Thomas Jefferson: American Humanist*. New York: Macmillan, 1947.

Lerner, Ralph. *The Thinking Revolutionary: Principle and Practice in the New Republic*. Ithaca. N.Y.: Cornell University Press, 1979.

Levy, Leonard. *Jefferson and Civil Liberties: The Darker Side*. Cambridge, Mass.: Belknap Press of Harvard University Press, 1963.

Licht, Robert A., ed. *The Framers and Fundamental Rights*. Washington, D.C.: American Enterprise Institute, 1991.

Locke, John, *Second Treatise of Government*. Ed. Richard Cox. Arlington Heights, Ill.: Harlan Davidson, 1982.

Lovejoy, Arthur O. *Reflections on Human Nature*. Baltimore, Md.: Johns Hopkins University Press, 1961.

Lucretius. *The Way Things Are*. Trans. Rolphe Humphries. Bloomington: Indiana University Press, 1969.

Macedo, Stephen. *Liberal Virtues: Citizenship, Virtue, and Community in Liberal Constitutionalism*. Oxford: Clarendon Press, 1991.

Machiavelli, Niccolò. *The Prince and the Discourses*. New York: Modern Library, 1950.

Magnet, Myron. *The Dream and the Nightmare: The Sixties' Legacy to the Underclass*. New York: Morrow, 1993.

Malcolm, Joyce Lee. *To Keep and Bear Arms: The Origin of an Anglo-American Right*. Cambridge, Mass.: Harvard University Press, 1994.

Mansfield, Harvey C. *America's Constitutional Soul*. Baltimore, Md.: Johns Hopkins University Press, 1991.

————. *Machiavelli's New Modes and Orders*. Ithaca, N.Y.: Cornell University Press, 1979.

————. *Machiavelli's Virtue*. Chicago: University of Chicago Press, 1996.

————, ed. *Thomas Jefferson: Selected Writings*. Arlington Heights, Ill.: AHM, 1979.

Marx, Leo. *The Machine in the Garden: Technology and the Pastoral Ideal in America*. New York: Oxford University Press, 1964.

Matthews, Richard. *The Radical Politics of Thomas Jefferson*. Lawrence: University Press of Kansas, 1984.

Mayer, David N. *The Constitutional Thought of Thomas Jefferson*. Charlottesville: University Press of Virginia, 1994.

McCoy, Drew. *The Elusive Republic: Political Economy in Jeffersonian America*. Chapel Hill: University of North Carolina Press, 1980.

McDonald, Forrest. *Alexander Hamilton: A Biography*. New York: Norton, [1979] 1982.

———. *Novus Ordo Seclorum*. Lawrence: University Press of Kansas, 1985.

McDowell, Gary L., and Sharon L. Noble. *Reason and Republicanism: Thomas Jefferson's Legacy of Liberty*. Lanham, Md.: Rowman and Littlefield, 1997.

McWilliams, Wilson Carey. *The Idea of Fraternity in America*. Berkeley: University of California Press, 1973.

Miller, John Chester. *The Wolf by the Ears: Thomas Jefferson and Slavery*. New York: Free Press, 1977.

Montesquieu. *The Spirit of the Laws*. Trans. Anne Cohler, Basia Miller, and Harold Stone. Cambridge: Cambridge University Press, 1989.

Morgan, Richard E. *Disabling America: The "Rights Industry" in Our Time*. New York: Basic Books, 1984.

Nedelsky, Jennifer. *Private Property and the Limits of American Constitutionalism: The Madisonian Framework and Its Legacy*. Chicago: University of Chicago Press, 1990.

Nichols, James H., Jr. *Epicurean Political Philosophy: The* De Rerum Natura *of Lucretius*. Ithaca, N.Y.: Cornell University Press, 1976.

Nylander, Jane C. *Our Own Snug Fireside: Images of the New England Home 1760–1860*. New York: Knopf, 1994.

Oates, Whitney J., ed. *The Stoic and Epicurean Philosophers: The Complete Extant Writings of Epicurus, Epictetus, Lucretius, Marcus Aurelius*. New York: Random House, 1940.

Onuf, Peter, ed. *Jeffersonian Legacies*. Charlottesville: University Press of Virginia, 1993.

Pangle, Lorraine Smith, and Thomas L. Pangle. *The Learning of Liberty: The Educational Ideas of the American Founders*. Lawrence: University Press of Kansas, 1993.

Pangle, Thomas L. *The Ennobling of Democracy: The Challenge of the Postmodern Age*. Baltimore, Md.: John Hopkins University Press, 1992.

———. *Montesquieu's Philosophy of Liberalism*. Chicago: University of Chicago Press, 1974.

———. *The Spirit of Modern Republicanism: The Moral Vision of the American Founders and the Philosophy of John Locke*. Chicago: University of Chicago Press, 1988.

Parrington, Vernon Louis. *Main Currents in American Thought: The Colonial Mind, 1620–1800*. New York: Harcourt, Brace, 1927.

Paul, Ellen Frankel, and Howard Dickman, eds. *Liberty, Property, and the Foundations of the American Constitution*. Albany: State University Press of New York, 1989.

Peterson, Merrill. *Adams and Jefferson: A Revolutionary Dialogue*. Athens: University of Georgia Press, 1976.

———. *The Jeffersonian Image in the American Mind*. New York: Oxford University Press, 1960.

———. *Thomas Jefferson and the New Nation*. New York: Oxford University Press, 1970.

Plato. *The Laws of Plato*. Trans. Thomas L. Pangle. New York: Basic Books, 1980.

————. *The Republic*. Trans. Allan Bloom. New York: Basic Books, 1968.

Pocock, J. G. A. *The Machiavellian Moment: Florentine Political Thought and the Atlantic Republic*. Princeton, N.J.: Princeton University Press, 1975.

Raab, Felix. *The English Face of Machiavelli: A Changing Interpretation, 1500–1700*. London: Routledge and K. Paul, 1964.

Rahe, Paul. *Republics: Ancient and Modern*. 3 vols. Chapel Hill: University of North Carolina Press, 1994.

Raphael, David Daiches. *The Moral Sense*. London: Oxford University Press, 1947.

Richard, Carl J. *The Founders and the Classics: Greece, Rome, and the American Enlightenment*. Cambridge, Mass.: Harvard University Press, 1994.

Rudolph, Frederick, ed. *Essays on Education in the Early Republic*. Cambridge, Mass.: Harvard University Press, 1965.

Salkever, Stephen G. *Finding the Mean: Theory and Practice in Aristotelian Political Philosophy*. Princeton, N.J.: Princeton University Press, 1990.

Sandel, Michael. *Democracy's Discontent*. Cambridge, Mass.: Belknap Press of Harvard University Press, 1996.

Sheldon, Garrett Ward. *The Political Philosophy of Thomas Jefferson*. Baltimore, Md.: Johns Hopkins University Press, 1991.

Smith, Adam. *Theory of Moral Sentiments*. Indianapolis: Liberty Classics, 1969.

Steele, Shelby. *The Content of Our Character: A New Vision of Race in America*. New York: Harper Perennial, 1991.

Stein, Susan R. *The Worlds of Thomas Jefferson at Monticello*. New York: Harry N. Abrams Publishers, in association with the Thomas Jefferson Memorial Foundation, 1993.

Storing, Herbert J., ed. *What Country Have I?: Political Writings by Black Americans*. New York: St. Martin's Press, 1970.

Stourzh, Gerald. *Alexander Hamilton and the Idea of Republican Government*. Stanford, Calif.: Stanford University Press, 1970.

Tarcov, Nathan. *Locke's Education for Liberty*. Chicago: University of Chicago Press, 1984.

Tocqueville, Alexis de. *Democracy in America*. Ed. J. P. Mayer. Garden City, N.Y.: Doubleday, 1969.

Twelve Southerners. *I'll Take My Stand: The South and the Agrarian Tradition* (New York: Harper and Brothers, 1930.

von Eckhardt, Ursula. *The Pursuit of Happiness in the Democratic Creed*. New York: Praeger, 1959.

White, Morton. *The Philosophy of the American Revolution*. New York: Oxford University Press, 1978.

Wills, Garry. *Inventing America*. Garden City, N.Y.: Doubleday, 1978.

Wilson, James Q. *The Moral Sense*. New York: Free Press, 1993.

————. *On Character*. Washington, D.C.: American Enterprise Institute, 1991.

Wiltse, Charles M. *The Jeffersonian Tradition in American Democracy*. Chapel Hill: University of North Carolina Press, 1935.

Wood, Gordon. *The Creation of the American Republic*. Chapel Hill: University of North Carolina Press, 1969.

————. *The Radicalism of the American Revolution*. New York: Knopf, 1992.

Scholarly Articles, News Reports, and Political Commentaries

Banning, Lance. "Jeffersonian Ideology Revisited: Liberal and Classical Ideas in the New American Republic." *William and Mary Quarterly,* 3rd ser., 43 (January 1986): 3-19.

Berns, Walter. "The New Pursuit of Happiness." *Public Interest,* no. 86 (1987): 65-76.

Brann, Eva T. H. "Concerning the Declaration of Independence." *Saint John's Review* 28 (July 1976): 1-16.

Brooks, David. "'Civil Society' and Its Discontents." *Weekly Standard,* February 5, 1996, pp. 18-21.

———. "The Rise of the Latte Town." *Weekly Standard,* September 15, 1997, pp. 17-22.

Dobbs, Darrell. "Natural Right and the Problem of Aristotle's Defense of Slavery." *Journal of Politics* 56 (February 1994): 69-94.

Dreisbach, Daniel L. "A New Perspective on Jefferson's Views on Church-State Relations: The Virginia Statute for Establishing Religious Freedom in Its Legislative Context." *American Journal of Legal History* 35 (1991): 172-204.

Freeman, Joanne B. "Slander, Poison, Whispers, and Fame: Jefferson's 'Anas' and Political Gossip in the Early Republic." *Journal of the Early Republic* 15 (Spring 1995): 25-57.

Galston, William A., and David Wasserman. "Gambling Away Our Moral Capital." *Public Interest,* no. 126 (Spring 1996): 58-71.

Ganter, Herbert Lawrence. "Jefferson's 'Pursuit of Happiness' and Some Forgotten Men." *William and Mary Quarterly* 16 (October 1936): 558-585.

Genovese, Eugene. "Eugene Rivers's Challenge: A Response." *Boston Review* 18, no. 5 (October/November 1993): 34-36.

Grant, Ruth W. "Locke's Political Anthropology and Lockean Individualism." *Journal of Politics* 50 (February 1988): 42-63.

Hamowy, Ronald. "Jefferson and the Scottish Enlightenment." *William and Mary Quarterly* 36 (1979): 503-523.

Henretta, James A. "Families and Farms: Mentalité in Pre-Industrial America." *William and Mary Quarterly* 35 (January 1978): 3-32.

Kaplan, Robert. "Cities of Despair." *New York Times,* June 6, 1996, p. A29.

Kessler, Sanford. "Locke's Influence on Jefferson's 'Bill for Establishing Religious Freedom.'" *Journal of Church and State* 25 (1983): 231-252.

Kloppenberg, James T. "The Virtues of Liberalism: Christianity, Republicanism, and Ethics in Early American Political Discourse." *Journal of American History* 74 (1987): 9-33.

MacDonald, Heather. "The Billions of Dollars That Made Things Worse." *City Journal,* Autumn 1996, pp. 26-42.

Mansfield, Harvey C. "Friends and Founders." *New Criterion* 13, no. 9 (May 1995): 69-72.

———. "Self-Interest Rightly Understood." *Political Theory* 23 (February 1995): 48-66.

Mathie, William. "God, Woman, and Morality: The Democratic Family in the New Political Science of Alexis de Tocqueville." *Review of Politics* 57 (Winter 1995): 7-30.

McCloskey, Donald. "Bourgeois Virtue." *American Scholar* 63 (Spring 1994): 177-191.

McMurtry, Larry. "How the West Was Won or Lost." *New Republic*, October 22, 1990, pp. 32–38.

Morton, F.L. "Sexual Equality and the Family in Tocqueville's *Democracy in America*." *Canadian Journal of Political Science* 17 (June 1984): 309–324.

Murray, Charles. "The Coming White Underclass." *Wall Street Journal*, October 29, 1993, p. A14.

———. "Limiting Government and the Pursuit of Happiness." *Cornell Journal of Law and Public Policy* 4 (1995): 449–455.

O'Brien, Conor Cruise. "Thomas Jefferson: Radical and Racist." *Atlantic Monthly*, October 1996, pp. 53–74.

Onuf, Peter. "Reconsidering an American Icon." *Washington Post Book World*, November 24, 1996.

———. "The Scholars' Jefferson." *William and Mary Quarterly* 50 (October 1993): 671–699.

Orwin, Clifford. "Civility." *American Scholar* 60 (Autumn 1991): 553–564.

Pangle, Lorraine Smith. "Liberal Education and Politics: Lessons from the American Founding." *Academic Questions* 8 (Winter 1994–95): 33–44.

Peeler, David P. "Thomas Jefferson's Nursery of Republican Patriots: The University of Virginia." *Journal of Church and State* 28 (Winter 1986): 79–93.

Rahe, Paul. "The Primacy of Politics in Classical Greece." *American Historical Review* 89 (April 1984): 265–293.

———. "Thomas Jefferson's Machiavellian Political Science." *Review of Politics* 57 (Summer 1995): 449–481.

Schaar, John. "And the Pursuit of Happiness." *Virginia Quarterly Review* 46 (Winter 1970): 1–27.

Shalhope, Robert E. "The Ideological Origins of the Second Amendment." *Journal of American History* 69 (December 1982): 599–614.

Sterngold, James. "For Some, It's Still a Wonderful Life." *New York Times*, December 8, 1996, p. 3.

Thomas, Andrew Peyton. "The Death of Jeffersonian America?" *Weekly Standard*, August 26, 1996, pp. 26–29.

Vickers, Daniel. "Competency and Competition: Economic Culture in Early America." *William and Mary Quarterly* 47 (January 1990): 3–29.

Will, George F. "Mr. Jefferson Comes to Town." *Public Interest*, no. 112 (Summer 1993): 50–59.

Wilson, Douglas L. "The American *Agricola*: Jefferson's Agrarianism and the Classical Tradition." *South Atlantic Quarterly* 80 (1981): 339–354.

———. "Counter Points: Jefferson Scholar Douglas L. Wilson responds to Conor Cruise O'Brien." *Atlantic Monthly On-Line*, http://www.TheAtlantic.com/atlantic/issues/96oct/obrien/response.htm.

Wilson, James Q. "Capitalism and Morality." *Public Interest*, no. 121 (Fall 1995): 42–60.

Winthrop, Delba "Tocqueville's American Woman and the True Conception of Democratic Progress." *Political Theory* 14 (May 1986): 239–261.

Wolfson, Adam. "Toleration and Relativism: The Locke-Proast Exchange." *Review of Politics* 59 (Spring 1997): 213–231.

———. "Two Theories of Toleration: Locke Versus Mill." *Perspectives in Political Science* 25 (Fall 1996): 192–197.

Wood, Gordon. "Inventing American Capitalism." *New York Review of Books*, June 9, 1994, pp. 44–49.

———. "Politics Without Party." *New York Review of Books*, October 11, 1984, pp. 18–21.

Yarbrough, Jean. "Race and the Moral Foundations of the American Republic: Another Look at the Declaration and the *Notes on Virginia*." *Journal of Politics* 53 (February 1991): 90–105.

———. "Republicanism Reconsidered: Some Thoughts on the Foundation and Preservation of Republican Government." *Review of Politics* 41 (January 1979): 61–95.

Index

251